D0294662

THE BIBLE AND BIBLES IN AMERICA

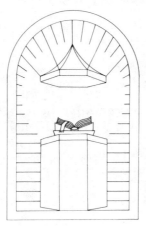

SOCIETY OF BIBLICAL LITERATURE

The Bible in American Culture

General Editors:

Edwin S. Gaustad
Professor of History
University of California, Riverside

Walter Harrelson
Distinguished Professor of Old Testament
Vanderbilt University

1. *The Bible and Bibles in America*
   Edited by Ernest S. Frerichs

2. *The Bible and Popular Culture in America*
   Edited by Allene S. Phy

3. *The Bible and American Arts and Letters*
   Edited by Giles Gunn

4. *The Bible in American Law, Politics, and Rhetoric*
   Edited by James T. Johnson

5. *The Bible in American Education*
   Edited by David Barr and Nicholas Piediscalzi

6. *The Bible and Social Reform*
   Edited by Ernest R. Sandeen

THE BIBLE AND BIBLES IN AMERICA

edited by

ERNEST S. FRERICHS

Scholars Press
Atlanta, Georgia

SOCIETY OF BIBLICAL LITERATURE

CENTENNIAL PUBLICATIONS

Library of Congress Cataloging-in-Publication Data

The Bible and Bibles in America.

(The Bible in American culture ; 1)
1. Bible--United States--History. 2. Bible--United States--Influence. 3. Bible--Publication and distribution--United States. 4. United States--Religious life and customs. I. Frerichs, Ernest S. II. Series.
BS447.5.U6B53   1988   220'.0973   87-9676
ISBN 1-55540-096-5 (alk. paper)

Printed in the United States of America
on acid-free paper

CONTENTS

Acknowledgements

The editor expresses appreciation to the contributors for their perseverance and patience; to my colleagues, Jacob Neusner and Wendell S. Dietrich for their friendship and encouragement; and to Sarah and our children for their tolerance and understanding.

Editor and Contributors

JOHN ALDEN, former Keeper of Rare Books at the Boston Public Library, is the author of numerous works on the history of printing and its social implications. At the time of his retirement in 1981, he was editor for Brown University's John Carter Brown Library of its ongoing *European Americana: A Chronological Guide to Works Printed in Europe Relating to the Americas, 1493–1976*.

F. FORRESTER CHURCH, Minister of The Unitarian Church of All Souls in New York City, has authored numerous books and articles dealing with New Testament studies, the history of Early Christianity, and the history of liberal religious thought.

KEITH R. CRIM, Editorial Director of Westminster Press, is a former Professor of Religion and Philosophy at Virginia Commonwealth University. He served as a translator with the American Bible Society and has published widely on biblical translation. He was the General Editor of the Supplementary Volume of the *Interpreter's Dictionary of the Bible* and *The Abingdon Dictionary of Living Religions*.

GERALD P. FOGARTY, S.J., is Professor of Religious Studies at the University of Virginia. In addition to articles on various aspects of American Catholic history, he is the author of *The Vatican and the Americanist Crisis: Denis J. O'Connell, American Agent to the Vatican (1885–1903)* and *The Vatican and the American Hierarchy from 1870 to 1965*.

ERNEST S. FRERICHS, Professor of Religious Studies and Judaic Studies at Brown University, serves as Director of Brown's Judaic Studies Program. He is the editor (with Jacob Neusner) of *"To See Ourselves As Others See Us:" Christians, Jews, "Others" in Late Antiquity*, and the author of articles dealing with the history of biblical interpretation.

KENT P. JACKSON is an Associate Professor in the Department of Ancient Scripture of Brigham Young University. He served previously as Assistant to the Publications Director of the American Schools of Oriental Research. In addition to his articles in biblical studies, he has published *The Ammonite Language of the Iron Age* as well as a study of the scriptural process among the Latter-day Saints.

ROBERT PEEL serves as writer and consultant on editorial and ecumenical matters to the First Church of Christ, Scientist in Boston. A frequent contributor to various journals, he is the author of *The Creed of a*

Victorious Pagan, Christian Science: Its Encounter with American Culture, and *Mary Baker Eddy: The Years of Discovery, The Years of Trial, The Years of Authority.*

JONATHAN D. SARNA is Associate Professor of American Jewish History, Hebrew Union College–Jewish Institute of Religion (Cincinnati) and Academic Director, Center for the Study of the American Jewish Experience. The author of numerous articles dealing with American Jewish history, he has published *Jacksonian Jew: The Two Worlds of Mordecai Noah, People Walk on Their Heads: Moses Weinberger's Jews and Judaism in New York,* and edited *Jews in New Haven.*

NAHUM M. SARNA is emeritus Dora Golding Professor of Biblical Studies of Brandeis University and a former faculty member of the Jewish Theological Seminary of America. President of the Association of Jewish Studies, he is a widely published author of studies on the Hebrew Bible, including *Understanding Genesis.* He served on the committee of translators for *The Writings: Kethubim* of the new Jewish Publication Society of America's translation of the Bible.

HAROLD P. SCANLIN is Translation Advisor, United Bible Societies, New York. In addition to articles in various journals, he serves as Associate Editor of *Religious and Theological Abstracts.*

Preface to the Series

To what extent are Americans a "people of the book"? To what degree is the history of their nation intermixt with the theology and story and imagery of the Bible? These and other questions are addressed in the several volumes of our series, The Bible in American Culture.

Initially conceived as part of the 1980 centennial celebration of the Society of Biblical Literature, this series explores the biblical influence—for good or ill—in the arts, music, literature, politics, law, education, ethnicity and many other facets of American civilization in general. It is the task of other series to examine biblical scholarship per se; these books, in contrast, search out the way in which the Bible permeates, subtly or powerfully, the very fabric of life within the United States.

The undersigned heartily commend the individual editors of each volume. They have persisted and pursued until all authors finally entered the fold. We also gladly acknowledge the wise counsel of Samuel Sandmel in an earlier stage of our planning, regretting only that he is not with us at the end.

Finally, we express our deep appreciation to the Lilly Endowment for its generous assistance in bringing this entire series to publication and wider dissemination.

EDWIN S. GAUSTAD
WALTER HARRELSON

Introduction

The Bible in America, judged by typical American success criteria, is assured of a prize. Viewed variously as a monument, an icon, a living presence, the Bible has continued to inspire and inform American life. If it is neglected as a work to be read, the Bible is nevertheless a predictable part of most home libraries. Indeed, for those homes that possess a Bible, more than one translation is common.

From the perspective of American publishers, sales of Bibles are big business. The cost of promotional campaigns for new translations is measured in millions of dollars and sales are projected in seven- and eight-digit numbers. Budgeting for a new translation is also planned in multimillion dollar terms.

Such large-scale planning is justified on balance sheets that show multimillion dollar sales. Estimates suggest annual sales of Bibles in excess of $170 million. If we add to sales of Bibles related items such as Bible study guides, gospel sheet music, and Bible recordings, total revenue begins to approximate the billion dollar mark.

The availability of the Bible in home, church, and synagogue is extended to insure that no American should ever be in a hotel, motel, hospital, or public transportation center without assured access to a Bible. The sale and distribution of Bibles is also increased by Christian congregations that are strongly devoted to the centrality of the Bible, especially when no ecclesiastical body dicates which translation should be used. The emphasis in such Christian bodies on personal Bible devotions, worship services in which each worshiper uses a personal Bible, and educational programs centered in a Bible curriculum—all promote the sales of Bibles.

Such a massive presence in American life stems from several sources. On one side stands the endurance of the Bible—the world's most translated book and the world's most frequently published book. All or some part of the Bible is available to the peoples of the world in nearly two thousand languages. This endurance relates in large part to the spiritual heritage that the Bible conveys for Judaism, Christianity, and Islam.

Viewed as an inspired work, Scripture for the great religious traditions of the West, the Bible has become a vital center for the religious life especially of Jews and Christians. No less does the Bible serve as a center of controversy as its users struggle with its interpretation. The issue is severe enough when the interpretation surrounds the "original" language of the Bible. Division without end is the consequence when the interpretation is centered in the accuracy and authenticity of a particular translation. For those who view the Bible as a treasured literary work, these divisions are unfortunate; for those whose lives are governed by the Bible, the issues are threatening to spiritual survival.

The unquenchable desire of Americans for the possession of the Bible and a willingness to accept a translated Bible combine to proliferate translations. A persistent American appetite for the Bible is abetted by American zeal and ingenuity that matches particular translations to every American taste. Every audience that might seek a special tendency in translation is given some recognition. Whether the needs of the Bible's audience are expressed in terms of language or style, doctrine or teaching, that audience is considered in the possible editions of an American Bible in English form. The premise of American Bible translations is that the reader does not know the original languages. The focus therefore of the translation is more frequently on the reader audience and less on the intention of the original language, author, or authors.

"Paraphrase" translations speak to the role of paraphrase in communication and not to the definition of paraphrase in translation theory or translation history. Exemplary of this voice in American Bible publishing is the Living Bible, a work of Kenneth N. Taylor, which sold some thirty million copies in fourteen years. Designed to appear as a novel, the Living Bible has stressed contemporary design, easy-to-read type, a one-column format, and a blue cover. Advertizing fervor has transformed the Living Bible into "The Book." In the intense competition which characterizes popular Bible sales in America, it is not surprising that the publishers of a New King James Version would dub that version "The Bible." "The Book" and "The Bible" are among twenty or more English-language versions of the Bible generally available today.

Clearly neither "The Book" nor "The Bible" exhaust the desire of American readers or publishers for the Bible. If the English vocabulary of a particular translation is too extensive or too obscure, there are limited-vocabulary versions and modern-speech versions. The Good News Bible, or Today's English Version, published by the American and United Bible Societies, is intended to be understandable to a person with a three thousand word vocabulary and a sixth grade education. Alternatively, a simple English translation with a thousand word vocabulary would be the Bible in Basic English. If the issue is length and compression of detail, a condensed version is prepared for the pressured American with limited time. To meet this need *Reader's Digest* produced a condensed version, forty percent shorter than the 850,000 word text of the Revised Standard Version on which it was based. In the reduction, the Old Testament was shortened about fifty percent and the New Testament some twenty-five percent. Condensation was seen as an antidote to length and what was perceived as a frequent repetitious style. Certain passages such as the Twenty-third Psalm and 1 Corinthians 13 survived intact.

Beyond issues of style, speech, and vocabulary, or questions of the authenticity of the translation lineage, stand translations representing many forms of special pleading. The pleading might be for any cause, though theological and doctrinal issues are common. The pleading is best understood as reflecting emphases in particular periods in the history of American society. An Olive Pell Bible (1852) reflects the vegetarianism of its sponsor by removing carnivorous references in the Bible as well as sex and violence. Slang translations may have limited readers and limited lives, but publishers have appealed to street gang jargon with the "God is for Real, Man" version.

An issue of high sensitivity in modern America is the alleged sexist character of the Bible, both in its original form and also in its translations. The dominating presence of men not only in the Bible itself but also in the history of translation is taken as an explanation for discrimination against women in the biblical text and in the translations. Such views were certainly part of Julia E. Smith's impetus to Bible translation in 1876, even if the more immediate occasion might have been the general movement in her time for women's suffrage. In what she did, however, she became the first woman to translate the whole Bible.

An effort in the same direction, though more of interpretation than translation, was *The Woman's Bible* (1895–1898), a work of some twenty women suffragists headed by Elizabeth Cady Stanton, a leader in the women's movement of the nineteenth century. Using a fresh translation, presumably without bias, the Stanton group wrote commentaries on selected sections intended to show that the Bible, a source of oppression for women, could be read differently.

Recently this concern for the removal of sexist language in Bible translation has shown itself in a lectionary of biblical readings sponsored by the National Council of Churches of Christ. The goal of the lectionary is to achieve "inclusive" rather than "exclusive" language. This new translation of the Bible in the lectionary removes references to God as solely male. Changes in the translation include references to God as both the Mother and Father of humankind. "Sons of God" has become "children of God" and the "Lord God" has become "God the Sovereign One."

Even more striking in the history of Bible translation in America has been the reflection of doctrinal or sectarian emphases. A concern for the form of baptism led to rendering the Greek term "baptize" as "immerse," a view upheld by the American Bible Union which was organized in 1850 and supported Baptist claims for this form of baptism. In such translations "John the Baptist" became "John the Immerser."

Such doctrinal and sectarian concerns might be conveyed in the language of translation. They might also be conveyed in other additions to the text. Annotations were an important means of achieving such ends and annotations have been used frequently in English Bibles since the seventeenth century. Particular annotators—John Brown, Thomas Scott, Matthew Henry—enjoyed favor across relatively long periods. Art and illustration became equally important ways of teaching. A new form of "illuminated Bible" emerged with the reproduction of the paintings by Hoffman and the statues by Thorwaldsen. Aids to study of all kinds were introduced into America Bibles—concordances, dictionaries, historical information. Typography was used to support theological and religious concerns, red print for the words attributed to Jesus, starred verses in the Old Testament for prophecies "fulfilled" in the New Testament. Color was superimposed in various hues to draw the Bible reader's attention to biblical passages important to central theological discussions of prophecy, sin, redemption, and the like.

Beyond the motivation of doctrinal or sectarian concern lie other explanations for the flow of Bible translations, a flow which has led our age to be characterized as "the age of translation," or the "fourth great age of Biblical translation" (Orlinsky, 1969:4–10) One explanation is the desire to correct the errors of earlier versions. The discoveries associated with archaeology in the nineteenth and twentieth centuries have given considerable opportunity for the review of the Greek and Hebrew textual base of translation. All of this has contributed to a series of publications of critical texts for the Hebrew Bible and the Greek New Testament. The recovery of cognate and other languages contemporary with the period of the origins of the Bible has provided further opportunity for changes in the translations of earlier periods. Beyond the recovery of languages and even ancient texts have been the further discoveries associated with archaeology that have given us a better-informed understanding of the daily life and customs of people from the time of the Bible.

Even when an earlier version was not incorrect, it was inevitably true that the language of any translation reflected the language and stylistic conventions of English in that day. As a work to be read and understood, it was imperative that the reader recognize the idiom of his day. Modern-speech translations emerged, especially with the beginning of this century, as a response to the desire of readers to recognize the speech patterns of their time. Depending on the rapidity with which such patterns change, the need for new modern-speech translations became an established expectation of translators. The danger in such translating is that the mode of speech used in the translation becomes too limited and is discarded after a brief time.

A further motivation in Bible translation has been the desire to make the Bible available to all peoples everywhere. This motivation has been especially apparent in the work of the Bible societies, here and abroad, and has contributed to the development of translation theory in our time. It is not surprising that leading translators in the Bible societies had been major figures in the modern movement of translation theory. Concerns such as the discussion between "formal equivalence" and "dynamic equivalence" has come from the work of a leading Bible translator, Eugene Nida (1964: 165–92). The distribution of the Bible to a world-wide readership is reflected in the story of the smuggling of more than a million Chinese-language Bibles to the People's Republic of China in 1981.

An additional characteristic of American Bible translation has been the growth of translation by committee. Precedents for this are available in such obvious instances as the committee preparation of the revered King James, or Authorized, Version. Understood as a pooling of collective knowledge or as protection against the unrestrained or idiosyncratic choices of an individual, committee translations have nevertheless born the brunt of accusations of translational mediocrity resulting from committee voting. The particular change in recent American examples, however, has been to extend to committee participation the ecumenical experience of the American churches. Historically, English translation of the Bible has been a particular province of Anglican and Protestant worlds; more recent translations show a clear desire to involve Roman Catholics, Eastern Orthodox Communicants, and Jews in the translation process. Such changes are slow, however, and there is still concern for translations officially sponsored or approved by Roman Catholic representatives.

Given the dominant role of the Bible in American life, it is to be expected that religious groups in the United States would extend the notion of sacred books to materials other than the Bible. Even in major forms of Christianity, differences occur in the definition of what is included in the Bible. In Judaism the notion of the Torah has extended beyond the Hebrew Bible to encompass narrow or broad definitions of a rabbinic canon.

A review of religious groups in the United States shows that they have been a fertile ground for the growth of movements that have their own sacred literature. Such groups include those that acknowledge an already established Scripture, such as the Bible, and add a supplementary scripture, often viewed as the product of the founder's inspiration. Other groups recognize the scriptural authority only of the revelation related to their founder. The scriptural supplements must be regarded as of divine inspiration and the particular group must hold the scriptural supplement to be authoritative in matters of faith.

The Scope of the Essays

In his account of "The Bible as Printed Word" John Alden gives a view of the role of the Bible in the great migration that recognizes the variety of motives—religious, political, economic—informing the settlement of America. The centrality of the Bible, however, not only in the religious communities, but also in the political pamphlets of the times, is paralleled by the importance of the Bible in the early history of American printing. The time of independence was not only an opportunity for political freedom from the British Crown, but also for the production of Bible printing and Bible translating. The growth of Bible societies and the extension of the view that saw the great migration as an "errand into the wilderness" led to a strong concern for the translation of the Bible into the languages of the American Indians.

Building on the rich heritage of the Bible in the life of colonial and postcolonial America, Keith Crim and Harold Scanlin treat in their separate essays the nature of biblical translations if they are viewed as a committee activity or as the work of an individual. The involvement of a committee leads, as Crim shows, to collective decisions on the choice of a textual base, issues of the meaning of the text, and questions of how to express the meaning of the text in the target language of the translation. Harold Scanlin traces the history of Bible translations by American individuals from the early nineteenth-century work of Charles Thomson, Secretary of the Continental Congress. This history has produced, as Scanlin notes, at least one new translation in every decade except that one following the Thomson translation of 1808. In these translations by individuals every issue contributing to the varieties of American Bible translations can be observed, whether the issue is language, style, or doctrine.

The history of Bible translation in the English-speaking world has been so often tied to Anglican and Protestant sponsorship that it is typical to view separately the role of American translations within the Jewish and Roman Catholic communities. The tradition of that separation, at least with respect to Roman Catholic participation, may be seen differently in the next century. Jonathan and Nahum Sarna show clearly the limits of the Jewish community in any attention to the Bible that isolates it from the larger Torah tradition of Judaism. A further question is the authoritative role of the Hebrew text of the Bible and the corresponding lack of authority for an English translation. At the same time, there is an important history in Jewish American translation of the Bible that extends from Isaac Leeser to the new Jewish Publication Society translation.

Gerald Fogarty explores the tradition of American Bible translations under Roman Catholic auspices, beginning with Bishop Carroll's letter to Mathew Carey in 1789. From the early concern of John Carroll and Francis Kenrick extended almost a century of experience producing a new understanding of the distinctions between a "Catholic" and a "Protestant" Bible. An important instance of change was the involvement in the translation leading to the 1970 publication of the New American Bible of various Protestant scholars. This was particularly significant in the publication of what was the first American Catholic translation of the entire Bible from the original languages.

Involved in all these questions is the continuing fascination of Americans not only with the Bible but also with notions of sacred writings. Forrester Church takes up in his essay the question of Thomas Jefferson's desire to produce his own "Bible," as he sought to find a view of Jesus in accord with his own rationalist principles. Questions of sacred literature for the Latter-day Saints are discussed by Kent Jackson. The Mormon perspective requires that sacred books stem from antiquity, but that revelation continues through church leadership to the present. The sacred texts of Latter-day Saints include not only the Bible but also the Book of Mormon as well as two collections of revelations to Joseph Smith and his successors, the Doctrine and Covenants and the Pearl of Great Price.

Robert Peel discusses the question of sacral writing among Christian Scientists by tracing the history of *Science and Health with Key to the Scriptures* from its publication under that title in 1885. Statements from Mary Baker Eddy attest to the central role of the Bible in the Christian Science tradition and the role of *Science and Health* as a "key" to the Scriptures. Peel's essay is a careful effort to explain the reality of such a linkage in the history of Mary Baker Eddy and the Christian Science movement.

American life has given a central role to the Bible through its history. That has been true even when the reading and the citing of the Bible have ceased to characterize the life of many Americans. So central has Scripture been that new religious groups in America affirm the Bible as Scripture, even when those new groups use additional scriptures within their traditions.

WORKS CONSULTED

Bailey, Lloyd R., ed. 1982 *The Word of God: A Guide to English Versions of The Bible*. Atlanta: John Knox Press.

Hatch, Nathan O. and Noll, Mark A., eds., 1982 *The Bible in America, Essays in Cultural History*. New York: Oxford University Press.

Lehmann-Haupt, Hellmut 1951. *The Book in America: A History of the Making and Selling of Books in the United States*. 2nd ed. New York: R. R. Bowker Company.

Hills, Margaret T., ed. 1961 *The English Bible in America*. New York: American Bible Society.

Lewis, Jack P. 1982 *The English Bible: From KJV to NIV*. Grand Rapids: Baker.

Nida, Eugene A. 1964 *Toward a Science of Translating*. Leiden: Brill.

Orlinsky, Harry M., ed. 1969 *Notes on the New Translation of The Torah*. Philadelphia: Jewish Publication Society of America.

Orlinsky, Harry M. 1974 *Essays in Biblical Culture and Bible Translation*. New York: Ktav.

Simms, P. Marion 1936 *The Bible in America: Versions that have Played Their Part in the Making of the Republic*. New York: Wilson-Erickson.

I

The Bible as Printed Word

John Alden

Of no nation can it as aptly be said as of the United States, that, in its settlement and development, the Bible has played a major role. It is true that ambition, greed, and sheer adventurism have also shared in the process, but they have been accompanied by and even over-shadowed by a genuine zeal for realizing a Christian faith and the promises embodied in the Bible. This is in contrast to the areas of the New World opened up by Columbus and subsequent Spanish en-trepreneurs in their search for the riches of the Indies. Here, how-ever, Christian though the Spaniards were, it was the Church rather than the Bible that inspired and accompanied them, in the person of the secular clergy or religious orders.

There is merit, perhaps, in examining the nature of that Bible and the means of its dissemination as a stimulus to both migration and settlement. Much of this is due to the accessibility of the Bible, predominantly in English, where the contributions of translators and editors are readily recognized. Less acknowledgment of debt is given to the printers, who in turn made such efforts fruitful, yet a considera-tion of how the Bible reached its audience offers a fuller dimension to its influence.

The Colonial Period

Of the swarming of the English to North America in the early seventeenth century Carl Bridenbaugh can say with justice: "In a real sense, the Holy Bible was the greatest piece of promotional literature of the era of the Great Migration . . ." (401). At the same time it should not be forgotten that the motives for that migration were also economic and political, as Bridenbaugh trenchantly also reveals: to overemphasize religious grounds is to deceive ourselves. For one thing, the decline in the frequency and severity of plagues had led to population growth and its consequences, consequences from which the vast if unknown area of North America offered a refuge.

Nor should we overlook a growing nationalism among the English, that sense of patriotic dynamism, stimulated on one hand by the collapse of the Spanish Armada in 1588, and on the other hand by the Reverend Richard Hakluyt's *Principall Navigations, Voiages, and Discoveries of the English Nation.* of the following year, exhorting, as it did, Englishmen to build for their nation's glory on the foundations already laid. (As it happened, Hakluyt encouraged such enterprise not only through the printed word but also with his purse as an investor in the Virginia Company of London that settled Jamestown in 1607.)

Even in the settlement of Plymouth, to see religious motives alone would be mistaken. It must be admitted that Robert Cushman, in his *Sermon Preached at Plimouth in New England December 9, 1621* (London, 1622), averred that the Pilgrims sought "first to settle religion here [in America], before either profit or populantirie," but the fact remains that in his magisterial *History of Plymouth Plantation* (1646), the colony's first governor, William Bradford, provides fuller reasons for the migration from Leyden, reasons other than religious. Thus Bradford enumerates grounds for removal to New England: "the hardness of the place and countrie" which deterred others from joining the Leyden group; the inability of some to endure the "great labor and hard fare, with other inconveniences," impelling a search for "a better and easier place of living." It is only after having acknowledged these material disadvantages that Bradford concludes: "Lastly, and which was not least a great hope, and inward zeall they had of laying some good foundation, (or at least to make some way thereunto) for the propagating, and advancing the gospell of the kingdom of Christ in those remote parts of the world; yea, though they should be but even as stepping stones, unto others for the performing of so great a work" (55).

In a similar manner, Edward Winslow, who too had been a member of the Leyden group, provided in his *Hypocrisie Unmasked* (London, 1646) parallel grounds for the Plymouth venture, emphasizing in conclusion how the Pilgrims sought "not onely to bee a meanes to enlarge the Dominions of our English State, but the Church of Christ also. . . . Hereby in their grave Wisdomes they thought wee might more glorifie God, doe more good to our Countrey, better provide for our posterity, and live to be more refreshed by our labours, then ever wee could doe in Holland where we were."

Addressed as Winslow's work was to the Earl of Warwick, governor-in-chief of the English plantations in America, his protestations of patriotism and a desire to maintain an English identity were indeed politic, but they do represent the complexity of the Pilgrims' aspirations. Only after having acknowledged these varied strands should we give weight to the religious element, the search, in Governor Bradford's words, for "the right worship of God, and discipline of Christ, established in the church, according to the simplicities of the Gospell, without the mixture of mens inventions. And to have and to be ruled by the laws of Gods word; dispensed in those offices, and by those officers of pastors, Teachers, and Elders, &c., according to the Scriptures."

That for the Pilgrims in general, and Bradford in particular, the "Scriptures" in question were those of the Bible first published in Geneva in 1560 there is ample evidence. According to its distinguished editor, Worthington C. Ford, all the Bible quotations in Bradford's *History* are from that version, and a copy that had belonged to him is today in Pilgrim Hall at Plymouth. It is likewise from the Geneva text that Deacon Cushman quoted in his 1621 sermon cited earlier. If John Alden did possess a copy of the King James version, now also in Pilgrim Hall, he possessed the Geneva version as well, found today in the Darthmouth College Library.

Overshadowed as the Geneva Bible has long been by the King James version, it is all too easy to overlook its importance in its own day. It was valued not only for its text, representing an effort to provide a newly authoritative translation of the Hebrew and Greek originals embodying current scholarship, but also as a physical object given a particular character by its printers. In the latter respect it marked a distinct departure from earlier English versions, notably the Great Bible first issued in 1539. Consideration of the 160 editions of the Geneva Bible that appeared between 1560 and 1640 reveals that all, with very few exceptions, were in quarto format. In addition, they were, again with few exceptions, printed in roman type rather than in Black Letter, the use of which perhaps reflected a lingering vestige of an earlier printer's convention that, whereas Latin texts were to be set in roman type, for vernacular texts Black Letter was to be used. May we not assume that, as with ourselves, the roman face of the Geneva versions was more readily legible? In any event, it was more economic, occupying less space. Another feature of the Geneva text was the fact that it introduced the numbering of verses, a practice subsequently incorporated in the Bishops' Bible of 1568 and later followed in the King James version of 1611.

It would be difficult to exaggerate the contribution of its format to the popularity and spread of the Geneva Bible. In contrast to the Great Bible and its successor, the Bishops' Bible, it constituted a compact and portable volume, whereas earlier Bibles in folio were designed primarily as lectern Bibles to be placed in a church's sanctuary. As a consequence, the Geneva Bibles were not only less unwieldy, they were also less expensive. Inasmuch as the quantity (as well as quality) of the paper employed was a major factor in production costs, here was a substantial saving: a Bible that the laity could more readily afford. Its success with its public is indeed manifest in the number of editions through which it passed, for though initially published at Geneva between 1576 and 1611, some ninety editions of the complete Bible (not counting those of the New Testament alone) were produced in England, in addition to others printed in Scotland or Holland. By contrast, during the same period, only eleven editions of the Bishops' Bible appeared. Only with the publication of the King James version in 1611 did the hegemony of the Geneva version decline; a mere nine editions of the latter were produced between the year 1612 and its last edition in 1644, while, during the same period, some 177 editions of the former were produced. It should be noted that though the first edition of the King James Bible was an imposing folio volume set in Black Letter, the year 1612 saw the issue of the new version in both quarto and even smaller octavo formats, both printed in roman type, silent testimony of the advantages of the Genevan version.

That, unlike the Pilgrims at Plymouth, the founders of the separate Massachusetts Bay Colony at Salem and Boston took for their guidance the King James version undoubtedly reflects rather more than what are seen as its literary merits. Sponsored as it was by the Church of England, it would have had for John Winthrop and his fellows an authority they continued to respect, and this was reflected in their *Humble Request of His Maiesties loyall Subjects, the Governor and Company late gone for Nevv-England; To the rest of their Brethren, in and of the Church of England* (London, 1630) wherein they made clear their sense of "honour, to call the Church of England, from whence wee rise, our deare Mother."

That the Puritans at Boston presently followed the Pilgrims into separation from the Church of England, which gave rise to Congregationalism, in no way, however, affected their loyalty to the King James version. An examination of the sermons published by Puritan clergy reveals that their citations are uniformly derived from it. See the writings of leaders such as John Cotton, Charles Chauncy, Thomas Hooker, John Norton, and Thomas Shepheard, and the 1649 *Platform of Church Discipline*.

In a stimulating essay, "Work and Order in Colonial New England," Harry S. Stout of the University of Connecticut has advanced even more significant reasons for a preference for the King James version, representing as it did a shift in focus. His thesis, set forth in *The Bible in America; Essays in Cultural History* (New York, 1982), is that the Geneva version was concerned chiefly with God's covenant with the individual, whereas the translators of the King James version had a larger vision of a Christian society: "Before the New World settlement English Puritans had moved beyond the Reformation emphases of the Geneva Bible and spoke increasingly of a special national covenant that existed alongside a personal covenant of grace. . . . Nowhere was the movement beyond the Geneva Bible more evidenced than in the Puritan-sponsored migration to Massachusetts Bay in 1630. This migration had as its overarching mission nothing less than the carving out of a new world order solely according to biblical precept" (26).

Evidence for the validity of Stout's concept is found perhaps in the comparatively rudimentary polity of the Plymouth colony, less structured in its social concerns. It is found, moreover, in the text chosen—from the King James version—by John Cotton for the sermon he preached at Gravesend on the eve of the departure of Winthrop's fleet for the New World: "Moreover I will appoint a place for my people Israel, and I will plant them, that they may dwell in a place of their owne, and move no more." The settlers of the Massachusetts Bay Colony were not solely to follow biblical precepts as individuals but as a people.

In view of the role of the Scriptures in the life of the colonists, it follows that they provided a significant market for Bibles printed in Britain and imported thence. Obviously English and Scottish publishers did in fact keep in view that market overseas, if one judges from the number of the editions of the Bay Psalm Book printed in Britain and found bound with copies of the Bible itself. The first edition of the Bay Psalm Book, the versified paraphrase of the Book of Psalms produced by Richard Mather and others and printed at Cambridge in 1640, is justly acclaimed as the first book (as such) produced in British North America. Less well recognized is that, in addition to the numerous American editions printed between 1647 and 1773, it was also reprinted at London, Oxford, and Edinburgh in some eighteen editions between 1652 and 1759 in formats that permitted its binding along with a Bible, as seen in extant examples. Although it is possible to believe in this context that there was an audience for the Bay Psalm Book in Britain itself—in competition with the vastly popular paraphrase by Sternhold and Hopkins—it is difficult to do so, and that these reprintings were destined for the colonies seems an inescapable inference.

That the Bibles of the American settlers were imported rather than printed here was of course due to the work's special status in possessing Crown Copyright rather than the ordinary copyright provided by the Stationers' Company in London. That is to say, the Bible could be reproduced only by royal license, normally accorded to the King's Printer of the day or to the Universities of Oxford and Cambridge. Whereas a normal copyright applied only within England itself—and American printers were exempt from it and reprinted English works as they saw fit—Crown Copyright was respected in the colonies.

To this there may have been two exceptions, if we are to credit statements made by Isaiah Thomas in his invaluable *History of Printing in America* (1810). Trained as a printer in Boston before removing to Worcester in anticipation of the Revolution, Thomas was intimately informed on the affairs of the trade there. According to Thomas there had been surreptitiously printed at Boston by the firm of Kneeland and Green, around the year 1750, an edition of the Bible with a false London imprint of the King's Printer Mark Baskett, as well as an edition of the New Testament in the shop of Rogers and Fowle. Thomas's source for his information, printers whom he had known, was admittedly second-hand but so knowledgeable was Thomas that it is difficult to discredit his account. The fact remains that, despite concerted searches by alert bookdealers over many decades, no such editions have been identified. In this context it may be noted, however, that though Thomas stated also that the Boston bookseller John Mein had published books which likewise falsely stated that they had been printed in London—to satisfy Bostonians' preference for English products—it was not until 1939 that the editions in question were traced, among them the first American edition of Sterne's *Sentimental Journey*, reprinted in 1767.

That in 1770 John Fleeming in Boston issued a prospectus for a projected edition of the Bible—on the condition that three hundred copies be subscribed—may indeed seem a violation of the Crown Copyright. That he felt free to undertake such an edition suggests, however, that he could call upon the support of royal officials in Boston. Politically a Loyalist who in 1776 was to quit Boston during its evacuation by the British, Fleeming and his partner John Mein had cooperated with the Commissioners for Customs at Boston in undermining the credibility of John Hancock and other patriots in their opposition to import duties. But, in any event, either because too few subscribers were found, or for other reasons, Fleeming's edition was not produced.

It is with nothing less than awe that one turns to what was the first

American Bible, produced at Cambridge in the year 1663 and translated into the language of the Massachusetts Indians by John Eliot. Whatever may be said adversely of the treatment of Indians by English colonists, the work stands out as an example of dedication and concern for them.

Armed with a linguistic aptitude fostered by studies of Greek, Latin, and Hebrew as an undergraduate at Cambridge Univesity, Eliot had become pastor of the church at Roxbury on coming to the New World. From the Indians he gained a knowledge of their language, which first enabled him to preach at the Indian settlements at neighboring Natick and elsewhere. After he published a catechism containing the Lord's Prayer and the Ten Commandments for the Indians' use, Eliot finally undertook the translation of the Bible itself.

Formidable as this undertaking was—it is difficult to imagine one as daunting, given conditions of the day—it may be said that transforming this biblical translation into a printed form was also an impressive achievement. It would not have been possible without the support of the Society for the Promoting and Propagating the Gospel of Jesus Christ in New England, set up in Britain to raise mission funds. Not only did the Society provide money and supplies of type and paper, it also sent out to New England a printer, Marmaduke Johnson, to work with Samuel Green at the press in Cambridge. Since the Bible comprised 1180 pages, each containing some four thousand characters, and since each piece of type was set individually (and was later to be returned to the cases from which it came), the task was a formidable one, compounded by the fact that though there may have been an Indian assistant—the evidence for this is not conclusive—the text was in a tongue alien to its compositors. The sixty copies that survive serve more than as a delight for bibliophiles: they are monuments to the dedication of Eliot himself—and to the craftsmen who under primitive conditions persevered in their task.

That many copies of the Bible were destroyed in the course of King Philip's War in the years 1675–1676 was inevitable, but once again Eliot—now approaching eighty—undertook preparation of a revised edition. The New Testament appeared in 1681 and the Old Testament in 1685.

It was not till 1743 that a Bible in a European language was published in America. The language was German and Christopher Sauer printed it at Germantown outside Philadelphia. A deeply pious individual who had migrated from Germany in 1724 at the age of thirty-one, and after trying his hand as a tailor, clockmaker, and farmer, Sauer finally found his vocation as printer and publisher, chiefly of religious or educational works in German. That Sauer in publishing his German Bible was motivated by religious zeal, rather than by thought of profit, is seen in his saying of it that its price would be eighteen shillings, "but to the poor and needy we have no price." Sauer's publishing of his Bible met a genuine need, demonstrated by the fact that his son of the same name who was his successor in the printing trade, was to publish a second and a third edition of the work in the years 1763 and 1776.

Thus, on the eve of the Revolution it can be said that the two major linguistic groups in the American colonies had access to the Bible in their own tongue: the English, albeit in imported editions, and the Germans, thanks to the two generations of Sauers. How widely disseminated copies of the Bible were among the population at large we have no way today of knowing, and how influential they were was dependent on the degree of literacy among the settlers. But subsequent events leave little doubt that even before the Revolution the Bible possessed paramount importance.

Independence and After

The full impact of the independence that the American colonies gained in 1783 was so broad that for us today it is all too easy to overlook its scope. It meant far more than the institution of self-government and freedom from parliamentary taxation. Released instead were energies, intiative, and skills hitherto inhibited as the new nation, led by figures of extraordinary distinction, abandoned sectional factionalism and implemented opportunities now revealed. Craftspersons and artisans found new stimuli and markets, which gave rise to invention and manufacture. Now the shipowners of New England and elsewhere could send their vessels to the four corners of the globe, while beyond the Alleghenies stretched vast resources to be explored and exploited.

Any doubt about the importance of the Bible for the American people elsewhere than New England is quickly dispelled by the concern shown for its availability following cessation of commerce with Britain at the outbreak of hostilities in 1775. No longer could copies be imported from England—and no longer need the crown copyright be observed. In July 1777 a petition was addressed to the Continental Congress urging it to order "a common Bible to be printed under their Inspection." Consideration of the petition was referred to a committee, headed by John Adams, which in due course received proposals from five Philadelphia printers outlining their financial requirements. But the committee reported, on 11 September, "that they have conferred fully with the printers, &c. in this city, and are of opinion, that the proper types for printing the Bible are not to be had in this country, and that the paper cannot be procured, but with such difficulties and subject to such casualties, as render any dependence on its altogether improper. . . ." Instead, the committee recommended "that Congress . . . order the Committee of Commerce to import 20,000 Bibles from Holland, Scotland [sic], or elsewhere" on the grounds that "the use of the Bible is so universal, and its importance so great." But the occupation of Philadelphia by the British and the removal of the Congress inland to Lancaster appear to have forestalled final action.

In the same year, though no American printer possessed necessary resources of type and paper to undertake publishing the entire Bible, an edition of the New Testament was produced at Philadelphia by Robert Aitken, followed, in 1779, by one issued at Trenton by Isaac Collins, while in Boston Thomas and John Fleet published one in 1780. Other similar New Testaments appeared in the years 1780 and 1781 until finally, in 1782, Robert Aitken published a complete Bible, a modest duodecimo volume, but America's first (if we ignore the hypothetical surreptitious Boston edition of ca. 1750). Of particular note is the fact that it included a recommendation on its behalf from the Continental Congress, an endorsement that might today engender controversy in terms of the Bill of Rights.

Although editions of the New Testament quickly followed Aitken's complete Bible, it was almost a decade later, in the 1790s, before further entire Bibles were produced. Notable among these was that published at Worcester, Massachusetts, by Isaiah Thomas, America's most enterprising and perhaps most distinguished printer of the day. An impressive folio edition, it was made even more so by the inclusion of fifty full-page copperplate illustrations, all by American artists; in the same year Thomas produced a quarto edition, also illustrated. These editions, to be sure, may be categorized as luxury items and perhaps more significant was the small duodecimo Bible that he issued in 1797. For this Thomas in 1790 had ordered, from the foundry of Joseph Fry and Son in London, both the casting of the type and the composition of the entire Bible, to be shipped on to Thomas in Worcester. This spared Thomas the need faced by most American printers of the Bible to distribute the type to free it for other uses, and enabled him to keep the type standing for use in further reprintings, altering only the imprint on the title page. This Thomas did, producing on an annual basis, except for the year 1805, eleven subsequent impressions between 1798 and 1809.

That Thomas's Bibles and those being published concurrently by other printers were the King James version is in no way surprising. More remarkable is the fact that in 1790 Mathew Carey produced an edition of the Douay Bible, though the number of Catholics then in America offered a limited market. Carey, who had fled Ireland for political reasons, was indeed to play an important role as a Philadelphia publisher and as an economist in the course of his long career. In an attempt to broaden advance interest in the Bible itself, Carey, in his *Address to the Subscribers for the Doway Translation of the Vulgate Bible* (Philadelphia, 1790), saw fit, in fact, to include a section appealing "To the Protestants of the United States" expressing the hope "that our subscription list, by uniting together the names of members of various and hitherto-hostile denominations of Christians, will afford one proof—among many that might be produced—of the rapid advances that America has made in the divine principle of toleration." That Carey's hopes were not met seems apparent from the fact that he secured only 471 subscribers, and the edition is the scarcest of all historic American Bibles. Apart from its position as America's first Catholic Bible, the work possesses particular typographic interest, since the type was specially cast by the firm of John Baine and his grandson. The pair had come to Philadelphia in 1787 from Scotland, where the grandfather had earlier provided the type employed in producing the first edition of the *Encyclopaedia Britannica* (Edinburgh, 1771). This contribution was curiously repeated at Philadelphia when the Baines produced, from matrices brought from Scotland, the type for the *Encyclopaedia; or A Dictionary of the Arts and Sciences* (Philadelphia, 1798), which was the first American work in this genre. Surely to few craftspersons can so impressive a function be assigned as to the Baines, in light of these three significant firsts.

That with independence the number of editions produced by American printers, in preference to imported texts, causes no surprise, but further impetus to their proliferation was to come in the first decade of the nineteenth century. This was the phenomenon known as the Second Great Awakening, in sequence to that earlier one of the 1740s, identified with Jonathan Edwards and George Whitefield. No satisfactory explanation of why this religious revival occurred has been advanced: one can only observe that it occasioned an outpouring of concern for religion. This was in contrast to the liberalism and the deism of previous decades, of which the excesses of the French Revolution may have appeared to contemporaries an example of their dangers. It may also be significant that the beginnings of the revival were found among college students, initially at Hampden-Sidney and Washington colleges in Virginia and later at Princeton and at Yale.

Out of this ambience of renewed zeal there developed a variety of institutions, national in scope, to further their causes. The earliest was the American Bible Society, founded in 1816. (In this the society followed the example of the British and Foreign Bible Society, founded in 1804 in London.) There had already existed numerous local Bible societies along the eastern seaboard, the earliest of which had been organized at Philadelphia in 1808, when Elias Boudinot, as president of the New Jersey Bible Society, called for a general meeting in New York on 8 May 1816. The convention was attended by delegates, some sixty in number, of twenty-eight local societies—among them James Fennimore Cooper. Here drawn up was a constitution that established the society, "of which the sole object shall be to encourage a wider circulation of the Holy Scriptures, without note or comment." In essence, the society's function—apart from its purpose—was to provide copies of the Bible for distribution through auxiliary societies.

That the society met an urgent need is apparent from its history as published in 1849, only thirty-three years after its founding. The author, W. P. Strickland, reported that by the end of 1848 "five millions eight hundred and sixty thousand, four hundred and ninety-three copies of Bibles and Testaments" had been distributed.

Though for the secular-minded Strickland's work, *History of the American Bible Society, from Its Organization to the Present Time* (New York, 1849), may appear as only of the most peripheral interest, for the social historian it offers a new dimension to our understanding of the period, since in its activities the society reached out to so many areas of this country's life. The scope of the society's distribution of Bibles is in fact impressive, placing them in prisons, among "seamen and boatmen" (the latter including workers on the building of the Erie Canal and its users), in the Army and the Navy, among Sunday schools, and the like. The fact that the society also distributed to European immigrants on their arrival Bibles in their native tongues perhaps symbolizes in a unique way the role the Scriptures were expected to play in their new life in the New World. Nor was the society restricted to an American audience alone, for Bibles were sent in appropriate languages far afield to all corners of the world. And at the same time support was given for translations of the Bible into foreign languages, their printing, and distribution. It is true that in all of this activity, there were shadows. Certain Baptist churches saw fit to withdraw from association with the Bible Society and to withdraw funds they had contributed. The society could not implement the wishes of the American Anti-Slavery Society to distribute Bibles to slaves in the South, nor could it agree to cooperate with the American Tract Society, despite its belief that the latter was "accomplishing a vast amount of good in substituting for the light, trashy, licentious, and infidel literature of the age, the substantial literature of an elevated morality and a pure Christianity." Although it was typical of the period, the virulence of the anti-Catholic antagonism expressed ("Romanism, the bitterest and most successful of all the enemies of the Bible, is tottering to its fall. The twelve hundred and sixty years of the reign of anti-Christ are drawing to a close") is nonetheless disconcerting. (However, the society has since distributed Catholic versions of the Bible).

That the society within a little more than three decades could so vibrantly establish itself was due, beyond the zeal and dedication of its participants, in good part to a recent technological development in the printing trade: the stereotype plate, which greatly facilitated the production of Bibles. By a process gradually developed by experiment in the eighteenth century and finally refined in England in 1804 by Earl Stanhope, from a text set in type a mold could be made of plaster of Paris. This in turn served as a matrix into which a molten alloy of tin, antimony, and lead was poured. When this cooled, it produced a plate which was then given a nickel surface suitable for printing. The advantages of the process are numerous: the avoidance of the need to tie up substantial quantities of type over a long period of time, the possibility of producing multiple plates, the creation of a printing medium of lighter weight, and one that could without undue risk be moved from place to place and even from city to city. The impact of stereotyping upon the whole printing industry in the nineteenth century was, in fact, a fundamental one.

It was certainly fundamental for the Bible Society, and in itself made possible its very first steps, a circumstance recognized in its constitution. There, after the initial statement of the society's purpose, the document continues: "II. This Society shall add its endeavours to those employed by other societies for circulating the Scriptures throughout the United States and their territories, and shall furnish them with stereotype plates or such other assistance as circumstances may require. . . ."

In recognizing the utility of the stereotype process for furthering

its aims, the society was, to be sure, simply following the example set
in 1812 by the Bible Society of Philadelphia, which was organized in
December 1808 and was the first to be founded in the United States.
That society had imported from London stereotype plates to produce
their Bibles, the earliest such edition in the country. (It might be
noted that the plates by special dispensation were exempted from
import duties, without reference to the First Amendment.) In 1815,
moreover, the firm of D. & G. Bruce in Philadephia published a Bible
from stereotype plates it had produced. David Bruce had gone to
Britain to learn the process, and to him can be credited the introduction of the technique within the United States.

The early history of the American Bible Society was indeed to be
largely that of its acquisition of stereotype plates, their use, and the
construction of a building, its Bible House in Nassau Street in lower
Manhattan. According to Strickland

> a set of stereotype plates of the French Bible was received from the
> British and Foreign Society . . .: this in conjunction with the six sets
> procured by the society, and the one presented by the New York Bible
> Society constituted all they had during the first year of the society's
> operations. At the end of the third year the managers report that they
> had in possession eight sets of stereotype plates for the whole Bible, and
> two sets for the New Testament, in addition to plates for the New
> Testament in Indian and Spanish. In 1822 the society procured two sets
> of stereotype plates of the New Testament in the brevier type and the
> 18mo size. In 1824 a set of stereotype plates was procured for an octavo
> edition of the New Testament in pica type. In 1833 plates were cast for a
> modern Greek Testament.

Though Strickland's catalog continues, the above should suffice to
demonstrate the contribution of stereotyping to the society's achievements. These continue in our own day, summarized in "A Historical
Sketch of the American Bible Society," which appeared in the society's annual report for 1975. Thus, one notes that during the Civil
War not only were 1,466,000 Bibles distributed to Northern soldiers
but also 300,000 to the Southern forces, and similar distributions have
also been made in subsequent wars. With an annual budget of some
thirty-five million dollars the society still pursues the aims for which it
was founded, "that all men and women may read and hear the saving
Word of God and find life in Jesus Christ." This it undertakes both by
providing Bibles for all who need them and by subsidizing translations where none have existed before. A further dimension to its work
is given by participating in the United Bible Societies, founded in
1946, international in scope, and active in 150 countries or territories.

Not the least of the society's undertakings in its early years were its efforts to reach the American Indian, taking up anew the heritage of John Eliot. As early as 1818 it published *The Three Epistles of the Apostle John* as translated by the Moravian missionary C. F. Dencke in the language of the Delaware Indians, and in the same year it reprinted one thousand copies of *The Gospel of Saint John* in the Mohawk language from the 1804 edition published at London by the British and Foreign Bible Society. In 1829 it issued *The Gospel of Saint Luke*, translated by T. S. Harris into the Seneca language.

But if the society was in the forefront in the production and distribution of the Bible, its aims were substantially furthered by those of missionaries, not least among peoples to whom they also brought the ability to read. With independence Americans had taken up, in the revivalist fervor that gave rise to the American Bible Society, a zeal for spreading the Gospel in their own terms. Of the numerous such organizations that were founded as a consequence of this movement, perhaps the most significant and enterprisng was the American Board of Commissioners for Foreign Missions, whose origins closely parallel those of the society.

An echo of the beginnings of the religious revival of the period among college undergraduates is found in that of the American Board, for it was a group of Williams College students, in Williamstown, Massachusetts, in the Berkshire Hills, who first conceived the idea that led to the Board's formation. The group was to go on to the Andover Theological Seminary and to petition the General Association of the Congregational Churches of Massachusetts for approval and support of a missionary society. The consequence of this was the formation in 1810 of the American Board, which was to become a vital force in American missionary activity throughout the world by expanding its original conception as a New England and Congregational institution to one national in scope, with Presbyterian support as well.

From its first undertakings overseas, in India and Ceylon, the Board made full use of the printing press. In fact, according to Clifton Jackson Phillips, in his *Protestant America and the Pagan World*, the Board's presses were initially its most effective instrument.

> In the first years, at least, the Board's educational and informational program was more successful than direct evangelism. Its agents set up presses in both Bombay and Jaffna, Ceylon, from which tracts and Bible translations commenced to pour forth. In 1832 the American Bible Society and the American Tract Society greatly enlarged this work by beginning to subsidize these publications. The printing establishment of the Board's mission in Bombay was for years the largest in India. . . . In the vernacular languages—Tamil and Maratha—the stations in India and

> Ceylon produced a whole library of volumes, including dictionaries and
> lexicons, as well as translations of tracts and the Sciptures. (45)

The printing press was indeed to prove a continuing factor in the
work of the American Board. The first missionaries sent out to the
Hawaiian Islands, in 1820, brought a press with them. Later, from
Hawaii, a press was shipped to the island of Ponape where the first
printing in Micronesia was produced, a rendering of the Lord's Prayer
in the vernacular. In a similar fashion, the earliest printing in the
Pacific Northwest came from a press at the Board's mission there,
again sent from Hawaii.

If the major thrust of the American Board was in its later days to
be overseas, it did not neglect opportunities closer at home and
indeed saw in the American Indian a proper object for attention. Only
five years after sending off its first missionaries to India, the Board
established a mission to the Cherokees at Brainerd, on the southern
boarder of Tennessee. The following year another mission was set up
among the Choctaws in Mississippi, while in 1821 one was established in Arkansas for Cherokees who had migrated there from Tennessee.

Though the missionaries to the Cherokees initially sought to
impose the use of English in the schools they established, this proved
impractical. It remained for a part-Cherokee named Sequoya—known
also as George Guess—with no knowledge of English, to devise an
alphabet for the Cherokee language, comprising eighty-six characters. Cumbersome though this may seem, Sequoya's system won the
approval of the Cherokee chiefs, and what was more important, that of
the American Board, which commissioned the casting of the special
types required, and provided a press. Thus was set up a printing shop
at New Echota, in northern Georgia, which produced the newspaper
the *Cherokee Phoenix*, edited by Elias Boudinot, an Indian who had
taken the name of the instigator of the American Bible Society.

It was in fact to the American Bible Societey that the New Echota
mission turned for assistance in producing a Cherokee translation of
the Gospel of Matthew and appropriated three hundred dollars for
that purpose in 1833. Finally, in 1857, the Society was able to publish
the entire New Testament in that language.

Notwithstanding the American Board's efforts among both the
Cherokees and Choctaws in the Southeastern states, the forced and
shameful removal of the two peoples to west of the Mississippi
brought the Board's activities there to an end. Undaunted, however,
the Board continued elsewhere among Indians. Having in the years

1826–1827 absorbed the functions of the United Foreign Missionary Society—founded by Presbyterians and Dutch and Associated Reformed Churches—the Board now founded missions to the Ojibwas, the Creeks, the Pawnees, the Nez Percés, the Dakotas (Sioux), and others, largely scattered between the upper reaches of the Missouri and Mississippi rivers and the Pacific.

Of these missions, that to the Dakota (Sioux) Indians was to be the most considerable, and its history to be was marked by the most turmoil, due to the intrusion of white settlers intent on seizing lands, which led to the massacre of both whites and Indians and the Sioux War of 1862. Sustaining the Board's efforts were two courageous men, Dr. Thomas S. Williamson and Stephen Riggs, who in 1837 set up a mission at Lac Qui Parle in southwestern Minnesota. They immediately undertook to learn the language of the Sioux with the help of a half-breed fur trader whom they found there, and within two years had translated portions of the Scriptures, which were printed at Cincinnati at the Board's expense. This work was followed again at Cincinnati by translations of Genesis and the Psalms in 1842 and of the Gospels of Luke and John in 1843, while in the latter year the complete Acts of the Apostles was issued by the American Bible Society. And, at long last, thanks to the perseverance of Williamson and Riggs, an edition "containing the greater part of the Old Testament and the New Testament in the Dakota language" appeared in 1877.

In a similar fashion it was the American Board who brought the Bible as well as printing to the Nez Percés Indians in the Pacific Northwest. As a missionary, Henry H. Spalding may not be as well known as his associate Marcus Whitman, whose efforts to preserve the area for the United States and from Catholicism has made him a legendary figure. It was, however, Spalding who was responsible for making the Bible available to his converts in their own language and, at the same time, for introducing printing to what is today the state of Idaho. No sooner had he set up his mission at Lapwai in 1838 than he requested that the American Board supply him with a printing press. To this the Board responded by having a press sent out to Hawaii in 1835 and transshipped to the Northwest, accompanied by a missionary printer, Edwin O. Hall and his wife, for whom Hawaii's climate had proved unsuitable. (The shipping of the press and its furniture was paid for by native Hawaiian women, among them the queen at that time.)

On this press in 1839, Hall initially printed a text in Nez Percé prepared by Spalding that was so unsatisfactory that the whole edition was destroyed. In no way daunted, the two now produced a larger work, *The Nez Percés First Book*, and Spalding and his wife Eliza turned to the translation of the Bible. The first fruit of this effort was the printing in 1845 of the Gospel of Matthew at Clearwater, then in Oregon Territory but today in Idaho. Of this the American Bible Society reprinted an edition in 1871.

* * *

The extent to which the Bible was able to permeate American life in the nineteenth century was of course due not solely to the American Bible Society and the American Board of Commissioners for Foreign Missions. On one hand, the Baptist Church had its own American Bible Union serving much the same ends as the Bible Society. On the other hand, denominations such as the Baptists and Methodists also engaged in missions to the Indians. Nor did the commercial publishers relinquish to the Bible Society the production of Bibles; these provided instead a wide variety of editions, often furnished with maps, illustrations, commentaries, concordances, or the like. Not the least of these features was, perhaps, blank leaves provided for a "family register," designed for the recording of genealogical information. This feature was introduced as early as 1802 by Isaiah Thomas and by Mathew Carey in editions of the Bible produced in that year and continued as an element in later editions from other publishers as well. It may indeed be possible to see in this a symbol of the way in which the Bible provided a nucleus for the American family and its life, for, notwithstanding doctrinal or sectarian differences, from its earliest days the Bible has provided impetus and incentive to the nation, made possible by the skills and enterprise of craftspersons at the printer's case and press and by the use of a continually evolving technology.

A Note on Sources

Of works relating to the Bible in America there is no lack. They tend, however, to fall into two camps, those inspired by theological considerations and those derived from a bibliophile's concern for, in the jargon of our day, the collectible. Of the former, that by the Reverend P. Marion Simms, *The Bible in America; Versions That Have Played Their Part in the Making of the Republic* (New York:

Wilson-Erickson, 1936) is the foremost. It amiably brings together a vast amount of information, but is less than critical of its sources. Nor does it completely supplant the Reverend Dr. John Wright's *Early Bibles of America* (New York: Thomas Whittaker, 1892), though this latter covers a narrower field. On the other hand, the book collector is more likely to turn to Edwin A. R. Rumball-Petre's *America's First Bibles, With a Census of 555 Extant Bibles* (Portland, ME: South-worth-Anthoensen, 1940). Rumball-Petre's approach is that of a knowledgeable antiquarian bookseller, who is concerned to be sure with scarcity, yet brings a healthy skepticism toward bookish myth and tradition.

It is fortunate that historians have at their disposal other objective approaches to the spread of the Bible in printed form. Most comprehensive is the *Historical Catalogue of the Printed Editions of Holy Scripture in the Library of the British and Foreign Bible Society*, compiled by T. H. Darlow and H. F. Moule (London: Bible House, 1903-11). Constituting two of four volumes, the first covers English texts and the second addresses "polyglots and languages other than English." Though limited to the society's own collectiions, so comprehensive are these that the work's usefulness is unsurpassed; however, the English volume has been supplanted by the *Historical Catalogue of Printed Editions of the English Bible, 1525–1961*, revised and expanded by A. S. Herbert from Darlow and Moule (London and New York: British and Foreign Bible Society and American Bible Society, 1968). Complementing this is Margaret T. Hills's *The English Bible in America, A Bibliography of Editions of the Bible and the New Testament Published in America, 1777–1957* (New York: American Bible Society and the New York Public Library, 1961). Both of these volumes are exemplary, combining not only bibliographical information but a wealth of historical annotation not otherwise readily accessible as well.

For the English background to American colonization, Carl Bridenbaugh, author of numerous fine works on the colonial period, has provided in his *Vexed and Troubled Englishmen, 1590–1642* (New York: Oxford University Press, 1968) a rich analysis of the forces that led to the westward migration.

For a full discussion of the Eliot Indian Bible, George Parker Winship's *The Cambridge Press, 1638–1692; A Reexamination of the Evidence Concerning the Bay Psalm Book and the Eliot Indian bible, as Well as Other Contemporary Books and People* (Philadelphia: University of Pennsylvania Press, 1945) is standard. Though originally published in 1810, Isaiah Thomas's *History of Printing in America* was reprinted with corrections and additions at Albany in 1874; of this edition a facsimile was printed in New York in 1967 by Burt Franklin, and an edition edited by Marcus A. McCorison was published by the American Antiquarian Society in 1975. The evidence concerning the surreptitious Bibles said to have been printed at Boston is discussed at length by Harry Miller Lydenberg in "The Problem of the pre–1776 American Bible" in *The Papers of the Bibliographical Society of America*, 48 (1954), 183–195.

The efforts to provide Bibles during the Revolution are described by William H. Gaines, Jr., "The Continental Congress Considers the Publication of a Bible, 1777," *Studies in Bibliography*, 3 (1950–1951), 274–81.

On the religious revival of the early nineteenth century William Warren Sweet's *Religion in the Development of American Culture* (New York: Scribner, 1951; repr., Gloucester, MA: Peter Smith, 1963) has been followed. Howsoever opinionated its author, W. P. Strickland's *History of the American Bible Society, from Its Organization to the Present Time* (New York: Harper & Bros., 1849) is invaluable as a social document; but for a subsequent account of the society's activities one is largely dependent upon its Annual Reports. By contrast, the American Board of Commissioners for Foreign Missions has published numerous works on its activities by geographical area, and a general survey is found in William E. Strong's *The Story of the American Board: An Account of the First Hundred Years of the American Board of Commissioners for Foreign Missions* (Boston: Pilgrim Press, 1910). This may be supplemented by Clifton Jackson Phillips's admirable *Protestant America and the Pagan World* (Cambridge, MA: East Asian Research Center, Harvard University; distr. by Harvard University Press, 1969). Its Chapter III, "The Heathen at Home," is particularly rewarding. The presses established by the Board in Hawaii, etc., are described by Richard E. Lingenfelter in his *Presses of the Pacific Islands* (Los Angeles: Plantin Press, 1967), while that set up in Idaho figures in Roby Wentz's *Eleven Western Presses* (Los Angeles: Los Angeles Club of Printing House Craftsmen, 1956).

For Indian translations of the Bible, along with those described by Simms in his *The Bible in America*, one has recourse to the second volume of Darlow and Moule's *Historical Catalogue,* which has entries by the different languages. More difficult to use with respect to the translations, since they are entered not as such but by name of the translator, is James Constantine Pilling's *Proof-sheets of a Bibliogra-*

phy of the Languages of the North American Indians (Washington: Government Printing Office, 1885; repr., Brooklyn, Central Book, 1968).

WORKS CONSULTED

Bradford, William 1646 *History of Plymouth Plantation*, ed., Worthington C. Ford. London.

Bridenbaugh, Carl 1968 *Vexed and Troubled Englishmen*. New York: Oxford University Press.

Carey, Mathew 1790 *Address to the Subscribers for the Doway Translation of the Vulgate Bible*. Philadelphia.

Hakluyt, Richard 1589 *Principall Navigations, Voiages, and Discoveries of the English Nation . . .* London.

Phillips, Clifton J. 1969 *Protestant America and the Pagan World*. Cambridge: Harvard University Press.

Stout, Harry S. 1982 "Work and Order in Colonial New England." *The Bible in America; Essays in Cultural History*. Nathan O. Hatch and Mark A. Noll, eds. New York: Oxford University Press, 19–38.

Strickland, William P. 1849 *History of the American Bible Society, from its Organization to the Present Time*. New York.

Thomas, Isaiah 1810 *History of Printing in America*. Worcester, MA.

Winslow, Edward 1646 *Hypocrisie Unmasked*. London.

Winthrop, John 1630 *The Humble Request of His Maiesties loyall Subjects, the Governor and Company late gone for Nevv-England; To the rest of their Brethren, in and of the Church of England*. London.

II

Bible Translation by Committees

Keith R. Crim

In the closing decades of the nineteenth century Bible translation in North America was dominated by the influence of scholars in Great Britain, and especially by the English Revised Version of 1881. Since that time translations by private individuals or unofficial groups and translations by committees sponsored by ecclesiastical organizations have created an impressive heritage of new translations and revisions and set new standards for Bible translation. Most of the work was done from the outset by Protestant scholars, but since the Second World War Jewish and Catholic translations have enriched the heritage. Nevertheless, throughout the entire period successive revisions of the King James Bible by committees have been the bench marks of Bible translation in North America.

The work begun by the American Standard Version (1901) was continued by two divergent streams, the Revised Standard Version (1946, 1952, 1955) and the New American Standard Bible (1971). Two similar but contrasting translations broke with the King James tradition in favor of entirely new translations from the original languages: Today's English Version (1968, 1976) sponsored by the American Bible Society, and the New International Version (1973, 1978), prepared under the supervision of the New York International Bible Society (now the International Bible Society). The Jehovah's Witnesses published their own translation, the New World Translation, in 1961, with revisions in 1970 and 1971.

In the 1850s a conservative committee headed by the Baptist scholar J. A. Broadus worked under the American Bible Union of New York to prepare a translation. Portions were published as early as 1852 and the entire New Testament appeared in 1863. Various parts of the Old Testament were also published subsequently: Genesis, Joshua through 2 Kings, Psalms, and Proverbs (Nida). This translation never achieved wide acceptance and is now only of historical interest.

The story of how these translations were produced has been told in various places, most recently in *The English Bible from KJV to NIV* (Lewis, 1981) and *The Word of God* (Bailey, 1982). Both of these works

provide extensive bibliographies and outline the principles and procedures of the respective committees. They also provide critical evaluation of the resultant versions. The major emphasis of this essay will
be placed on criteria by which the translations may be described in
comparable terms, so that each can be evaluated in the light of its
stated purpose and the use for which it is most appropriate. (See
Crim, 1976.) It may never be possible to surmount the practice of
evaluating translations on the basis of the critic's own shibboleths, but
greater scholarly rigor in establishing principles of evaluation is an
attainable goal.

Each translation is made in a specific historical setting and seeks
to meet specific needs of Christian communities. Both the setting and
the felt needs are relevant to an evaluation of the translation. At the
same time, the steps in translation, no matter how much they may
differ in detail, are essentially the same. Identifying criteria implicit
in each of these stages will serve the cause of objectivity.

A. Criteria for Evaluating Bible Translations

The first state involves the determination of the textual basis on
which the translation is to be made. The accumulated evidence of
newly-discovered Greek manuscripts of the Bible was a major stimulus to the British efforts that produced the English Revised Version
of 1881 and the subsequent ASV and RSV, and new Hebrew textual
witnesses had similar impact from the middle of this century forward.
Thus it is necessary to ask how a given version used the available
resources in deciding what text it was translating. The various ancient
translations, especially the Septuagint for the Old Testament, have
also been drawn on in the attempt to determine the textual basis for
the translation.

The next step in translation is establishing the meaning of the text
that has been decided upon. At least three issues are involved. First,
the translator must determine the meaning of individual words and
phrases, taking into consideration the evidence of context, of cognate
languages, and of assumed etymologies, perhaps the most untrust-
worthy evidence of all. The evidence of ancient versions and nonbiblical texts is also used. The second issue is the identification of
basic units of the text and the analysis of the significance of the
transition or lack of transition from one unit to the next. Third, the
governing ideology by which the translation was shaped must also be
taken into account.

Only when the textual basis and its meaning have been decided upon can the translator turn to the question of how best to express that meaning in the target language, in this case English. It is beyond dispute that the form of the original conveys part of the meaning and must therefore be respected in translation. Respect is best shown, however, not by a mechanical reproduction of a Hebrew or Greek literary form. All linguistic and literary forms are language specific, and a familiar form may have an entirely different meaning when it is found in another language. Respect is shown by the identification and adoption of an analogous form in the target language. This is especially evident to those who have lived in bilingual or multilingual situations and are familiar with several cultures.

The best illustration of this is found in the translation of poetry. The translator can rest content with identifying a passage of the Hebrew Bible as poetic, Or, on the other hand, the translator may ask what function the poetic form served in ancient Hebrew and then seek to determine what form in the target language performs that function. The answer may indicate the use of English prose for passages that are poetic in Hebrew. For example, the threats and ultimatums delivered by the Old Testament prophets are far from the content and mood of modern English poetry. At the other extreme, the satirical poem in Isa 23:16 calls for verse form in English, preferably with a jaunty rhyme, and verse form is also demanded by highly lyrical passages, such as many of the passages in Isaiah 40–55. Much of biblical Hebrew poetry, however, is difficult to turn into poetical English. In many instances, to translate poetry as poetry may well involve unfaithfulness to the meaning of the text. It may also mean translating into a form that is not at all poetic in the resultant text. Merely arranging lines on a page in imitation of Hebrew parallelism does not turn rambling prose into English poetry, especially for the average Bible reader, who cannot be expected to know what Hebrew poetry is like.

Form also involves the level of language and historic stage of a given language. When, if ever, are deliberate archaisms appropriate? Is there such a thing as "timeless language"? These issues raise many questions, and in the case of a revision that requires a majority vote to change an earlier translation, these questions are almost insoluble. It must also be asked whether the level of language—varying from formal to informal or even colloquial—should reflect the original, or the needs of the intended audience, or some combination, or both?

Although translators have not always raised these questions explicitly, critics should. Yet once these and similar questions have been posed and answered, there remains a final question to ask of each

translation: Does the translation communicate to its intended readers
the same emotional, volitional, and cognitive message that the original communicated to its readers and hearers? The answer can never
be a simple yes or no, and a fair assessment will always take into the
account the needs of the intended readers and the magnitude of the
task of translation. It is certain that in the present day the communication of the biblical message is best served by the existence of a variety
of translations, by an understanding of what each translation is best
suited to do, and by modesty in criticizing a translation made by
someone else.

The above program for evaluating translations demands fuller
explication than is possible in a single chapter, but it is the theoretical
basis for the following discussion.

B. Revisions of the King James Bible

1. The American Standard Version

The American Standard Version of 1901 cannot be understood
apart from the English Revised Version (1881–1885). A committee to
prepare a revision of the King James Bible was authorized by the
upper house of the Convocation of Canterbury in 1870 and non-
Anglicans were later added to it. An invitation was issued to American
divines to "cooperate," but because of the distance involved the
Americans under the leadership of the brilliant and energetic Phillip
Schaff had little impact on the British committee's work. Some alternate translations preferred by the American committee were included
in an appendix to the English Revised Version when it was published
in 1881, but the American translators were dissatisfied with the way
these alternatives were presented. Eventually the results of the
American committee's work were made available in the American
Standard Version of 1901. It departed from the ERV at many points,
but essentially it shared the ERV's strengths and weaknesses. Schaff
(1883) has described the work of the two committees and the issues
that divided them.

The textual studies of Westcott and Hort, though highly influential, had not gained total acceptance. Both committees were eclectic
in their approach and tried to judge each passage on its merits. In the
Old Testament they were loyal to the Masoretic Text, and only rarely
did they prefer one of the ancient versions to the MT. Throughout
their work they acted responsibly in dealing with the best evidence
available.

As for the interpretation of meaning, they were conservative.

Extensive marginal notes supply alternate renderings, which in a less cautious time might well have been incorporated into the text. The ERV and the ASV strove for "concordant consistency," the principle by which a given lexeme is always translated by the same English term, regardless of context. This tended not only to make the translation harder to read enjoyably, but also to skew the meaning.

It is in the realm of English usage, however, that the ASV failed to win lasting approval. Too great fidelity to the syntax and style of the Greek and Hebrew languages produced an English that gave the reader little pleasure and at times required such close attention to the wording that it is difficult to keep the progression of thought in mind. Many archaisms found in the KJV were avoided, but the reluctance to find natural English equivalents for biblical words and phrases reinforced the archaic language that remained. Two examples among many where the KJV is freer and expresses the meaning more faithfully and in more natural English are Matt 27:44 and Gal 2:20. In both instances the KJV departed from a literal rendering in the interests of clarity and force, but the ERV and its successors reverted to a literal rendering.

One significant point of difference between the ERV and the ASV was the rendering of the divine name. ERV retained the traditonal "LORD," while ASV used "Jehovah" throughout. Quite apart from etymological and other linguistic considerations, the name "Jehovah" has not appealed to the majority of Bible readers.

2. The New American Standard Bible

The ASV served its purpose, but it has given way to two contrasting revisions in the KJV tradition, the New American Standard Bible and the Revised Standard Version. The NASB is much closer to the ASV than is the RSV. This was deliberate. The Lockman Foundation of La Habra, California, sponsor of the NASB, sought to preserve the best features of the ASV while extending its usefulness through limited modernization and simplification of its language. Care has been taken not to reveal the names of the translators, in order that the value of the translation not be judged by the reputation of those who prepared it.

Lewis (168–174) cites extensive evidence for the textual base of NASB, for its interpretation of the meaning of the text, and for its wording. Newman (74–97) gives a negative evaluation of the NASB, illustrating his conclusions by numerous quotations. Taken together, the careful work of these two scholars provides a balanced picture.

The NASB's popularity is largely as a study Bible for those who want a literal rendering that reflects linguistic features of Hebrew and Greek and almost always uses the same English translation for any given lexeme. The impact of the NASB extends beyond the English-speaking world because the Lockman Foundation has used it as a standard for similar translations in other languages as well.

3. The Revised Standard Version

During the half century that elapsed between the publication of the ASV in 1901 and that of the RSV New Testament in 1946, private translations had prepared the way for more radical departure from the KJV. In addition there was a greater willingness on the part of the Bible-reading public to accept changes in language. The revisers could not know that they were working at the beginning of a period of even greater change, and that by the end of the 1980s the RSV would seem the bulwark of conservative translation practice.

Separate committees worked on the Old Testament and on the New, and another committee on the Apocrypha. Their methods of work have been described elsewhere (Weigle; Branton). These committees included many of the ablest and best-known biblical scholars in North America, and the statements of their principles in the preface to the 1946 edition of the NT and the 1952 edition of the Bible show a sound grasp of the issues they confronted. *An Introduction to the RSV of the OT* (1952) was compiled by the chair, Luther A. Weigle, and several members of the committee contributed. Over the years younger scholars have been added to the committees as vacancies occurred.

In the New Testament the translators used the latest textual evidence, but felt free to decide each passage on its merits. Footnotes are a helpful guide to their procedures. They printed the longer ending to the Lord's Prayer (Matt 6:13), the ending of Mark's Gospel (Mark 16:9–20), and John 7:53–8:11 in footnotes in small italics. The Catholic edition of the RSV (1965) restored the latter two passages to the text. Later editions of the RSV also restore these passages, but set them off in such a way as to indicate that they rest on inferior textual evidence. Throughout the Bible the evidence of the ancient translations was considered, and in many passages "other authorities" are cited in footnotes.

Footnotes in the OT indicate passages where the ancient versions are preferred to the Masoretic Text, where conjectural emendations are made, and where the meaning of the Hebrew is "uncertain." In both Testaments, notes present possible alternate readings, and there are miscellaneous notes. For example, the revisers regularly identified Jesus by name in preference to the "he" indicated by the Greek in instances where the antecedent was not immediately clear. When they did so they felt obliged to point this out in a footnote. This of course is not a textual issue, but an indication of loyalty to the structure of the original language, where the relationship of a pronoun to its antecedent is often quite different from that demanded by English usage.

In dealing with the meaning of the text the revisers were conservative. Heated criticism of the RSV to the contrary, the revisers were conscientious in presenting what the text seemed to them to mean rather than what they or their critics wished it meant. In particular they were careful not to force the Old Testament into uniformity with the New (e.g. Isa 7:14). In addition, evidence from the Ugaritic literature was used sparingly, and the careful reader of the RSV gets the impression that pet theories of interpretation were not welcomed, but that the revisers sought to be in the mainstream of biblical interpretation.

The greatest strength of the RSV when it first appeared—the way in which it used the English language—has over the years become its greatest drawback, as translations employing more nearly contemporary language have appeared. The preface (1952) made much of the avoidance of archaisms, and yet the RSV retained the archaic second person singular pronouns and the accompanying verb forms in speaking to the deity. The preface also said, "We have resisted the temptation to use phrases that are merely current usage, and have sought to put the message of the Bible in simple, enduring words that are worthy to stand in the great Tyndale–King James tradition." Thus as a revision rather than a fresh translation, the RSV, like all revisions, has to leave much intact while making specific changes. The resultant language fluctuates between the seventeenth century and the early twentieth century, but belongs fully to no period in the history of the language.

Again and again the revisers relied on the form of the Hebrew at the expense of idiomatic English, even in passages where familiarity with the old wording was not an issue. Judg 3:6 is an example of the use of pronouns without benefit of antecedents. In 1 Kgs 7:25, "all their hinder parts were inward" is an unidiomatic way of saying, "they were facing outward." Such examples could be multiplied.

Poetic passages were printed in a distinctive form, unlike any widely used form of English poetry, but a general approximation of the form of Hebrew poetry. Because this practice was followed throughout the OT, some forty percent of the text is given in this form. In the NT, poetic passages quoted from the OT are printed in the same form, and so are such NT hymns as Rev 4:11; 5:9–10; and 7:15–17 and the hymns in Luke 1–2.

From its first publication to the present day the RSV has been immensely popular, appearing in numerous editions and formats. As already noted, some specific changes were made for the Catholic edition (1965) and a few alterations were introduced in all editions. An extensive revision has been in preparation for many years. In the 1980s the most serious criticism to be raised is that the RSV used "sexist language," that is, male-oriented, noninclusive language, both for humans and for the deity. The committee has been taking this into account in its ongoing revision. In addition, a version of the lectionary, based on the RSV but seeking to use more nearly inclusive language, was prepared by a special committee of the National Council of Churches, which holds the copyright to the RSV, and the *Inclusive Language Lectionary, Readings for Year A* was published in 1983. The lectionary has been criticized on doctrinal grounds and also for awkwardness in the use of the English language.

The RSV has established itself as the version routinely cited by writers in the field of biblical studies and the version most widely used in public worship. No modern translation has challenged the RSV's dominance in these areas.

C. New Translations

1. Today's English Version

By the early 1960s the American Bible Society had become interested in preparing "common language" versions in several modern languages. These were to be new translations based on the best modern scholarship in both biblical studies and linguistics. The level of language was to be that which is common to the vast majority of users of the language, avoiding literary language at one extreme and colloquial language at the other. The first such translation was the Spanish *Version Popular,* published in 1965. The following year *Good News for Modern Man,* a translation of the New Testament known as Today's English Version, made its appearance and proved to be highly popular. This was the work of one person, Robert G. Bratcher, but for the Old Testament a committee of six was formed, with Bratcher as the chairman. A smaller committee later translated the deuterocanonical books. The OT appeared in 1976 and the deuterocanonicals in 1978.

The TEV was the first Bible translation into English to be preceded by a linguistic rationale for its methods. Eugene A. Nida, long concerned with the theory of translation, developed a model based primarily on transformational grammar (1966). A subsequent series of volumes applied Nida's principles not only to English but to German, French, and other languages as well. The translators of TEV were chosen for their adherence to those principles and for their experience in multilingual cultures as much as for their biblical expertise. A consultant from the British and Foreign Bible Society worked with the committee and prepared the basis for the subsequent British edition of the TEV Bible.

Although during this same period the Bible Societies were also involved in textual projects related to both the Old Testament and the New, TEV did not seek to break new ground textually. The textual basis for the NT was the United Bible Society's Greek New Testament (1968). The Old Testament translators seldom departed from the Masoretic Text, but they noted those instances in which they did. In some difficult passages such as Ezek 27:17–19; 17:5; 16:15, they omitted one or more words whose meaning is unclear rather than resorting to conjecture. In other places they relied on versional evidence.

In interpreting the meaning of the text, TEV also was cautious and claimed no new insights. Where this translation sought to be distinctive was in presenting the meaning in English. A basic principle was that meaning is paramount and form must follow and reinforce meaning. A translation that sought to reproduce the form of the Greek and Hebrew has been called a "formal correspondence" version in contrast to the attempt of TEV to achieve "dynamic equivalence." This term may be paraphrased as the attempt to communicate the biblical message in such a way that it will have the same impact on its readers today that it had on its original readers and hearers.

No arbitrary limits were placed on vocabulary, but preference was given to simpler and more common words and phrases. Traditional religious vocabulary was often expressed in less complex language, for example, "to be justified" was rendered as "to be put right with God" (Rom 3:21–31 etc.). The translators tried to find a clear and natural way to express the message in contemporary English, while adding nothing to and taking nothing away from the meaning. Unusual words were explained in a footnote or in a glossary. Long sentences were broken into smaller units, and transitional devices were supplied to mark the relationship between sentences and from one paragraph to the next.

Especial attention was paid to the translation of poetry. In the prophetic books whenever the subject matter was not considered appropriate to contemporary canons of English poetry the passage was rendered as prose, regardless of the form of the Hebrew original (e.g., Isa 9:8–21 et passim). The aphorisms in Proverbs 10–30 were translated as proverbs, not as verse. The Psalms were given poetic form, with the needs of public worship in mind. In Job and the Song of Songs special care was taken to ensure that all passages sounded rhythmic and poetical when read aloud, and in Job the members of parallel lines were rearranged to avoid the monotony that can result when long passages are rendered with strict literal imitation of Hebrew parallelism. The translators reasoned that parallelism as a poetic device is specific to Hebrew and creates quite another effect when used in English, where the conventions of poetry are so different. This was consistent with the principle of dynamic equivalence.

The NT went through three revisions before the publication of the entire Bible in 1976, and various minor changes have been made since that time. As the issue of male-oriented language came more and more to the fore, the committee modified the translation to achieve a more nearly inclusive language, but no such changes were made in reference to the deity.

The TEV has been especially popular among children and young people, new Christians, and people who use English as a second language.

2. The New International Version

The New International Version is a new translation prepared by conservative Protestant scholars, selected largely from the faculty of seminaries and universities and representing a number of denominations. The New York Bible Society (later the New York International Bible Society and now the International Bible Society) sponsored the work of translation and gave direction and oversight to its progress. Since publication the NIV has achieved wide acceptance in conservative Protestant circles and seems destined to displace most other translations in those circles. Its main advantages are conservative backing and a readable but dignified style.

The preface to the Bible (1978, viii) states that "the translators were united in their commitment to the authority and infallibility of the Bible as God's Word in written form." Bratcher has given a detailed analysis of the principles that guided the translators (153–157). Of particular note is the classic Reform stance indicated by the appeal to the "high view of scripture as set forth in the Westminster

Confession of Faith, the Belgic Confession, and the Statement of Faith of the National Association of Evangelicals."

In dealing with the textual questions the translators stayed well within the mainstream of recent scholarship. In the OT, versional evidence was followed in a number of passages, whereas in the NT there are indications that the textus receptus was not totally ignored (1 John 5:7–8). Perhaps also the preference for the "easier reading" in John 7:8, "not yet" instead of the more widely accepted "not," is a sign of preference for the textus receptus, though it may be due to the stress on the "unity and harmony" of the Bible. Taken as a whole the NIV represents a responsible and careful consideration of textual issues.

In its approach to understanding the meaning of the Bible, NIV was guided by the belief in the harmony of the OT and the NT. Thus the OT was translated to agree with the wording of the NT. A classic test may be found in Isa 7:14, which reads in part, "the virgin will be with child." There are three footnotes to this verse, but none of the three deals with the issue of "virgin" versus "young woman." The Greek of Matt 1:23 was determinative for the understanding of this verse in Isaiah. Psalm 16:10 reads, "nor will you let your Holy One see decay." A footnote gives the alternate reading "faithful one" (cf. RSV "godly one"). "Holy One" illustrates two points: literal agreement with the text of Acts 2:27 and the capitalization of both words to mark the term as a prophecy of Jesus Christ. The same commitment to the Messianic interpretation of the OT can be discerned in the capitalization of terms in Psalm 2. Although it is not particuarly good translation practice to let spelling conventions carry major components of meaning it is probably effective for students of the Bible who are familiar with that practice through their reading of other religious books.

The quality of the language is consistent. It is contemporary, free of archaisms, and slightly solemn. Peter's rebuke of Simon the Sorcerer (Acts 8:20) and Saul's angry outburst against Jonathan (1 Sam 20:30) are almost identical with RSV in their restraint. Bratcher comments on this similarity (163–65). He also points out the similarity to RSV in the misleading literalism involved in "daughter of Sidon" (Isa 23:12 et passim) and "horn" as a symbol of strength. He also calls attention to the strange translation of 1 Sam 14:19, "Withdraw your hand." Hardly any native speaker of English could understand what that means.

In most places, however, the translators felt free to abandon literalism and express the meaning clearly. The long sentence in 1 John 1:1–3 is broken into four sentences and the clause "this we proclaim" has been moved from v 3 to v 1. The troublesome term "flesh" was translated as "sinful nature" (Rom 8:3–5; Gal 5:16–24; Col 2:13), "outward and physical" (Rom 2:28), "body" (Eph 2:11), "race" (Rom 9:3) and "man" (Matt 16:17; Gal 1:16). But the literal "flesh and blood" is retained in 1 Cor 15:50; Eph 6:12 and Heb 2:14, where the meaning is not clear. And in John 1:14, "The word became flesh" and John 3:6, "flesh gives birth to flesh," no use was made of the translation skills evident in other passages in NIV. This fluctuation between literalness and dynamic equivalence may be the result of a difference in policy and practice from one group of translators to another.

3. The New World Translation

In 1961 the Watchtower Bible and Tract Society of New York, one of the corporate bodies of the Jehovah's Witnesses, published the New World Translation of the Holy Scriptures prepared by a committee whose members were not identified. The word "Testament" and "covenant" are avoided when referring to the two divisions of the Bible, which are called the "Hebrew-Aramaic Scriptures" and the "Christian Greek Scriptures." The NWT of the latter first appeared in 1950, and that of the former division appeared in five successive volumes between 1953 and 1960. A revision was published in 1970.

According to the foreword of the 1961 edition, the translation was made from the original languages. It is not always possible to determine the textual bases of the NWT, but Matt 6:13; Mark 16:9–20; and John 7:53–8:11 are dealt with the same way as they are in the RSV. In the OT, the translators followed the MT closely, even where it is difficult to make sense out of it (e.g., Ezek 16:15, 16, 30).

Because Witnesses reject many traditional beliefs and usages, the translators expressed their interpretation of the text in striking ways. The word "church" has been consistently replaced by "congregation." In Phil 1:1 the church officers are "overseers" and "ministerial servants." An appendix discusses the translation of "soul," and the abode of the dead, which is rendered as "Sheol," "Hades," or "Gehenna," depending on the original text. Especial care is devoted to the name of God, in order to show that *ha'elōhîm* should be rendered as "the [true] God." "Jehovah" is used, not only for the tetragrammaton but also for *kyrios* in the NT whenever it refers to God. Matt 22:44 reads "Jehovah said to my Lord . . ." An appendix lists a total of 237 occurrences of "Jehovah" in the NT. The passage most strikingly influenced by doctrinal presupposition is John 1:1, "the Word was with God, and the Word was a god."

The Psalms, Job, Lamentations, and a few isolated poetic passages are printed in parallel lines. The first line of each verse begins immediately after the verse number and subsequent lines are indented. This alerts the reader that the Hebrew original is poetic in form, but the prevalence of awkard sentence structures keeps the translation from sounding poetic.

The NWT is essentially a concordant translation, each lexeme being translated by the same word or phrase in every instance. It also attempts to reflect subtleties of syntax, such as inceptive and progressive aspects of verbs. Genesis 1 and Ephesians 6 are good examples of the awkward language that results. In many instances the word order is unnatural. Job 20:3 reads, "An insulting exhortation to me I hear." And intensives such as "my very flesh," "even I," "my very eyes" occur so often as to become annoying.

Periodicals published by Jehovah's Witnesses regularly quote other modern versions, and there seems to be a tendency to play down the NWT in dealing with outsiders. Perhaps this version will eventually cease to play a major role even for Witnesses.

WORKS CONSULTED

Bailey, Lloyd, ed. 1982 *The Word of God*.

Branton, James R. 1962 "Versions, English. *Interpreter's Dictionary of the Bible*, 4:760–71.

Bratcher, Robert 1982 "The New International Version," in Lloyd Bailey, ed., *The Word of God*, 152–136.

Crim, Keith 1976 "Versions, English," *The Interpreter's Dictionary of the Bible*, Suppl. vol, 933–38.

Lewis, Jack 1981 *The English Bible from KJV to NIV*.

Newman, Barclay 1982 "The New American Standard Bible," in Lloyd Bailey, ed., *The Word of God*, 74–97.

Nida, Eugene, ed. 1972 *The Book of A Thousand Tongues*, United Bible Societies, rev. ed.

Schaff, Phillip 1883 *A Companion to the Greek Testament and the English Version*.

The United Bible Societies 1968 *The Greek New Testament*.

Weigle, Luther 1952 *An Introduction to the RSV of the Old Testament*.

III

Bible Translation by American Individuals

Harold P. Scanlin

In the long history of the translation of the Bible, the most influential and enduring translations are those done by committees or groups of scholars. So, for example, the Septuagint, the first translation of the Hebrew Bible into Greek, begun in the third century B.C., was named for the seventy translators on the "committee." The virtue of this kind of translation was emphasized by Aristeas in his famous letter to Philocrates. The seventy (LXX) carried out their work, "making all details harmonize by mutual comparisons" (Hadas: 219). Yet many individuals, under a variety of motivations, have disregarded the evident advantages as well as the restraints of committee work and made their own translations. Sometimes historical circumstances made it necessary for translation pioneers to work independently. Martin Luther did much of the work for producing his German New Testament while cloistered in Wartburg. William Tyndale revised and perfected his New Testament while exiled from his native England during his travels on the Continent.

With the exception of Luther's Bible and some other Reformation-motivated translations into a variety of Indo-European languages, the efforts of individual translators are better known for the influence they had on the work of major committee translations. Individuals were quicker to respond to immediate needs for new and better translations. Not bound by tradition or ecclesiastical restraint, they were able to break new ground in applying the results of biblical study to translation. They were often the first to use principles of translation that only later found their way into the major translations.

With the freedom and creativity of individual translators come the excesses and failures of their work. Some translations are based on mistaken notions of biblical exegesis or some peculiar theory regarding the original languages of the Bible. Other translations are produced for the sole purpose of promoting some particular doctrine or system of religious views. These efforts are rightly relegated to the role of minor idiosyncracies in the long history of Bible translation. Yet these, and all individual American translations are testimony to a

vigorous and variegated history of religion in America. In the following necessarily brief sketch of more than seventy individual translations of at least an entire Testament done by Americans since 1808,
the impact of the Bible in American can be seen. The number, if not
the variety, of individual translations would be expanded beyond the
scope of this survey if translations limited to individual books of the
Bible or translations made in conjunction with Bible commentaries
were included. A few pioneering efforts of this sort will be mentioned
in connection with the influential role they played.

First Efforts in Bible Translation

A response to the unique needs of the New World produced the
first translation of any part of the Bible and the first book published in
English-speaking America. The metrical Psalter rendered by the
Separatist Henry Ainsworth, which was popular with some colonists,
was not quite satisfactory for use in the Massachusetts Bay Colony. So
"the chief Divines" of the Bay Colony decided to do their own
translation. The result of their labors, the famous *Bay Psalm Book*,
was "an expression of the Colony's own brand of Calvinism—as a
gesture designed to demonstrate that its people were congrega-
tionalists and, at the same time, loyal members of the Church of
England" (Haraszti: 6–9). The work of translation was divided among
the chief clergy of the colony, including Richard Mather, John Cotton,
and John Eliot, all of whom were able to work directly with the
Hebrew text. Eliot later achieved fame as a translator by producing
the first American missionary Bible translation in the language of the
Massachusetts Indians (1663).

The translators of the *Bay Psalm Book* were well aware of the
major problem that confronts all translators: balancing exegetical
accuracy with naturalness in the receptor language. They explained
how they treated the problem in the preface: "Neither let any think,
that for the meetre sake wee have taken liberty or poeticall licence to
depart from the true and proper sence of Davids words in the hebrew
verses, noe; but it hath beene one part of our religious care and
faithful indeavour, to keepe close to the original text. . . . As for our
translations, wee have with our english Bibles (to which next to the
Originall wee have had respect) used the Idioms of our owne tongue
in stead of Hebraismes, lest they might seeme english barbarismes"
(**3). Their application of this latter principle led them to render the
same Hebrew word with different English words when dictated by
contextual meaning or metrical requirements. This included the fre-

quent use of "Jehovah" for "LORD." Modern critics have generally agreed that they were not altogether successful in producing natural English poetry. Yet the popularity of the *Bay Psalm Book* is attested by the fact that it remained in use for many years.

In light of the intense interest in the Bible among the English colonists, it is surprising that over 150 years passed before the first Bible translation prepared by an American individual appeared in 1808. But with the publication of the Charles Thomson Bible, except for the 1810's, every decade since has seen the appearance of at least one new translation.

Charles Thomson's (1729–1824) translation of the Bible is notable in many ways, perhaps the least of which is its place as the first translation by an American. Thomson had no formal theological or linguistic training. Although he considered himself to be a Christian, he did not express any strong commitment to the church or espouse any special doctrinal belief. A translator may lack one of these two ingredients, but rarely both. Thomson began his career as a Latin teacher in a school run by Benjamin Franklin. He later became a prosperous Pennsylvania businessman. He took an active part in the political concerns of the colonies, which ultimately led him to be elected secretary of the Continental Congress in 1774. "For fifteen years he sat at the secretarial table, listening to the debates, minuting the birth-records of a nation." (Reumann: 124) Those turbulent years left little time for pursuing the study of Greek and translating the Bible, but when he retired in 1789, he devoted the next two decades to the preparation of his Bible translation, first published in 1808 when he was nearly eighty.

Thomson continued to pursue his interest in Bible study by preparing a *Synopsis of the Four Evangelists*, published in 1815 (Philadelphia: Wm. M'Culloch). Thomas Jefferson commended Thomson's *Synopsis:* "This work bears the stamp of that accuracy which marks everything from you, and will be useful to those who, not taking things on trust, recur for themselves to the fountain of pure morals" (Reumann: 130).

Thomson's translation of the Old Testament lays claim to another first: it is the first translation of the Greek Septuagint into any modern European language. To this day only one other English translation of the Septuagint has been published. It is not certain why Thomson chose to translate from the ancient Greek text rather than the Hebrew. However, Thomson observed that the New Testament writers generally quoted the Old Testament in a form more closely resembling the Septuagint than the Hebrew Bible. Thomson's primary interest in the New Testament and its moral teachings probably led him to translate from the Septuagint, since he could not find an English translation of this ancient version (Reumann: 128–29). Thomson used the Field edition of the Septuagint (Cambridge, 1665) for his Old Testament translation. This edition arranged the books in the order of the Hebrew canon and lacked the Apocrypha.

Thomson's Old Testament has been reprinted twice, by S. F. Pells (London: Skeffington, 1904) and by C. A. Muses (Indian Hills, Colorado: Falcon's Wing Press, 1954); the former is a reprint, whereas the latter includes some revisions by the editor. Both reprints were motivated by the view that the Septuagint is a more accurate representation of the original text of the Old Testament than the Massoretic Text of the Hebrew Bible. This view is rejected by virtually all modern textual scholars, even though it is recognized that the Septuagint may preserve some readings superior to those in the Massoretic Text, and as Thomson himself observed, is frequently the form of the text cited by the New Testament writers.

Thomson's translation was published by Jane Aitken, who succeeded her father Robert, the Philadelphia printer who produced the first English Bible published in America. The British crown did not charter any colonial printers to produce the King James Version. But the United States Congress, under the signature of Charles Thomson, secretary, authorized Robert Aitken to publish the Bible in the King James Version, which appeared in 1782, though the "authorization" came apparently after the publishing project was already underway.

Many Americans recognized that a revision of the King James Version was necessary. This need was based primarily on two factors: first, the English language had undergone many changes since 1611; second, evidence regarding the Greek text of the New Testament, based on the study of manuscripts and a refinement of the canons of textual criticism, which would ultimately lead to the overthrow of the textus receptus, needed to be applied to translations. Among some, there was also the feeling that certain theological matters were inadequately or inappropriately handled in the King James Version.

Abner Kneeland (1774–1844), a minister of the Universalist Church, made an effort to deal with all of these issues by publishing a two-volume, Greek-English New Testament in 1823. In the same year, he also issued his English translation separately. His Greek text was essentially that of J. J. Griesbach, whose critical edition of the Greek New Testament marked the beginning of scientific textual criticism of the New Testament. Griesbach enclosed in brackets passages such as John 5:3b–4 and John 7:53–8:11 and relegated other texts such as 1 John 5:7b to footnotes. Kneeland was not the first to publish the Griesbach edition in America; Wells and Hilliard of Cambridge, Massachusetts, produced a manual edition in 1809. But Kneeland's diglot edition undoubtedly served to introduce the discoveries of contemporary textual scholars to a much wider audience. Kneeland's English translation, although it differed little in style from the King James Version, reflects the textual base of Griesbach's edition. A special concern of the translator was his belief that certain Greek terms were inaccurately translated in the other versions. Notably, *haîdēs*, *aiōnios*, and *diabolos* were generally translated "hades," "aionian" (instead of "everlasting"), and "impostor."

John Gorham Palfrey (1796–1881), an ordained Unitarian minister and professor of Sacred Literature at Harvard, published a revised New Testament in 1828 as a response to the need of his students to have before them an English translation that reflected the advances in the study of the Greek text. Palfrey says in the advertisement of his New Testament: "the editor . . . has exactly reprinted the Common Version, except in places where the Greek text, from which that version was made, is now understood to have been faulty. In other words, he has aimed to present the Common Version precisely as it would have been if the translators could have had access to the standard text of Griesbach, instead of the adulterated text of Beza. In the translations which he has introduced to correspond to the amended Greek, it has been his careful endeavor to imitate the style of the received version . . ."(8). This seems to be an accurate description of Palfrey's work. The text differs little from the King James Version.

Rodolphus Dickinson (1787–1863), a rector of the Episcopal Church, sought to make the New Testament more readable in content and form in his translation issued in 1833. It was based on Griesbach's Greek text and in that way differed little from the work of Kneeland and Palfrey. However, his translation attempted to break significantly from the tradition of the King James Version. In his preface, Dickinson declared "The lapse of centuries has produced a revolution in the English language, requiring a correspondent change in the version of the scriptures; and I may add, that the errors in grammar and rhetoric, the harsh and indelicate expressions, dispersed through the generally adopted text, demand amendment" (vii). Dickinson's translation is significant more for his success in articulating the need for a fundamental departure from the style of the King James Version than for his ability to produce a good translation. The *American Monthly Review* (March 1833) pronounced "a verdict of unqualified condemnation," on the basis of Dickinson's style (Cheek: 110). Several examples from his translation will confirm this early verdict: ". . . when Elizabeth heard the salutation of Mary, the embryo was joyfully agitated. . . ." (Luke 1:41); "Be not therefore inquisitive, what you shall eat, or what you shall drink: nor be in unquiet suspense" (Luke 12:29).

Dickinson undoubtedly considered his florid style the literary standard of the day, though it hardly communicated effectively. One sentence in his preface (xi–xii) contains 601 words, although he did manage to render Ephesians 1:3–14 in one sentence of 268 words, as compared with the two sentences in the King James Version.

Noah Webster (1758–1843), the famous lexicographer whose name is virtually synonymous with the American dictionary, considered his revision of the King James Version "the most important enterprise of my life." Webster, a Congregational layman, had advocated a revision of the King James Version, attempting to gain the support of distinguished American scholars such as Moses Stuart, as well as the American Bible Society. Discouraged by an apparent lack of interest on their part, he undertook the project on his own, resulting in the publication of his translation of the Bible in 1833.

Webster clearly set forth the threefold aim of his revision in the preface. Changes in the English language required substitution for archaic words and phases that "are not understood by common readers, who have no access to commentaries, and who will always compose a great proportion of the readers." Errors in grammar also needed correction. His revision also called for "the insertion of euphemisms, words and phrases which are not very offensive to delicacy, in the place of such as cannot, with propriety, be uttered before a promiscuous [i.e., heterogeneous] audience." Webster's bowdlerizing, for example, changed "they bruised the teats of their virginity" to "they were first corrupted" in Ezekiel 23:3. Apparently, the book did not sell as well as Webster hoped, since he authorized price reductions from $3.00 to $2.00 and later to $1.50, although the city schools of New Haven adopted his text.

"Immersion" Versions and Other Alterations to the KJV

Several other translations published in the nineteenth century were essentially revisions of the King James Version, aiming at modernization of style, and occasionally introducing a particular theory of the individual translator. For example, David Bernard and "several biblical scholars" published a Bible in 1842 that included the following revisions: proper names were spelled consistently in both Old and New Testaments, archaic and "indelicate" words were changed, errors in grammar in the King James Version were corrected, and "several most important words" that were left untranslated in the King James Version were "translated." This is a reference to a debate that was current in the nineteenth century about *baptizō*. Immersionists argued that earlier translators simply transliterated the Greek *baptizō* into "baptize." Since they held that *bapitzō* could only mean "immerse," translations should render the Greek accordingly. This is the policy followed in the Bernard translation.

Several other "immersion" versions appeared in this era. Perhaps the most significant and influential one was by Alexander Campbell (1826). Since the significance and impact of the Campbell version went beyond the immersion issue, it will be considered later in greater detail. Other nineteenth-century New Testament "immersion" versions were produced by Nathan N. Whiting (1849), Spencer H. Cone and William H. Wyckoff (1850), H. T. Anderson (1864), Samuel Williams (1881), Cortes Jackson (1883), and J. W. Hanson (1884-1885). Two other "immersion" versions appeared in the twentieth century: Adolphus S. Worrell (1904) and George N. Le Fevre (1928).

Nathan Whiting, an Adventist, followed the greek text of J. A. H. Tittmann, as revised by Augustine Hahn and edited by Edward Robinson. This was a popular manual edition of the Greek New Testament in mid-nineteenth-century America. The translation shows little, if any, influence of Whiting's Adventist beliefs. In fact, it is essentially a revised King James Version in paragraph form with "controverted" texts placed in brackets.

The "immersion" version prepared by Spencer H. Cone (1785–1855) and William Wyckoff (1807–1876) was intended to serve as an example of a New Testament that would meet the needs of those who wanted an "immersion" translation until a completely new translation could be produced. Cone was Corresponding Secretary of the American Bible Society from 1833 to 1836, when he withdrew to form the American and Foreign Bible Society. This he did when the American Bible Society refused to publish an "immersion" version, which they considered sectarian. Later, when the American and Foreign Bible Society would not authorize the preparation of a new "immersion" translation, Cone was instrumental in founding the American Bible Union in 1850. Cone and Wyckoff hastily produced an "immersion"-modified King James Version that same year to supply the need until the American Bible Union Version could be produced. The story of this committee-produced translation is told in the essay by Keith Crim in this volume, (x ref).

Although Henry Tompkins Anderson (1812–1872) declared that his "immersion" translation was a completely new translation, rather than a revision, he went on to say: "In revising his work, he re-examined the common version, and wherever that version has expressed the sense of the Original in good English, he has adopted it" (Preface: 3). The latter statement of the translator more closely describes his work. The grip of the familiar King James Version still influenced the translation style of Anderson's New Testament as well as most other revisions produced in this era.

Two "immersion" versions appeared in the 1880s as a result of dissatisfaction with the newly-published English Revised Version of 1881–83. Samuel Williams not only placed the reading of the American committee of the English Revised Version into the text, contrary to the policy of that translation, but also substituted "immerse" for "baptize" in the text as well (1881). John Wesley Hanson expressed dissatisfaction with the English Revised Version because the translators adhered too closely to the King James Version tradition. In addition to producing an "immersion" version (1884–1885), which, in fact, was a modern-speech version, with the exception of prayers, he rearranged the New Testament text by rendering the four Gospels in one continous narrative and placed the rest of the books of the New Testament in chronological order. Hanson's notes present his interpretation as a Universalist.

The appearance of dozens of new translations by individuals in nineteenth-century America failed to erode the popularity and influence of the King James Version. This continued popularity caused the King James Version to be the text used by some who wished to make the Bible more accessible or readable. Two New Testaments appeared in 1848 that promoted revisions in the orthography of the English language. Jonathan Morgan (1848) was a lawyer and inventor from Portland, Maine, who was an advocate of spelling reform. His New Testament incorporated numerous spelling revisions such as "thru," "lik," "brot," and "tung" (Simms: 233). More radical was the New Testament of Andrew Comstock (1848), which was printed, except for a brief preface, entirely in a phonetic alphabet described on the title page as "Komstok's Purfekt Alfabet" (Hills: 202–3). Another King James Version of the New Testament in a phonetic alphabet was published in Cincinnati by Longley Brothers (Hills: no. 1596), reprinted in 1864 and again in 1885 with some orthographic revisions.

Revisions of spelling and orthography of the King James Version were not limited to these two efforts. In fact, the American Bible Society, one of the main publishers of the King James Version in the United States, undertook a revision and standardization of their text of the KJV. Ever since 1611, a surprisingly large number of minor spelling, punctuation, and other variants crept into the often reset and reprinted King James Version. In Great Britain, some degree of standardization was achieved through the efforts of F. S. Paris, Cambridge (1762; Herbert: no. 1142) and Benjamin Blayney, Oxford (1769; Herbert: no. 1194). Scrivener has detailed the many minor textual variants that occur in the major English editions of the King James Version. The American Bible Society appointed a committee in 1847 to review the text of the King James Version that the Society published to make recommendations for a "standard" text, dealing with matters of spelling, capitalization, and punctuation. In 1850, the first New Testament of the American Bible Society incorporating the new "standard" text appeared (Hills: no. 1443) and the entire Bible was published in 1852 (Hills: no. 1504). The Committee reported that they had found twenty-four thousand variations among the six texts of the King James Version that they examined, but hastened to assure the public that "there is not one, which mars the integrity of the text, or affects any doctrine or precept of the Bible."

It is apparent that many critics were not reassured. They examined the new "standard" text of the American Bible Society and concluded that the revisions were too radical, even though all standardizations and spellings were limited to matters of orthography in the text; however, some changes were made in chapter summaries and running heads. The ensuing controversy ultimately resulted in the resignation of the original committee and the appointment of a new committee that recommended more modest and less extensive changes, which were first incorporated in an American Bible Society edition of the Bible in 1857. Hills, in her entry number 1643, for this edition, lists a number of the pamphlets and other documents related to this controversy. The revised standard edition continued to be the standard text for American Bible Society publications of the King James Version until 1932, when a new standard text was published. Another standardized text was issued by the American Bible Society in 1962 when it published a King James Version in which the text was set in paragraphs, the poetry was divided into poetic lines, and the spelling of proper names was standardized.

Others, in issuing editions of the King James Version, also incorporated numerous minor revisions. In 1897, Horace E. Morrow issued a New Testament in the King James Version that incorporated several different type faces to mark various kinds of emphasis, either based on his understanding of the underlying Greek text or on a desire to emphasize certain utterances of Jesus or didactic portions of the Epistles (Hills: no. 2085). C. I. Scofield introduced a number of revised renderings for archaic words and phrases in his *Reference Bible* (1909; Hills: no. 2192). The *New Scofield Reference Bible* (1967) has placed many of these revised renderings in the King James Version text and relegates the earlier translation to marginal notes.

The desire to make available the King James Version, realized in an extensive variety of publications, attests to its enduring popularity among Bible readers throughout the nineteenth century. Only the impact of the acceptance of a number of major translations since 1946 has jeopardized the position of the King James Version as the most widely-used English translation.

Nineteenth-Century Modern-Language Versions

The modern-language translation that commends itself to the reading public because it presents the biblical message in clear, natural English can trace its early roots in America to the work of Alexander Campbell (1788–1866). Campbell was born in Ireland and came to America in 1809 as a Presbyterian minister but soon affiliated with the Baptists and later founded the Disciples of Christ. In his effort to provide a modern translation for the restoration movement, he attempted to have published in America a New Testament translated by George Campbell, James MacKnight, and Philip Doddridge and published in London in 1818. When this did not materialize, he edited the work of the three translators, adopted the readings of the Greek text of Griesbach, and added notes that helped to explain the cultural background of the text and some of the striking examples of translations that diverged significantly from the King James Version.

In his general preface to the first edition, published in 1826, Campbell explained the reasons why he believed a new translation was needed. He recognized that any living language is continually changing, requiring new and revised translations. He disputed the notion that "the common version was an exact representation of the meaning of the original at the time in which it was made" (5). Further, he believed that only an individual would be able to produce the needed translation. The dominance of the King James Version in his day was so great that "it is probable that a new translation into our language will never again be undertaken by public authority" (6).

With advances in understanding of the Greek language and with better manuscripts of the Greek New Testament available, Campbell believed "we are now in possession of much better means of making an exact translation than we were at the time when the common version appeared" (6). Cecil Thomas, after a detailed study of Campbell's work, has concluded: "In the use of textual criticism, the emendation of archaic language, and, in several cases, the reading of passages, Campbell, in a remarkable way, anticipated much that has been done in modern-language translations since his times" (82). And Luther Weigle, chairman of the Revised Standard Version translation committee, in the Introduction to Thomas's book, agrees with the author that Campbell "was aware of the basic principles of interpretation and translation which were accepted by the best scholars of his day and which have been proved valid by the testing of over a century of critical study" (13).

Campbell's revision of the Campbell-MacKnight-Doddridge translation is admitted, even by its supporters, to lack good English style. But his perception of what constitutes good principles of translation and his influential role in the developing native American churches resulted in wide distribution of a "modern" translation based on a critical Greek text and paved the way for its many successors. Campbell reported that, by 1842, forty thousand copies of his New Testament were sold or distributed. His version remains in print today.

Characteristic elements of "modern" translation were introduced only gradually into translations of the Bible and the New Testament. The traditional diction of the King James Version, with its seventeenth-century vocabulary and phraseology, had become the accepted means of presenting the biblical message. Hezekiah Woodruff presented his translation (1852) "to benefit the rising generation, by presenting them the Holy Scriptures . . . in an idiom with which they are familiar." His work was hardly more than a revision of the King James Version with a few notable exceptions, such as "was the father of" instead of "begat" in Matthew 1 (Cheek: 110).

Perhaps the first American translation to break significantly with the archaisms of the King James Version was the rendering of the Gospels by Andrews Norton (1786–1853), published posthumously in 1855. It appeared in two volumes, the first containing the translation and the second his notes. It is apparent that for the first time in any English translation, "thou" was consistently changed to "you" (Pope: 546). In the preface, his son, Charles Eliot Norton, says: "A translation was needed which, while corresponding to the original as nearly as the idiom of our language would permit, should not be a mere verbal rendering, but should clearly express the meaning of the text, preserving, as far as possible, the simplicity which characterizes the style of the Evangelists" (iii). The text is generally clear, natural, nineteenth-century American English, but the influence of the King James Version style is still apparent: "And when the angels had ascended from them to heaven, the shepherds said to one another, Come, let us make our way to Bethlehem, and see that which has come to pass, what the LORD has made known to us" (Luke 2:15).

The first complete "modern-language" New Testament of the nineteenth century was produced by Leicester Ambrose Sawyer (1807–1898). Sawyer left the Presbyterian ministry in 1832 to affiliate with the Congregational and later the Unitarian Church. He considered himself to be a "Christian Rationalist." Sawyer adopted a thoroughly modern style, including the abandonment of archaic forms of personal pronouns, although "thou" was retained in prayers. He also divided the text into an entirely new system of chapters and verses, according to the sense of the text as he rendered it. While this kind of division enhanced readability, it was too radical an innovation for anyone who wished to find a particular passage. The traditional verse numbering, which originated in the work of the famous printer Robert Stephanus for his 1551 edition of the Greek New Testament, had become a universal system with only minor variations.

Typical of Sawyer's straightforward style is his translation of Matt 13:44 (XI.7a in Sawyer's system): "The kingdom of heaven is like a treasure hid in a field, which a man found, and concealed, and went away with joy, and sold all that he had and bought that field." In commending the work of individual translations such as his own, he said, in the preface to his New Testament:

> It is an unfortunate result of King James's translation of the Bible by an imposing council of learned men, that it has tended to discourage individual effort in respect to a labor of this kind, and to create a prejudice against it as necessarily incompetent and untrustworthy. . . . But there are great works which individuals can perform better than multitudes or councils. . . . As individuals, therefore, have generally been the prosecutors of literary enterprises, in the department of Bible translation no less than in other departments, and as individuals have been eminently successful and useful in this department of labor heretofore, both in England and other countries, let it be hoped that they may be again (vi–vii).

Sawyer also published his translation of parts of the Old Testament beginning in 1861. His Old Testament was never completed, but he published a revised edition of the New Testament in 1891, in which he reverted to the traditional chapter and verse numbering. But he rearranged the book order according to the order in which he believed them to be written. This order is a reflection of his advanced critical views. According to Sawyer, Period I (A.D. 53–64) was characterized by a dialectic between the thought of Peter and Paul, which resulted in a "third compromise school" in Rome about A.D. 62. Period II (A.D. 135–150) includes fourteen New Testament Epistles such as 2 Thessalonians, Ephesians, and Hebrews. The Gospels, Acts, and Revelation were written in Period III (A.D. 150–165). It is hardly surprising that Sawyer's innovative translations and critical views failed to gain popular acceptance.

George Rapall Noyes (1798–1868), a Unitarian and professor of Hebrew and biblical literature at Harvard, actively engaged in Bible translation throughout his academic career. Beginning in 1827 (Hills: no. 592) with the publication of his translation of Job, with notes, and continuing through the posthumous publication of his New Testament in 1869, he produced a translation of most of the Bible except for the Pentateuch and Historical Books of the Old Testament. His work is marked by its high level of scholarship and a generally high quality of English. His style differed somewhat from the "modern-language" translations of Norton and Sawyer. In his preface to the New Testament, he says: "I have endeavored . . . to retain what may be called the savor and spirit of our old and familiar version so far as is consistent with the paramount duties of a translator . . ."(iv–v).

Noyes was one of the first translators to base his work on the Greek text edited by Constantin von Tischendorf in his eighth major edition. This text incorporated the evidence of the famous Codex Sinaiticus, which Tischendorf himself had discovered. Although he generally accepted Tischendorf's readings, Noyes on occasion expressed his disagreement with the famous Greek scholar. Some of the independent judgments of Noyes have been confirmed by later discoveries and studies.

Frank Schell Ballentine's (1859–1936) translation of the New Testament (1899–1901), more than any of its nineteenth-century "modern-language" predecessors, succeeded in producing a translation in "modern American idiomatic English" (introduction to Mark: iii). In addition, standard typographic arrangement of dialogue and poetry was utilized throughout. His first publication of the Gospels in 1897 carried the title *Good News: The Four Gospels in a Modern American Dress*. The first edition of the entire New Testament, published in five separate volumes, was called *The Modern American Bible*. Ballentine reprinted his translation in 1909 and 1922, each time with a different title. He also incorporated some revisions that tended toward more traditional phraseology.

Additional Mid-nineteenth-Century Translations

Nineteenth-century America was marked by a diversity of religious interests that created a variety of religious writings. Considered by their adherents as Scripture, some of the writings of such groups as the Mormons are described in chapter seven of this volume. Part of this creative, pluralistic concern was demonstrated in the production of special translation projects whose primary concern had a different thrust from most versions of the period, which aimed at producing a more readable and more accurate translation within the King James Version tradition.

Though it was predominantly Protestant, mid-nineteenth-century America saw a marked increase in Roman Catholic and Jewish populations. They, too, needed readable and accurate translations. Francis Patrick Kenrick (1797–1863), while he was Bishop of Philadelphia, published his translation of the Gospels in 1849, followed by the rest of the New Testament as well as most of the Old Testament. A one-volume edition of the New Testament was published in 1862. Toward the close of the nineteenth century, another Roman Catholic scholar, Francis Aloysius (born Seymour Hobart) Spencer (1845–1913), translated the New Testament, first from the Latin Vulgate and later from the Greek. Only his translation of the four Gospels was published in his lifetime (from the Vulgate, 1898; from the Greek, 1901). His entire New Testament translation was first published in 1937. The full story of these significant Roman Catholic translations is presented in the essay in this volume by Fogarty.

The Jewish scholar, Isaac Leeser (1806–1868), concerned for the scriptural needs of the Jewish community in the United States, produced a translation of the Hebrew Scriptures that began to appear in 1845 and was completed in 1853. The role of Leeser in Jewish translation work done in the United States is discussed in the essay by Nahum and Jonathan Sarna in chapter four of this volume. In the early part of the twentieth century, Alexander Harkavy (1863–1939) emended the King James Version, making revisions and emendations. "Among the passages emended are all those which have been mistranslated or colored to suit Christian dogma. . . ." (1916: preface).

Two other productions of the midnineteenth century are presented as translations, but they actually modify the biblical text in its ancient canonical form under the authority of divine revelation to those who prepared the translation. Joseph Smith, Jr. (1805–1844), founder of the Church of Jesus Christ of Latter-day Saints, based his version of the Bible on a "direct revelation," which he first received in June 1830. Smith's manuscript remained unpublished during his lifetime. Following his death, the manuscript was retained by his widow, and was eventually prepared for publication by the Reorganized Church of Jesus Christ of Latter-day Saints, and it appeared in 1867. According to Smith, this revision of Holy Scripture was necessary because "Ignorant translators, careless transcribers, or designing and corrupt priests have committed many errors. . . . From sundry revelations which had been received, it was apparent that many important points touching the salvation of men, had been taken from the Bible, or lost before it was compiled" (Matthews: 2, 3). Typical of the additions to Smith's version are the additions of references to Jesus Christ in the Old Testament. Gen 5:2 is expanded to include "And as many as believed in the Son, and repented of their sins, should be saved." Gen 6:67–68 describes the baptism of Adam, who was "born of the Spirit, and became quickened in the inner ·man." Noah's call to repentance (Gen 8:11) includes a challenge to "be baptized in the name of Jesus Christ." Certain other texts dealing with the nature of God and humanity and the power of Christ were also changed (Matthews: 6–9).

A New Testament appeared in 1861 that carried the subtitle, *As Revised and Corrected by the Spirits.* The actual translation is preceded by "Introductory Remarks and Explanations by the Spirit of Jesus Christ," which tell the reader that Jesus and the Apostles came in spirit and revised and corrected the books of the New Testament. The net result is an abridgment of the King James Version: Romans contains only seven chapters, Revelation three chapters, and Hebrews is omitted entirely. An additional brief section contains a "New Dispensation by the Spirit of Christ," intended for spiritualists. The work was probably prepared by Leonard Thorn, who held the copyright for the publication.

Two little-known translations appeared in this period that deserve wider recognition. James Murdock (1776–1856) published his translation of the New Testament from the Syriac Peshitta in 1851. Retiring from teaching in 1828, he devoted himself to the study of church history and ancient languages, including Syriac. Murdock wanted to provide a literal translation of the Syriac New Testament. The first translation of the Syriac New Testament into English had been published only a few years earlier by J. W. Etheridge in London, 1843–1849. Murdock's translation closely follows the Syriac text, providing in the margin the underlying Syriac word for certain theological and technical terms. Where Syriac idiomatic phrases would be unnatural or unintelligible in English, a literal translation of the idiom is also given in the margin. Murdock's work provides a useful source for gaining some appreciation for the Syriac New Testament. The books of the Greek New Testament canon not included in the Peshitta were supplied from other Syriac versions. Murdock's New Testament was reprinted in 1893 with a biographical sketch of the translator and a historical introduction to the Syriac New Testament.

Another notable achievement in Bible translation was the publication of the first translation of the complete Bible done by a woman. Julia Evelina Smith [later Parker] (1793–1886) first studied Greek in 1843 to help her evaluate the predictions of William Miller regarding the end of the world. She and her sisters were well known for their active participation in the women's suffrage movement. In their weekly Bible study, Julia and her four sisters were struck by the marginal notes in the King James Version, giving the literal meaning of the Hebrew or Greek. "We saw by the margin that the text had not been given literally, and it was the literal meaning we were seeking" (1876: preface). Motivated by the desire for a "literal" translation, she "studied it [Hebrew] thoroughly, and wrote it out word for word, . . . endeavoring to put the same English word for the same Hebrew or Greek word; everywhere. . . ." (preface). Smith's translation was published at her own expense in 1876. The books of the Old Testament were arranged in Jewish canonical order. The New Testament is an "immersion" version. Since she consistently applied the principle of concordant, literal translation, the English is unnatural. Although Smith's translation did not achieve popularity, the desire for a "literal" translation would produce several new versions in the next fifty years.

Methods: Better Texts and Translation Theory

In 1881, the famous British New Testament textual scholars B. F. Westcott and F. J. A. Hort published their Greek New Testament. They combined careful examination of recently-discovered Greek New Testament manuscripts with their newer theory of textual criticism to produce this new critical edition. Much of their work had formed the basis of the New Testament translation of the English Revised Version. Several individual translators in America wanted to take advantage of this latest research on the text of the New Testament to present these results to their readers. John Wesley Hanson, a Universalist minister, produced the first American translation based on the Westcott and Hort Greek text. It was a modern-language version with the text arranged in paragraphs and poetic lines (1884-1885). Robert Dodd Weekes (1819–1898), a Congregational layman, attempted to retain the "more familiar style of the older [King James] version," although he generally based his revision work on the Greek text of Westcott and Hort.

Perhaps the most outspoken advocate of recent manuscript discoveries was William B. Godbey (1833–1920). Godbey was a popular Holiness preacher affiliated with the Southern Methodist Church. In the introduction to his *Translation of the New Testament from the Original Greek* (1902?), Godbey noted that the year of his college graduation in 1859 coincided with the discovery of the famous Greek Codex Sinaiticus manuscript of the Bible by Constantin von Tischendorf. Godbey believed that "the revelation of God's precious truth . . . survived in primitive purity in this manuscript" (Bills: 3). Although he relied too heavily on Codex Sinaiticus, a tendency supported by many in an earlier generation, Godbey's willingness to mediate the results of textual criticism to audiences that were generally reluctant to accept such claims is significant. He explained the gloss in Acts 15:34 as an attempt to solve a historical difficulty in the text. Regarding the famous passage in 1 John 5:7, which adds a reference to the Trinity in the text, he said that this verse was added during the Arian controversy and concludes "They made a mistake, as we have no right to add anything to the Bible . . . ," even if what is added is true. (1902?: preface). Godbey's literal rendering of the Greek is typical of a number of translations from that period that seem to reflect a reaction to the "modern-language" translations.

Toward the close of the nineteenth century, a number of translations appeared that consciously attempted to extol the virtues of literal translation. We have already noted Julia Smith's intention to produce such a translation. The desire to produce a literal translation was, in part, a reaction to the many "modern-language" versions that were appearing. A cyclical pattern of "literal" versus "free" translation has been part of the history of biblical translation (Sjölander: 15–16). In fact, this issue was debated in antiquity. From earliest times some objected to the rendering of the Hebrew Bible into Aramaic. Others, such as Aquila, considered the Septuagint Greek translation of the Hebrew Bible too free, and produced other Greek translations that adhered much more closely to the formal features of Hebrew vocabulary and syntax.

On the other hand, freer translation principles were defended by Hebrew sages such as Rabbi Judah, who said, "anyone who translates a biblical verse [strictly] according to its form [that is, 'literally'] misleads" (*b. Qidd.* 49g, cited by Weingreen: 268). Maimonides also defended this translation technique.

> Let me premise one canon. Whoever wishes to translate and purposes to render each word literally, and at the same time to adhere slavishly to the order of the words and sentences in the original, will meet with much difficulty. This is not the right method. The translator should first try to grasp the sense of the subject thoroughly, and then state the theme with perfect clarity in the other language. This, however, cannot be done without changing the order of the words, putting many words for one word, or vice versa, so that the subject be perfectly intelligible in the language into which he translates (cited in Brock: 570–1).

The advocates of "literal" translation maintain that a translation should reflect as many of the formal features of the original language as possible. This means that the same English word is used consistently to render a single Hebrew or Greek word. This principle is called "concordance." Further, the sentence word order, idioms, and other formal features of style in the original language should be reproduced in the receptor language, even though the result will be awkward and unnatural English. This style is sometimes called "translationese." This kind of "literal" translation should be distinguished from translations following "traditional" vocabulary and phraseology that became part of the Church's language under the pervasive influence of the King James Version. In fact, the King James Version is actually a rather free translation when compared with the "literal" translations of the nineteenth-century, though by modern linguistic standards it is a literal translation.

In contemporary linguistic terms, these two types of translation theory are called "formal correspondence" vs. "dynamic equivalence." The most famous formal correspondence translation is a German translation of the Hebrew Scriptures made by Martin Buber and Franz Rosenzweig. The result is difficult German that is hard to understand, but does reproduce for the reader the flavor and idiom of the Hebrew original. Few, if any, literal English translations have achieved the same measure of success or literary quality.

The "dynamic equivalence" approach to translation maintains that faithful and accurate translation is achieved by rendering the meaning of the original text in the closest natural equivalent in the receptor language. The focus is on the act of communication; intelligibility of a translation is not measured by the correspondence of formal features, but by whether the message understood by the reader of the translation closely corresponds to the message the original writer intended to communicate to the readers.

The stated intention of the *Emphatic Diaglott* translation prepared by Benjamin F. Wilson (1817–1900) was to take the reader back to the Greek text through a literal translation coupled with a system of typographic features that attempt to highlight certain features of Greek grammar and syntax that cannot be duplicated in the word-for-word translation itself. Wilson believed that his work would place "in the hands of the intelligent English reader the means of knowing and appropriating for his own benefit, with but little labor on his part, what it has cost others years of study and severe toil to acquire" (1865: iv). Although his motive may be commendable, the result is a translation that neither communicates the meaning of the text in clear English nor really enables the reader to understand Greek.

Emphasizing the principle of concordant translation, W. D. Dillard (1885) expressed the same desire for a literal translation. In spite of Dillard's intention, his translation is mainly a reworking of the text of the King James Version (Hills: 310). The concordance principle is applied far more extensively in Adolph Ernst Knoch's *Concordant Version, The Sacred Scriptures*. The New Testament appeared in separate pamphlets from 1919 to 1926(?). The entire New Testament has been reprinted frequently, as well as an interlinear Greek text, using Greek capital letters (uncials) in a typeface specially designed for this publication. Portions of the Old Testament, including Genesis, Exodus, Isaiah, Ezekiel, Daniel, and the Minor Prophets, have also appeared. The work begun by Knoch (1874–1965) continues today, with the intention of publishing the entire Bible. Knoch was fond of a similar British translation prepared by Rotherham because "he did not shrink from using 'impossible' English in the service of truth." Two examples of this concordant translation demonstrate Knoch's "impossible" English: "And make you will I into a great nation, and bless you will I and make your name great and become must you a blessing" (Gen 12:2); "Now at their hearing these things, He spoke, adding a parable because He is near Jerusalem, and they are supposing that the kingdom of God is about to be looming up instantly" (Luke 19:11).

Early Twentieth-Century Developments

Two other versions were produced based on a numerical system that the editors perceived in the biblical text. Frederick W. Grant (1834–1902) published his *Numerical Bible* (1891–1931), which was essentially a revision of the King James Version using the symbolism of numbers and numerical structure as an aid to interpretation. Ivan

Panin (1855–1942) edited a Greek New Testament based on his perception of a numeric system in the Bible, which included word and letter counts. This numerical scheme formed the basis of determining the original text. He produced The *New Testament from the Greek Text as Established by Bible Numerics* (1914) based on his edition of the Greek text, although his Greek New Testament was not published until 1936.

Very little additional translation work was done in the first two decades of the twentieth century. The only other translation that appeared in this period was the New Testament published by Johannes Rudolph Lauritzen, which was presented as an English rendering of the German translation of Luther. Lauritzen, a Lutheran minister, produced his New Testament in a number of formats for his pastoral work among prisoners. The translation is essentially a minor revision of the King James Version and continues to follow its underlying Greek textus receptus, even where Luther followed a different Greek text. (See, for example, 1 John 5:7 and Rev 22:19, "book" instead of "tree" of life.)

Instead of producing new translations, a number of people published several influential editions of existing translations in different formats and arrangements. For example, Richard Green Moulton (1849–1924) published *The Modern Reader's Bible* (1895–1906; Hills: no. 2066), in which the text of the English Revised Version is arranged in paragraph form, with poetic passages in the form of poetry, and other features designed to present the Bible as a work of literature. Charles Foster Kent (1867–1925) produced a six-volume *Student's Old Testament Logically and Chronologically Arranged* (1904–1927; Hills: no. 2158). Kent did his own translation for this publication. C. C. Torrey and F. C. Porter collaborated in the preparation of the final volume. Kent's work was designed to introduce to the general reader the conclusions of modern biblical study. Kent, together with Frank Knight Sanders, published *The Message of the Bible* (New Testament, 1918, Hills: no. 2242; and Old Testament, 1921, Hills: no. 2253), which was an abridged text subtitled *The Shorter Bible*. Eleven of twelve projected volumes were published. Kent and Sanders also prepared *The Children's Bible* in simplified English (1922). Perhaps no other individual produced as many different Scripture publications in an effort to appeal to many different audiences.

Modern-Language Versions

After experiencing little progress in the production of "modern-language" translations for several decades, new impetus was provided by the highly successful *The New Testament: An American Transla-tion*, translated by Edgar Johnson Goodspeed (1871–1962). Good-speed's translation in good idiomatic American English benefitted from several factors that the well-known Greek scholar from the University of Chicago was able to build on in his work. Goodspeed combined an appreciation for good literary style with a recognition of the changes in American English, which had taken place since the modern-language translations of the previous century, to produce a very readable translation. As a Greek scholar, he knew firsthand the value of continuing discoveries of Greek New Testament manuscripts. Perhaps of equal significance was the discovery of many nonbiblical Greek documents from about the time of the New Testament and written in an everyday, common (Koine) dialect of Greek that in many ways was similar to the Greek of the New Testament. With these discoveries, documentary evidence demonstrated that the New Testa-ment was generally written in the language of the people, not in some elevated or artificial style of religious language. If the first readers of the Greek New Testament had a "modern-language" text, contempo-rary readers should have the opportunity of reading the Scriptures in natural, contemporary English.

Goodspeed, in his autobiography, devotes a chapter to his experi-ences as a translator. He was well aware of the problems faced by anyone who wanted to translate the Bible: ". . .in language study . . . so often almost no attention is paid to English, and all attention is riveted on the language studied. Translation English is mostly no English at all. . . . The most difficult thing, I found, was to forget the old translations. . . ." (161, 162). Yet he succeeded better than any of his predecessors in overcoming these obstacles: "I wanted my transla-tion to make on the modern reader something of the impression the New Testament must have made on its earliest readers, and to invite the continuous reading of a whole book at a time" (162). Goodspeed also kept in mind the need for the public reading of the Scriptures, even though his friend, James Moffatt, disdained the public reading of his own translation (Goodspeed: 158). Both Goodspeed and Moffatt later served on the translation committee of the Revised Standard Version.

Goodspeed's translation was subjected to a good deal of unwar-ranted criticism by the public and in the popular press. Many critics took exception to his following Greek manuscripts that did not contain verses and phrases found in the later manuscripts the King James Version translators used. They were especially critical of the shorter text in the familiar Lord's Prayer. This type of criticism is surprising in the light of the fact that dozens of earlier translations had generally followed the same Greek manuscripts that Goodspeed used. Apparently, the reading public was made aware of these matters only through this modern-language version, the first to be published by a major publisher, the University of Chicago Press. Regarding the criticism of his translation, Goodspeed said: "The fault was basically ours of the biblical profession, for we had so long been silent about the progress of biblical studies and discoveries that the general public was unaware of what was going on . . . ." (156).

The enthusiasm for Goodspeed's New Testament translation prompted a translation of the Old Testament, under the direction of J. M. Powis Smith of the University of Chicago. He was assisted in the translation by Theophile J. Meek, Alex R. Gordon, and Leroy Waterman, all well-known biblical scholars. The Old Testament was published in 1927, and the complete *American Bible* was first issued in 1931. Based on the same principles as Goodspeed's, it became quite popular, though the Old Testament, too, was criticized for reflecting the trends of modern biblical study.

Goodspeed also translated the books of the Apocrypha, published in 1938. After examining the translation of the Apocrypha in the English Revised Version, he concluded that it was evidently based on the King James Version of the Apocrypha without revising the text in accordance with the original texts. He concluded that the *American Bible* with his translation of the Apocrypha was the first complete Bible translated entirely "from the original tongues" (188–90).

Two other modern-language versions appeared in the 1920s, one by William G. Ballantine (1923) and another by Helen Barrett Montgomery (1924). Ballantine (1848–1937) was a Congregational minister who served as president of Oberlin College from 1891-1906. Although subtitled *Into the English of To-Day*, his translation is more literal than most modern-speech versions. Montgomery's *Centenary Translation of the New Testament* was published in commemoration of the American Baptist Publication Society, which was the direct successor of the American and Foreign Bible Society. They had withdrawn from the American Bible Society when the latter organization would not publish "immersion" versions. The immersion controversy had subsided long before the publication of the Montgomery translation, which translated *baptizō* as "baptism." Mrs. Montgomery (1861–1934), a licensed Baptist minister, was the first woman to independently produce a translation of the New Testament in modern speech. It was based on the same Greek text used in the English Revised Version.

Since the 1920s, a number of other modern-language translations have been published. In 1937, Charles B. Williams (1860–1952) published his New Testament translation, subtitled, *A Translation in the Language of the People*. Williams attempted to combine the principle of using natural American English to express the thought of the original with a conscious effort to reproduce the diction and style of the original. He based his translation on the Greek text of Westcott and Hort, and used paragraph style for the text and included brief introductions to each book. This Williams translation should not be confused with one done by the Australian, Charles Kingsley Williams, whose translation uses a restricted vocabulary and was published in 1963 by William B. Eerdmans.

In 1945, Gerrit Verkuyl (1872–1967) published *The Berkeley Version* of the New Testament, named for the city where it was first published. Verkuyl was motiviated by the twofold purpose of utilizing the evidence of recently-discovered Greek manuscripts of the New Testament and of employing current vocabulary in his translation. In this he was reflecting similar motivations of many other translators who wanted to produce modern-language translations. Verkuyl based his translation on the eighth edition of von Tischendorf's Greek New Testament, with reference to Nestle's edition. However, a number of verses and phrases not found in earlier manuscripts and relegated to the critical apparatus in the critical editions of the Greek New Testament that he used are included in the text of the translation and placed in parentheses. Beginning in 1950 *The Berkeley Version* was published by Zondervan, who also published the entire Bible in 1959. Verkuyl served as chair of a translation committee for the Old Testament. This version has now been retitled *The Modern Language Bible*.

In 1954, James A. Kleist and Joseph L. Lilly, two Roman Catholic scholars who translated directly from the Greek text, published their New Testament translation in contemporary, literary English. (See the essay by Gerald Fogarty,   , for further information on their work.) The need for a modern-language translation among the Greek Orthodox in the United States prompted Metropolitan Fan S. Noli to publish his translation in 1961. As one would expect, Noli followed the Byzantine Greek text in his translation, rather than one of the critical editions of the Greek New Testament. The Byzantine text is close to, but not identical with, the textus receptus.

In 1972, the Watchtower Bible and Tract Society of New York, the publication arm of the Jehovah's Witnesses, published *The Bible in Living English*, translated by Steven T. Byington (1868–1957), even though Byington was not affiliated in any way with this organization.

One feature that apparently prompted the Jehovah's Witnesses to publish the modern-language translation of Byington was his rendering of the divine name as "Jehovah" in the Old Testament, although other renderings conflict with the interpretations found in *The New World Translation of the Holy Scriptures* (1961; see Crim,   ). Byington's translation illustrates the tendency of individual translations to reflect the idiolect and peculiar style of the individual, which, though interesting, limits its usefulness and general acceptability.

Richmond Alexander Lattimore (1906–1984) produced a modern-language translation in two volumes: the Gospels and Revelation appeared in 1979 and the remainder of the New Testament, in 1982. Lattimore, "struck by the natural ease with which Revelation turned itself into English," decided to translate the entire New Testament into literary English "in the belief that fidelity to the original word order and syntax may yield an English prose that to some extent reflects the style of the original" (vii). Lattimore was a classics scholar who translated a number of other ancient Greek texts along the same principles.

The most recent of the modern-language translations was published in 1984 by the Reverend Julian G. Anderson: *New Testament into Simple, Everyday, American English: A New, Accurate Translation of the Greek*. Anderson was motivated by the recognition that there is still no perfect translation of the original Greek into English. Although he does not claim that his translation is perfect, he believes that the King James Version and its direct descendent revisions have translated the Greek incorrectly. Anderson believes that technical vocabulary should be avoided, and short, simple English words used instead. Complex Greek sentences have been restructured into short English sentences. Anderson has rearranged the order of the Epistles in their presumed chronological order, beginning with James (ca. 45–50), and ending with 3 John. He also designates 2 Corinthians 1–9 as "3 Corinthians."

Special-Purpose Translations

Olaf Morgan Norlie (1876–1962) translated the New Testament "in Modern English," with outlines and marginal notes, in 1951 in mimeographed form. Ten years later a commercial publisher released Norlie's translation as the *Simplified New Testament in Plain English—For Today's Reader*. This edition (1961) included a translation of the Psalms by R. K. Harrison of Toronto, Canada. Later retitled *The Children's Simplified New Testament*, Norlie's concern was for a readable translation in simplified English designed to appeal to a young audience that was "not familiar with many of the obscure, archaic and complicated terms used in other and older versions" (1971 edition: preface). While "espoused" (Matt 1:18, KJV) was rendered "betrothed" in the 1951 edition and later changed to "engaged," "propitiation" (1 John 2:2, KJV) was translated "atonement," and other technical vocabulary is still retained.

Frank C. Laubach (1884–1970), who dedicated much of his life to world literacy, produced a translation, *Inspired Letters of the New Testament in Clearest English* (1956) as part of his graded series aimed at teaching people to read the Bible. In order to achieve the intended clarity, Laubach sometimes added words or phrases, abandoned any effort to preserve the style of the original, and changed difficult words into well-known words or phrases. Laubach considered his text as preparation for reading the Bible in a translation such as the Revised Standard Version.

Don Klingensmith produced *Today's English New Testament* (1972) "with only one idea in mind—to make the message of this book understood by all people who read and listen to its message in the English language" (introduction). Klingensmith exhibits a tendency in some modern-language translations to use short sentences and simple syntax. Klingensmith served as a minister among North American Indians and immigrants in North Dakota. His translation seeks to use English that would be intelligible to them.

Gleason H. Ledyard had a similar audience and language level in mind when he published his translation of the New Testament in 1969. It was published under the title *The New Life Testament* by the Christian Literature Foundation, Canby, Oregon, and as the *Children's New Testament* by Word Books of Waco, Texas, in the same year. Apart from the title and the inclusion of pictures in the children's edition, there are no differences in the two editions. Ledyard served as a missionary to the Eskimos in the Canadian Central Arctic as well as to American Indians. From this ministry came his conviction that a translation was needed that would present the text in easy-to-read form. An additional feature is a word list that gives traditional biblical vocabulary in the King James tradition with the equivalents used by Ledyard.

William Frederick Henry Beck (1904–1966) recognized the function of English as a world language. His New Testament translation in contemporary language (1963) aimed to be a translation that could be understood by children as well as adults. Beck believed that "Today our language carries a world responsibility. . . . God wants to use our language to talk to the world—before the end!" (viii–ix). Beck also translated most of the Old Testament before his death in 1966. His translation, after some revisions, both of the Old Testament manuscript and the published edition of the New Testament, was published as *The Holy Bible: An American Translation* in 1976.

In 1978 the World Bible Translation Center, Arlington, Texas, produced a translation designed to meet the reading needs of the deaf. Some of the features intended to enhance comprehension for the deaf are short sentences and sparing use of relative pronouns. This same translation was also published under the title *The New Testament, A New Easy-to-Read Version*. This organization also produced *The New Testament: International Children's Version* in 1983. Based in part on their earlier translation, this version was developed for children at a third-grade reading level. The translators recognized that this is a special translation and ". . . it is not designed for adult level exegesis" (iv). A further revision of the same translation appeared in 1984, entitled *The Word: New Century Version*. Aiming at a more general audience, the revisions include greater use of personal pronouns and more flexibility in sentence structure.

Stanley Morris was the principal translator of the *Simple English Bible: New Testament* published in 1981. Morris aimed at a grade five reading level of English. He reintroduced the use of italics to indicate words considered to be only implied in the original Greek text. No distinction is made between these types of additions and English words needed to express the meaning of the Greek text in natural English equivalents. This translation also revives the use of "immerse" for "baptize."

Jay Green launched a series of publications in 1960 when he issued *The Children's "King James" Bible: New Testament*. His work is basically a revision of the King James Version with some words and phases changed to improve readability for a twentieth-century audience. Although the archaic pronouns such as "thou" were changed, and other minor revisions have been made, it is essentially a King James Version revision similar to those done in the first half of the nineteenth century. Green's King James Version revision has been reprinted, with few additional changes, under a number of different titles, most recently the *King James II Version*, presumably not referring to the monarch who succeeded Charles II.

Some translations have been produced in conjunction with biblical studies. Frequently, those who write commentaries on individual books of the Bible produce their own translations as a basis for their comments. Rarely, however, does one individual produce a commentary with a translation of an entire Testament. For example, dozens of individuals have contributed to the Anchor Bible (Doubleday, 1964–). If the translations done for this series are eventually published separately, it will be a significant interfaith and interconfessional translation, although the diversity of approaches to translation will be evident.

Apparently, only one American, Richard Charles Henry Lenski (1864–1936), has ever produced a commentary-related translation of the entire New Testament. His twelve-volume series appeared from 1931 to 1946. Lenski served as a professor at the Evangelical Lutheran Theological Seminary in Columbus, Ohio. A brief list of translations appearing in commentaries is given in Herbert (492–501). This list, which is predominantly British, does include Americans. Hills's "Index of Editors and Commentators" in her book, *The English Bible in America*, is another useful reference for access to these translations.

William Wallace Martin (1851–1947) attempted to reflect in his translation of the New Testament (1937?) and a large part of the Old Testament (1928; Hills: no. 2302) the results of his research on the literary sources of the Bible. While professor of Hebrew at Vanderbilt University, he was asked to devote his full attention to his investigation of the Old Testament. He had previously published two books on the documents of the Pentateuch, in which he proposed an alternate view to the Wellhausen school. His further study led him to advocate a theory of two documents traceable throughout the Old Testament. Martin's translation presents his reconstructed "Ephramean" and "Judean" versions not only in the Pentateuch but in the poetry and prophets as well. His New Testament translation also presents his distinct views. It divides the New Testament into thirty-six books, and assigns certain canonical material to Apollos, Barnabas, and John the son of Zebedee.

Ervin Edward Stringfellow, professor of New Testament at Drake University, translated the New Testament in conjunction with a textbook he prepared. It presented his translation, based on the Greek text of Westcott and Hort, together with a Gospel harmony, historical notes, and questions for discussion (1943–1945).

Although he never translated the entire New Testament, Charles Cutler Torrey (1863–1956), for many years professor of Semitic languages at Yale University, published *The Four Gospels, a New Translation* (1933) and *The Apocalypse of John* (1958), which contained his translation of those books based on his theory of the Aramaic origin of the New Testament. Other scholars had emphasized the Semitic background and Aramaic influence on portions of the New Testament, but Torrey believed that the Gospels and Revelation were actually written in Aramaic and later (mis)translated into Greek. By reconstructing the assumed original Aramaic, Torrey believed that numerous problems of interpretation and translation could be solved. Although his work was skillfully executed, most of his conclusions have not found wide acceptance.

Even less convincing was the effort to demonstrate that the Syriac Peshitta version best represents the original text of the Bible. This theory was the basis of the English translation made by George M. Lamsa (1892–1976). He published *The Four Gospels according to the Eastern Version* in the same year Torrey's *Four Gospels* appeared. This was followed by the publication of the New Testament in 1940 and the entire Bible in 1957. Lamsa followed the format and English style of the King James Version, altering the text generally, but not always, according to the readings of the Peshitta (Frank).

Jay Adams translated the New Testament (1977) with the needs of persons engaged in Christian counseling in mind. Adams prepared a new translation reflecting "important counseling nuances [which] have been missed by other translators. . . ." (vii). Texts of particular interest to counselors are overlined in yellow with marginal references and explanatory notes added.

The desire to tailor a translation to reach a Jewish audience has prompted two recent publications that modify existing translations to reflect the "Jewishness" of the Bible. *May Your Name Be Inscribed in the Book of Life* (1981) makes several verbal changes in the New Testament text of the *New King James Version*. For example, "Jesus" is changed to "Yeshua," and footnotes explain Jewish cultural features such as "border of garments" as "tzitzit or fringes," and proper names are given in their Jewish form. The same principle of adaptation was applied to the *Living Bible* in the production of *The Living Scriptures* (1982) edited by David Bronstein, although the verbal changes are not always the same.

Three translations have been made that were also motivated by the desire to restore the Jewish character to the Bible. Their primary concern is the consistent use of the divine name, YHWH, generally spelled "Jehovah" in most translations from the King James Version to the American Standard Version but usually represented by the traditional "LORD." Some modern translations such as the *Jerusalem Bible* use the more likely form "Yahweh" throughout.

Angelo B. Traina (1889–1971) produced the *Sacred Name Version*

New Testament (1950), in which he revised the King James Version by giving Semitic forms of proper names and by using "El," "Elohim," and "Yahwheh" for God. Applying the same principles, he published the entire Bible in 1963 with a revised title, *Holy Name Bible*. A similar publication, *The Restoration of Original Sacred Name Bible*, appeared in 1970, also based on the King James Version. The verbal alterations are more extensive than Traina's, and the divine name is spelled YAHVAH. Both Traina and the *Restoration* version translated "immersion" for baptism. *The Sacred Scriptures*, (Bethel edition) was published in 1981 under the editorship of Jacob O. Meyer, who based his work on the American Standard Version. It uses "Yahweh" and "Elohim," and *ekklēsia* ("church") is translated "assembly." Unlike the other sacred-name versions, pronouns referring to the deity are not capitalized.

Two "spiritual" translations of the New Testament were published in the twentieth century. Arthur E. Overbury's New Testament, whose subtitle includes the phrase, *Translated from the Meta-Physical Standpoint* (1925?) "is based on the premise of 'Scientific Statement of Being' as given in 'Science and Health' by Mary Baker Eddy" (7). It was never considered an official Christian Science translation. In 1937, Johannes Greber (1876–1944), a former Roman Catholic priest who came to believe in communication with divine spirits, published his translation of the New Testament based on the Greek Codex Bezae, with corrections given to him by the spirits. Greber translated John 4:24 as "God is a spirit, and those who worship Him must therefore be under the guidance of a spirit of God and of the divine truth when they come to do Him homage."

A number of individuals produced translations that followed more traditional lines of vocabulary and style. Edgar Lewis Clementson wanted to produce a translation that would "avoid paraphrase and periphrase." The result was a rather literal translation well within the King James Version tradition (1938).

George Swann (born 1882) first published his translation of the New Testament in 1947. A unique feature was the arrangement of the entire New Testament text in 1,782 numbered paragraphs with a key word from the text printed in boldface at the head of each paragraph. An index of these key words provides access by topic to the text. In later editions, traditional chapter and verse numbers were added to the paragraphs.

The *Authentic Version* appeared in 1951, the work of an anonymous translator who believed that he had "been given authority through the Holy Spirit to bring the true translation of the original Greek text. . . ." He used "American language," but gave "as near as possible a word for word translation" (preface).

George Albert Moore (born 1893), a retired colonel, found that no existing translation exactly suited him, so he decided to publish his own translation, which was issued serially in mimeographed form (1953/1954?). To accomplish this, he compared the Greek text with several ancient and modern versions to produce his "independent, individual, unsponsored" translation (preface).

James L. Tomanek published his New Testament translation in 1958, hoping to meet the need for a "clearer rendering of some parts . . . of the New Testament." His translation is a rather literal rendering of the Greek. A few distinct features of his translation are the use of "Anointed" for "Christ" and the use of the pronoun "It" in reference to the Holy Spirit.

Chester Estes (1903–) published *The Better Version of the New Testament* (1973), believing that his "Better Version is an interpretation, according to the author's understanding, of what the inspired writers of the New Testament said" (viii). Estes believed he offered a better version by using simple sentence structure and improved punctuation. Generally, however, the translation followed traditional lines.

Expanded Translations and Paraphrases

One of the greatest challenges for any translator is to express in the receptor language all the information that is explicit or implicit in the original text, while adding nothing or failing to include any information evident to the original hearers. Because of the difference in language structure and the historical and cultural gap of two thousand and more years, the ideal is often difficult to achieve. A translator may resort to several approaches to provide information not readily built into a natural translation. Notes can be added that explain the cultural background or the meaning of a particular text. This type of information is an important feature of annotated editions and study Bibles. Another approach is the expanded translation or paraphrase.

Wuest's Expanded Translation of the Greek New Testament, published in three volumes (1956–59), was the version Kenneth S. Wuest (1893–1961) produced to escape the "linguistic straitjacket" of "standard translations" such as the King James Version and the American Standard Version. His expanded translation was promoted as "the *only* translation which gives the *full* English equivalent of Greek text in modern speech." Wuest was especially concerned with expressing the nuances of the Greek tense system. Expansion also provided an opportunity to offer fuller explanations of words and phrases. Wuest's translation of the first beatitude is typical: "Spiritually prosperous are the destitute and helpless in the realm of the spirit, because theirs is the kingdom of heaven" (Matt 5:3). Although this expansion offers Wuest's understanding of the words "blessed" and "poor," the dramatic conciseness of the original, which surely impressed the original hearers, is lost. Wuest recognized that an expanded translation such as his should be used as a companion to one of the standard versions.

The *Amplified New Testament* (1958), primarily prepared by Frances E. Siewert, provides expanded meanings for thousands of words and phrases. Some expansions are included in brackets and parentheses or are given in italics, according to the translator's understanding of the relation of the expanded text to the original. The first beatitude is translated: "Blessed—happy, to be envied, and spiritually prosperous [that is, with life-joy and satisfaction in God's favor and salvation, regardless of their outward conditions]—are the poor in spirit (the humble, rating themselves insignificant), for theirs is the kingdom of heaven!" (Matt 5:3). The Old Testament was prepared by a committee and published with the New Testament in 1965 as *The Amplified Bible*. The extent of amplification in the Old Testament is substantially less than in the New.

Kenneth Taylor was confronted with the need for a translation of Paul's Epistles that his own children could understand. To help them, he took his *American Standard Version* as he commuted to Chicago and paraphrased Romans in a vocabulary and style that would communicate to children. Romans begins: "Dear Boys and Girls, Fathers and Mothers there in Rome: This letter is from Paul, your old missionary friend and a slave." This paraphrase of Romans, first published in 1959 by Moody Press, his employer, later developed, with revisions, into *Living Letters*. For this and all subsequent publications, he founded his own publishing house, Tyndale House. The entire New Testament appeared in 1967, followed by the *Living Bible* in 1971.

The weaknesses of Taylor's translation have frequently been pointed out by reviewers: It is a secondary version, being a paraphrase based on an English translation, the *American Standard Version*. Consequently, Taylor did not make use of the latest manuscript evidence. His theological orientation is too evident—for example, in his rendering of "salvation" as "get to heaven." In light of Taylor's theological conservatism, it is also surprising that he takes many liberties with the text by adding and deleting material from the text. (Jack Lewis lists over forty published reviews of the *Living Bible* and provides his own analysis [237–60].) Despite these criticisms, the *Living Bible* remains "an appealing and readable paraphrase" (Kubo and Specht: 241). It has been read with enthusiasm by many for whom traditional translations are difficult. The publication of a *Complete Catholic Edition, Including the Deuterocanicals* with the imprimatur (1978) suggests the breadth of its influence. Perhaps the *Living Bible* demonstrates better than any other version both the weaknesses and the potential for success of a translation by an individual. It lacks the discipline of committee review, but it meets a need for a version that people can understand and enjoy reading. As a paraphrase, with additional background information and the interpretations of the translator built into the text, it has become the most popular English version by an individual ever published.

As mentioned above, some translators have attempted to bridge the culture gap of two millennia by adding cultural and interpretive notes to the translation. Another approach is to transfer the cultural background to a modern cultural setting. This method is sometimes called transculturation. Clarence Jordan (1912–1969) used this approach in his *Cotton Patch Version*, published in four volumes from 1963 to 1970. He translated the entire New Testament with the exception of Mark, John 9–21, and Revelation. The subtitle on the cover describes Jordan's work as "A colloquial modern translation with a Southern accent, vigorous and fervent for the gospel, unsparing in earthiness, rich in humor" (1968). The southern accent makes Rome, the capital, Washington; Corinth, the great commercial center, becomes Atlanta; the poor, struggling church at Philippi becomes "the Alabaster African Church, Smithville, Alabama." Jordan, however, says that the place names were chosen at random (1968: 11). Other transculturations render "Jew and Gentile" as "white man and Negro," and "eating meat sacrificed to idols" becomes "working on Sunday" (1 Cor 8:4). This type of translation can be helpful to a specific audience if one keeps in mind that such a version is not "a historical text," a point that Jordan stresses. It is evident that the subjective element will be far more extensive here than in other individual translations.

A transculturation even more extensive than Jordan's is *The Word Made Fresh* by Andrew Edington. It was published privately in 1972 and was reprinted in 1976 in three volumes by John Knox Press. The judge Othniel is called "Mac the Knife." In the Lord's sign to Gideon in Judges 6, "fire came out and cooked the TV dinner as if by laser beam." Edington also adds footnotes such as his comment on "I never departed from any of his commandments" (2 Sam 22:22), "I think the local PR men added this." By any definition, Edington's very readable work passes well beyond translation.

From modest reworkings of the King James Version to translations that use the most contemporary, idiomatic American English, Bible translations by American individuals demonstrate the diversity, creativity, and excesses of seventy or more persons who chose to share their work with the reading public. The audiences for some translations were quite small. Press runs of less than one thousand copies were not uncommon. Other individuals found their claim to fame elsewhere than in their translation, as in the case of Charles Thomson and Noah Webster. Still others produced translations that were not famous in their own right, but did reflect the state of biblical scholarship in America and profoundly influenced the major translations of the past two centuries. A few translations even achieved a level of popularity in their own right. They all contribute to the story of the influence of the Bible in America.

NOTES

/1/   Personal appreciation is expressed to Dr. Erroll Rhodes and other members of the library staff of the American Bible Society in New York. They graciously made available the often obscure publications discussed in this essay. The extensive Bible collection of the American Bible Society is an invaluable resource for the study of the Bible in America.

/2/   Occasionally, reference is made to a revision of the New Testament by John McDonald published in Albany, New York, (1813, 1816). However, even though the title page of the 1816 edition says that the text has been "carefully revised and corrected, by The Rev. John McDonald of Albany," it is actually the King James Version with a few minor changes in punctuation and orthography.

/3/   See the essay by Keith Crim in this volume (x ref) for a discussion of the English Revised Version and the contribution of the American Committee.

APPENDIX
Translations by American Individuals
(in Chronological Order)

Generally, only translations of at least an entire Testament made by Americans, or others whose translations were done while residents of the United States, are included here. Translations marked * are mentioned in this chapter but are less than a Testament in length.

Dates given are for the first edition of a complete Testament.

Later (or earlier) appearances of other portions of the Bible are also indicated in a note.

The Hills bibliographic numbers are from *The English Bible in America, A Bibliography of Editions of the Bible and the New Testament Published in America 1777–1957*, edited by Margaret T. Hills (New York: American Bible Society and The New York Public Library, 2d ed., 1962).

1808 Thomson, Charles. *The Holy Bible, Containing the Old and New Covenant, Commonly Called the Old and New Testament: Translated from the Greek*. Philadelphia: printed by Jane Aitken.

1823 Kneeland, Abner. *The New Testament; Being the English Only of the Greek and English Testament; Translated from the Original Greek According to Griesbach. . . .* Philadelphia: William Fry, printer; published by the editor and sold by him and also by Abm. Small (Hills, no. 478).

1826 Campbell, George, James MacKnight, and Philip Doddridge. *The Sacred Writings of the Apostles and Evangelists of Jesus Christ, Commonly Styled the New Testament: Translated from the Original Greek*. Buffaloe, Brooke County, VA: Printed and published by Alexr. Campbell (Hills, no. 567).

1828 Palfrey, John G. *The New Testament in the Common Version, Conformed to Greisbach's Standard Greek Text*. Boston: Press of the Boston Daily Advertiser; W. T. Lewis, printer (Hills, no. 643).

1833 Webster, Noah. *The Holy Bible . . . In the Common Version: With Admendments of the Language*. New Haven: Durrie & Peck (Hills, no. 826).

1833 Dickinson, Rodolphus. *A New and Corrected Version of The New Testament; or, a Minute Revision, and Professed Translation of the Original Histories, Memoirs, Letters, Prophecies, and Other Productions of the Evangelists and Apostles*. Boston: Lilly, Wait, Colman, & Holden (Hills, no. 839).

1842 *The Holy Bible; Being the English Version of the Old and New Testament, Made by Order of King James I: Carefully Revised and Amended, the meaning of the sacred original being given, in accordance with the best translations and the most approved Hebrew and Greek lexicographers*, by Several Biblical Scholars. Philadelphia: published for David Bernard, by J. B. Lippincott (Hills, no. 1134).

1848 Morgan, Jonathan. *The New Testament . . . Translated from the Greek, Into Pure English. . . .* Portland, ME: S. H. Colesworthy (Hills no. 1389).

1849 Whiting, Nathan N. *The Good News of Our Lord Jesus, the Anointed; from the Critical Greek Text of Tittmann*. Boston: published by Joshua V. Himes (Hills no. 1411).

1850 Cone, Spencer H., and Wm. H. Wyckhoff, eds. *The Commonly Received Version of the New Testament . . . With Several Hundred Emendations*. New Orleans: Duncan, Hurlbutt (Hills no. 1444).

1851 Murdock, James. *The New Testament; or, The Book of the Holy Gospel of our Lord and our god, Jesus the Messiah. A Literal Translation from the Syriac Peshito Version*. New York: Stanford & Swords (Hills no. 1477)

*1852 Woodruff, Hezekiah. *An Exposition of the New Testament: or The New Covenant of Our Sovereign Saviour. . . .* Auburn, NY: Henry Oliphant (Hills no. 1515). Of the Gospels, only Matthew is included.

1853 [5614] Leeser, Isaac. *Torah Nebi'im weKetubim: The Twenty-Four Books of the Holy Scriptures: Carefully Translated According to the Massoretic Text, on the Basis of the English Version, after the Best Jewish Authorities.* Philadelphia: L. Johnson; published at 371 Walnut Street (Hills no. 1540).

*1855 Norton, Andrews. *A Translation of the Gospels: With Notes.* Boston: Little, Brown (Hills no. 1601).

1858 Sawyer, Leicester Ambrose. *The New Testament, Translated from the Original Greek, with Chronological Arrangement of the Sacred Books, and Improved Divisions of Chapters and Verses.* Boston: John P. Lewett; Cleveland: Henry P. B. Jewett; London: Sampson Low, Son (Hills no. 1687). Portions of the Old Testament were published in 1861, 1862, and 1864. See Hills no. 1745.

1861? *The New Testament . . . As Revised and Corrected by the Spirits.* Entered in the year 1861, by Leonard Thorn. New York: published by the proprietors (Hills no. 1749A).

1862 Kenrick, Francis Patrick. *The New Testament: Translated from the Latin Vulgate, and Diligently Compared with the Original Greek Text. With Notes, Critical and Explanatory;* 2d. ed., revised and corrected. Baltimore: Kelly, Hedian & Piet (Hills no. 1761). The Gospels and most of the Old Testament were also published separately. See Hills no. 1414.

1864 Anderson, H. T. *The New Testament: Translated from the Original Greek.* Cincinnati: published for the author (Hills no. 1785).

1865 Wilson, Benjamin. *The Emphatic Diaglott: Containing the Original Greek text of what is commonly styled the New Testament, according to the recension of Dr. J. J. Griesbach, with an Interlineary word for word English Translation.* Geneva, IL: published by the author (Hills no. 1792).

1867 Smith, Jr., Joseph (the Seer). *The Holy Scriptures, Translated and corrected by the Spirit of Revelation.* Plano, IL: Church of Jesus Christ of Latter-Day Saints (Hills no. 1817).

1869 Noyes, George R. *The New Testament: Translated from the Greek Text of Tischendorf.* Boston: American Unitarian Association (Hills no. 1845).

1876 Smith, Julia E. *The Holy Bible . . . Translated Literally from the Original Tongues.* Hartford: American Publishing (Hills no. 1918).

1881 Williams, Samuel. *The New Testament . . . Revised A.D. 1881. (Amended).* New York: Fords, Howard & Hulbert (Hills no. 1975).

1883 Jackson, Cortes. *The New Testament . . . Translated out of the original Greek . . . with Apostolic References.* Denver: Collier & Cleaveland (Hills no. 2002).

1884–85 Hanson, J. W. *The New Covenant: Containing I. An Accurate Translation of the New Testament. II. Harmony of the Four Gospels. III. A Chronological Arrangement of the Text. IV. A Brief and Handy Commentary . . .* Boston and Chicago: Universalists Publishing House (Hills no. 2008).

1885 Dillard, W. D. *The Teaching and Acts of Jesus of Nazareth and His Apostles: Literally Translated Out of the Greek* (NT). Chicago: privately printed (Hills no. 2023).

1891–1931 Grant, Frederick W. *The Numerical Bible. Being a Revised Translation of the Holy Scriptures with Expository Notes: Arranged, Divided, and Briefly Characterized according to the Principles of their Numerical*

Structure. New York: Loizeaux Brothers (Hills no. 2044).

1897   Weekes, Robert D. *The New Dispensation: The New Testament Translated from the Greek*. New York and London: Funk & Wagnalls (Hills no. 2084).

1899–1901   Ballentine, Frank Schell. *The Modern American Bible . . . The Books of the Bible in Modern American Form and Phrase with Notes and Introduction* (NT). New York: Thomas Whittaker (Hills no. 2102). Ballentine also published his translation of the New Testament under several other titles, including *The Bible in Modern English* (1909) and *A Plainer Bible for Plain People in Plain America* (1922).

1902?   Godbey, W. B. *Translation of the New Testament from the Original Greek*. Cincinnati: Office of God's Revivalist (Hills no. 2142).

1904   Worrell, A. S. *The New Testament Revised and Translated*. Louisville: A. S. Worrell (Hills no. 2161).

1914   Panin, Ivan, ed. *The New Testament from the Greek Text as Established by Bible Numerics*. New Haven: Bible Numerics (Hills no. 2220).

1916   Harkavy, Alexander. *The Twenty-Four Books of the Old Testament: Hebrew Text and English Version with Illustrations*. New York: Hebrew Publishing (Hills no. 2227A).

1917   Lauritzen, Johannes Rudolph. *The New Testament . . . Translated out of the Original Greek by Martin Luther; Former Translations Diligently Compared* (revised by author). Knoxville, TN: J. R. Lauritzen.

1919–26   Knoch, Adolph E. *Concordant Version. The Sacred Scriptures. Designed to put the English reader in possession of all the vital facts of Divine revelation without a former knowledge of Greek by means of A Restored Greek Text with Various Readings, A Consistent Sublinear, based upon a Standard English equivalent for each Greek Element, and An Idiomatic, Emphasized English Version with notes* (NT). Los Angeles: The Concordant Publishing Concern (Hills no. 2250). Portions of the Old Testament have also been published.

1923   Goodspeed, Edgar J. *The New Testament: An American Translation*. Chicago: University of Chicago Press (Hills no. 2260).

1923   Ballantine, William G. *The Riverside New Testament: A Translation from the Original Greek Into the English of To-Day*. Boston and New York: Houghton Mifflin; Cambridge: Riverside (Hills no. 2261).

1924   Montgomery, Helen Barrett. *Centenary Translation of the New Testament Published to Signalize the Completion of the First Hundred Years of Work of the American Baptist Publication Society*. Philadelphia: American Baptist Publication Society (Hills no. 2276).

1925?   Overbury, Arthur E. *The People's New Covenant . . . Scriptural Writings Translated from the Meta-Physical Standpoint* (NT). Monrovia, CA: Arthur E. Overbury (Hills no. 2280).

1927   Smith, J. M. Powis, Theophile J. Meek, Alex. R. Gordon, and Leroy Waterman, translators, J. M. Powis Smith, ed. *The Old Testament: An American Translation*. Chicago: University of Chicago Press (Hills no. 2290). The Smith (OT) and Goodspeed (NT) translations were published as *The Bible: An American Translation* in 1931.

1928   LeFevre, George N. *The Christian's Bible—New Testament: A Translation from the Greek, Chiefly of the Codex Sinaiticus and Codex Vaticanus*. Strasburg, Pennsylvania: George N. LeFevre (Hills no. 2303).

*1931–46   Lenski, R. C. H. *The Interpretation of the [New Testament] . . .

Columbus, OH: Lutheran Book Concern (Hills no. 2323). Lenski prepared an independent translation of the entire New Testament for his commentaries. The translation has never been published separately.

*1933 Torrey, Charles Cutler. *The Four Gospels, a New Translation*. New York and London: Harper & Brothers (Hills no. 2339). Torrey also published his translation of Revelation in *The Apocalypse of John* (New Haven: Yale University Press, 1958).

1937? Martin, William Wallace. *The New Testament critically reconstructed and retranslated*. Nashville: Parthenon (Hills no. 2360). Martin also translated several books of the Old Testament. See Hills no. 2302.

1937 Greber, Johannes. *The New Testament: A New Translation and Explanation Based on the Oldest Manuscripts;* part I, translation. New York: John Felsberg (Hills no. 2361).

1937 Williams, Charles B. *The New Testament: A Translation in the Language of the People*. Boston: Bruce Humphries (Hills no. 2362).

1937 Spencer, Francis Aloysius, trans; Charles J. Callan and John A. McHugh, eds. *The New Testament . . . Translated into English from the Original Greek*. Francis Aloysius Spencer. Edited by Charles J. Callan, and John A. McHugh. New York: Macmillan (Hills no. 2363). Spencer translated the Gospels both from the Vulgate and from the Greek (1898). See Hills no. 2099.

1938 Clementson, Edgar Lewis. *The New Testament: A Translation*. Pittsburgh: Evangelization Society of the Pittsburgh Bible Institute (Hills no. 2368).

1940 Lamsa, George M. *The New Testament According to the Eastern Text Translated from the Original Aramaic Sources*. Philadelphia: A. J. Holman (Hills no. 2389). Lamsa published his translation of the entire Bible in 1957. See Hills no. 2568.

1943–45 Stringfellow, Ervin Edward. *A Translation, Harmony and Annotations* (NT). St. Louis: John S. Swift (Hills no. 2416).

1945 Verkuyl, Gerrit. *The Berkeley Version of the New Testament from the Original Greek with Brief Footnotes*. Berkeley, CA: James J. Gillick (Hills no. 2437). The *Berkeley Version* of the Bible was first published in 1959. Recently it has been retitled *The Modern Language Bible*.

1947 Swann, George. *The New Testament . . . Translated from the Greek text of Westcott and Hort*. Louisville, KY: Pentecostal (Hills no. 2464).

1950 Traina, A. B. *The New Testament of our Messiah and Saviour Yahshua: Sacred Name Version* (preface by Philip B. Wisman). Irvington, NJ: Scripture Research Association (Hills no. 2495). The entire Bible was published in 1963 as *The Holy Name Bible*, revised by A. B. Traina.

1951 Norlie, Olaf Morgan. *The New Testament . . . in Modern English translated from the original Greek*. Northfield, MN: published by the author (Hills no. 2502). Norlie's *Simplified New Testament* was published in 1961 (Grand Rapids: Zondervan) with a translation of the Psalms by R. K. Harrison.

1951 *The New Testament of Our Lord and Savior Jesus Christ: The Authentic Version*. Plattsburg, MO: Brotherhood Authentic Bible Society (Hills no. 2504).

1953–54? Moore, George Albert. *The New Testament: A New, Independent, Individual Translation from the Greek*. Chevy Chase, MD: Country Dollar (Hills no. 2528).

1954   Kleist, James A. *The New Testament Rendered from the Original Greek with Explanatory Notes;* part one, *The Four Gospels.* Milwaukee: Bruce (Hills no. 2543)

Lilly, Joseph L. *The New Testament Rendered from the Original Greek with Explanatory Notes;* part two, *Acts of the Apostles, Epistles and Apocalypse.* Milwaukee: Bruce (Hills no. 2543).

1956–59   Wuest, Kenneth S. *Wuest's Expanded Translation of the Greek New Testament.* (3 vols.) Grand Rapids: Eerdmans.

1956   Laubach, Frank. *Inspired Letters of the New Testament in Clearest English.* New York: Thomas Nelson. Laubach did not translate the Gospels because he felt that they were generally translated into clear English.

1958   Tomanek, James L. *The New Testament of our Lord and Savior Jesus Anointed.* Pocatello, ID: Arrowhead.

1958   Siewert, Frances E. *Amplified New Testament.* Grand Rapids: Zondervan. The entire Bible was published by Zondervan in 1965. The Old Testament was the work of a committee.

1960   Green, Jay P. *The Children's "King James" Bible* (NT) Evansville, IL: Modern Bible Translations. The entire Bible was published in 1962 by McGraw-Hill. Green later published this revision of the King James Version under several titles, including King James II Version of the Bible.

1961   Noli, Fan S. *The New Testament of our Lord and Savior Jesus Christ, translated into English from the approved Greek text of the Church of Constantinople and the Church of Greece.* Boston: Albanian Orthodox Church in America.

1963   Beck, William F. *The New Testament in the Language of Today (An American Translation).* Saint Louis: Concordia. Beck's translation of the Bible was published posthumously in 1976.

*1963–70   Jordan, Clarence. *The Cotton Patch Version . . . A Colloquial (Modern) Translation with a Southern Accent.* New York: Association. Jordan's translation was published in four volumes and includes the entire New Testament except Mark, John 9–21, and Revelation.

1967   Taylor, Kenneth N. *The Living New Testament Paraphrased.* Wheaton, IL: Tyndale House. The *Living Bible* was published in 1971.

1969   Ledyard, Gleason H. *The Children's New Testament.* Waco, TX: Word.

1970   Missionary Dispensary Bible Research, revisers. *The Restoration of Original Sacred Name Bible.* Buena Park, CA: Missionary Dispensary Bible Research.

1972   Byington, Steven T. *The Bible in Living English.* Brooklyn: Watchtower Bible and Tract Society.

1972   Klingensmith, Don. *Today's English New Testament.* New York: Vantage.

1973   Estes, Chester. *The Better Version of the New Testament: Based on the Greek Text according to Eminent Scholars and according to Certain Fundamental Principles and Rules of Biblical Interpretation.* Muscle Shoals, AL: Chester Estes.

*1976   Edington, Andrew. *The Word Made Fresh.* (3 vols.). Atlanta: John Knox.

1977   Adams, Jay E. *The Christian Counselor's New Testament: A New Translation in Everyday English.* Nutley, NJ: Presbyterian and Reformed Publishing.

1978	*The New Testament: English Version for the Deaf*. Grand Rapids: Baker. Also published as *The New Testament, a New Easy-to-Read Version*.
1979–82	Lattimore, Richmond. *New Testament: Newly Translated from the Greek*. Vol. 1, *The Four Gospels and Revelation;* Vol. 2, *Acts and Letters of the Apostles*. New York: Farrar, Strauss, Giroux.
1981	Meyer, Jacob O. *The Sacred Scriptures* (Bethel edition). Bethel, PA: Assemblies of Yahweh.
1981	Morris, Stanley. *The Simple English Bible, New Testament* (American edition). New York: International Bible Publishing.
1981	*May Your Name Be Inscribed in the Book of Life: A Messianic Version of the New Covenant Scriptures* (NT). Washington, D.C.: Messianic Vision.
1982	Bronstein, David, ed. *The Living Scriptures*. Wheaton, IL: Tyndale House.
1983	*New Testament: International Children's Version*. Fort Worth: Swete Publishing.
1984	*The Word: New Century Version*. Fort Worth: Swete Publishing.
1984	Anderson, Julian G. *New Testament into Simple, Everyday, American English: A New, Accurate Translation of the Greek*. Naples, FL: privately published.

WORKS CONSULTED

Bills, V. Alex 1968 "The Godbey New Testament." *The Bible Collector* 14:3–4.

Brock, S. P. 1974 "The Phenomenon of Biblical Translation in Antiquity." In *Studies in the Septuagint: Origins, Recensions, and Interpretations*, Sidney Jellicoe, editor, pp. 541–571. New York: KTAV.

Cheek, John 1953 "New Testament Translation in America." *Journal of Biblical Literature* 72:103–114.

Frank, Richard M. 1958 "Review of *The Holy Bible from Ancient Eastern Manuscripts*." *Catholic Biblical Quarterly* 20:384–89.

Goodspeed, Edgar J. 1953 *As I Remember*. New York: Harper.

Hadas, Moses 1951 *Aristeas to Philocrates (Letter of Aristeas)*. New York: Harper & Brothers.

Haraszti, Zoltan 1956 *The Enigma of the Bay Psalm Book*. Chicago, University of Chicago Press.

Herbert A. S. 1968 *Historical Catalogue of Printed Editions of the English Bible 1525–1961*. London and New York: British and Foreign Bible Society and American Bible Society.

Hills, Margaret T., ed 1962 *The English Bible in America*. New York: American Bible Society and New York Public Library.

Kubo, Sakae and Walter Specht 1983 *So Many Versions? Twentieth Century English Versions of the Bible*. Revised edition. Grand Rapids: Zondervan.

Lewis, Jack P. 1981 *The English Bible: From KJV to NIV*. Grand Rapids: Baker.

Matthews, Robert J 1969 "Joseph Smith's Revision of the Bible." *The Bible Collector* 17–18:2–12.

O'Callaghan, E. B. 1861 *A List of Editions of the Holy Scriptures and Parts Thereof, Printed in America Previous to 1860*. Albany: Munsell & Rowland.

Pope, Hugh 1952 *English Versions of the Bible*. Revised by Sebastian Bullough. St. Louis: B. Herder.

Reumann, John H. P. 1965 *The Romance of Bible Scripts and Scholars*. Englewood Cliffs, NJ: Prentice-Hall.

Rumball-Petrie, Edwin A. R. 1940 *America's First Bibles with a Census of 555 Extant Bibles*. Portland, ME: Southworth-Anthoensen.

Scrivener, F. H. A. 1884 *The Authorized Edition of the English Bible (1611)*. Cambridge: University Press.

Simms, P. Marion 1936 *The Bible in America: Versions that Have Played Their Part in the Making of the Republic*. New York: Wilson-Erickson.

Sjölander, Pearl 1979 *Some Aspects of Style in Twentieth-century English Bible Translation*. Umeå: privately published.

Skilton, John Hamilton 1961 "The Translation of the New Testament into English." Ph.D. dissertation, University of Pennsylvania.

Thomas, Cecil K 1958 *Alexander Campbell and His New Version*. St. Louis: Bethany.

Weingreen, J. 1982 "Dib^{e}rah Tôrah Kil^{e}šôn b^{e}nê-ādām." In *Interpreting the Hebrew Bible*, J. A. Emerton and Stefan C. Reif, editors, pp. 267–275. Cambridge: Cambridge U. Press.

Wyckoff, William H. 1842 *The American Bible Society and the Baptists*. New York: John R. Bigelow.

IV

Jewish Bible Scholarship and Translations in the United States

Jonathan D. Sarna
and
Nahum M. Sarna

For two thousand years, the Hebrew Bible has been studied by Jews not simply as a self-contained, sacred work on its own terms, but largely as a body of religious literature that has been filtered through a continuous process of rabbinic interpretation and reinterpretation within the community of practice and faith from which its immediate authority derived. Already in 553 C.E., the emperor Justinian (527–565 C.E.) took note of this fact in his *novella constitutio* concerning the Jews to whom he granted permission to read their sacred scriptures in Greek, Latin, or any other language. He stipulated, however, that they should "read the holy words themselves, rejecting the commentaries," by which he clearly meant rabbinic exegesis. As he put it, "the so-called second tradition *(deuterosis)* we prohibit entirely, for it is not part of the sacred books nor is it handed down by divine inspiration through the prophets, but the handiwork of men, speaking only of earthly things and having nothing of the divine in it" (Baumgarten: 37).

Justinian's motives and intentions are irrelevant to the present theme, for they belong within the category of medieval Jewish-Christian polemics. But his specified restriction does illustrate a historic fact of cardinal importance that differentiates the Jewish study of the Scriptures from the Christian approach, which, of course, has its own venerable tradition of theological reinterpretation of the Bible of the Jews. The educated, committed Jew to whom study of the Bible is at one and the same time a religious obligation, a spiritual exercise, a mode of worship, and a moral as well as an intellectual discipline, is confronted with a vast array of texts which, if not of equal authority, and most have no authority at all, yet command his attention, his concentrated thought and study. It is a literature that has long been endowed with a life and energy of its own, and in its independent existence the light of the Hebrew Bible has become refracted through a thousand prisms. In discussing the role of the Bible in any Jewish community, this circumstance must be taken into account.

Another factor that requires recognition is the term "American Judaism." It is an appellation that well-nigh defies meaningful definition. The variable, restless, frequently chaotic, and always kaleidoscopic configurations of American Jewish life do not easily yield to procrustean generalizations. American Judaism is not, strictly speaking, simply a peer group of the Protestant and Catholic faith communities, for it encompasses a considerable number of individuals who possess no affiliation with religious institutions but whose sense of Jewish self-identity is strong and for whom "Judaism" carries with it a humanistic, secular nuance and/or nationalistic orientation. Nevertheless, it appears to be an incontrovertible fact that the ultra-Orthodox and the ultra-Reform, as well as those who represent the variegated shadings of religiosity between these poles, together with the secular Jew, all accept the Hebrew Scriptures as the bedrock of Jewish civilization, and all share a common recognition and conviction that the Hebrew Bible is a living force within the community of self-identifying Jews from which the structure of values to which Judaism subscribes ultimately derives. That this *consensus omnium* may also be accompanied by a commonality of ignorance of the biblical text itself is beside the point. What is pertinent is that the peculiar makeup of American Judaism distinguishes it from Protestantism and Catholicism in a very significant way.

Still another, no less important, singularity is that the received Hebrew text forever remains the sole authentic and valid basis for Jewish study and interpretation. Translations of the Bible have no authority for Jews. Particular English versions, like those of Isaac Leeser and of the Jewish Publication Society of 1917, achieved universal acceptance by English-speaking Jews, as will doubtless the new JPS translation. However, in no instance was the version initiated, sponsored, authorized or sanctioned by any official Jewish ecclesiastical body. In each case, the English version was a decidedly lay production even though learned rabbis representative of the three organized wings of American Judaism actively participated in the work.

The Leeser Translation

American Jewish Bible translations date back to the foremost Jewish religious leader in early America: Isaac Leeser (1806–1868).

Born in Westphalia and orphaned as a child, Leeser studied both at the gymnasium in Muenster and with Rabbi Abraham Sutro (Grossman). He arrived in this country in 1824 to work with his uncle, Zalma Rehine, a storekeeper in Richmond, Virginia. There he learned English, assisted on a volunteer basis at Congregation Beth Shalome, studied with Richmond's three most learned Jews, and in 1829 undertook to defend Judaism in print against the strictures of a British critic. Shortly thereafter, Congregation Mikveh Israel called him to Philadelphia to serve as its *ḥazan*. He spent the rest of his life in Philadelphia, first at Mikveh Israel, later on his own, and still later at Congregation Beth El Emeth. He never married and never made much money. His time, energy, and resources went exclusively to the congregation and the Jewish community, which he served faithfully as spiritual leader, writer, organizer, translator, and publisher. The magnitude of his achievements defies easy summary. Merely to read Bertram Korn's list of Leeser's "firsts," however, is to gain some appreciation of his formative role in American Judaism:

> The first volumes of sermons delivered and published by an American Jewish religious teacher (1837); the first complete American translation of the Sephardic prayer book (1837); the first Hebrew primer for children (1838); the first Jewish communal religious school (1839); the first successful American Jewish magazine-news journal (1843); the first American Jewish publication society (1845); the first Hebrew-English Torah to be edited and translated by an American Jew (1845); the first complete English translation of the Ashkenazic prayer book (1848); the first Hebrew "high school" (1849); the first English translation of the entire Bible by an American Jew (1853); the first Jewish defense organization—the Board of Delegates of American Israelites (1859); the first American Jewish theological seminary—Maimonides College (1867). Practically every form of Jewish activity which supports American Jewish life today was either established or envisaged by this one man. Almost every kind of publication which is essential to Jewish survival was written, translated, or fostered by him. (1967: 133)

Leeser's scholarly equipment was somewhat limited. The more learned and often more religiously radical Jewish religious leaders who followed him to America's shores had no trouble confounding him with intricate Talmudic arguments. Leeser's energy, however, was boundless, and likewise boundless was his desire to strengthen the Jewish community against assimilation and protestantization. Reanimating Jews' "almost expiring desire for critical inquiry into the sacred text" formed part of Leeser's program for stimulating Jewish revival (Leeser, 1856: vii). His other activities—educational, religious, philanthrophic and political ones—similarly related to his broad mission, that of preserving Jewish identity in the face of Christian conversionism and Jewish apathy.

While Isaac Leeser's decision to translate the Bible largely stemmed from these domestic concerns, it was also partly influenced by Moses Mendelssohn's translation of the Pentateuch from Hebrew to German (1780–1783), an epoch-making event whose reverberations spread throughout post-Emancipation Jewry (Weinberg; Billingheimer; Altmann). Mendelssohn served as one of Leeser's early role models, and when he first contemplated a Bible translation, the young *hazan* may have wanted to carry forward the master's work in a new language. But by the time he actually began his work in 1838, Leeser was less enamored with Mendelssohn, and he had a better conception of his own community's needs. Mendelssohn had translated the Bible as part of his program to enlighten the Jews of his day. Leeser's translation, by contrast, aimed to fight too much enlightenment; it sought to help Jews preserve their own identity intact.

The average American Jew in Leeser's day did not read Hebrew and, therefore, studied the Bible, if at all, from the venerable King James Version obtained cheaply or at no charge either from missionaries or from the American Bible Society. These Bibles contained the Hebrew Scriptures and New Testament bound together, in one volume, according to the Christian canon, and in a thoroughly christological format. Every page and every chapter of the Bible society's Bible bore a brief summary heading, many of which read Christian interpretations into the text. Jews who used these Bibles often condemned, as Leeser did, the "unfairness" of those who chose such headings as "the Prediction of Christ" (Psalm 110), "A Description of Christ" (Song of Solomon 5), and "Christ's Birth and Kingdom" (Isaiah 9) (1867: 41). Innocent Jews seeing these headings had, Leeser feared, "no means of knowing what is Scriptural and what is not" (1867: 42)

Format aside, the King James Bible translated many verses in a manner that Jews found thoroughly objectionable. As Leeser saw it, (*Occident*, 1851: 480) "wherever it was possible for the translators to introduce Christianity in the Scriptures, they have uniformly done so," in order, he said on another occasion, (1853: iii), "to assail Israel's hope and faith." He found particularly galling what he called the "perversions" introduced into the standard English text of the Prophets and the Psalms.

Leeser was not alone in his wrath. English Jews, as early as David Levi, had penned critiques of the Authorized Version, while Selig Newman's *Emendations of the Authorized Version of the Old Testa-*

ment (1839) filled seventy-two closely-printed pages with examples of where "the translators were either decidedly wrong, or . . . have not given the happiest rendering" (iv). Particularly troubling from a Jewish point of view were such readings as "virgin" for the Hebrew *'almâ* (Gen 24:43, Isa 7:14), or young woman; repeated capitalization of the word "saviour," and the like.

Had Leeser's objections to the King James Version only been confined to these kinds of Christological biases, he might have composed a Jewish revision without undue difficulty, simply by deleting the headings, repairing offensive verses, and rearranging the order of the books to conform with Jewish tradition. Just as the Ferrara Bible of 1553 appeared in a Christian edition where *'almâ* in Isa 7:14 was translated "virgin," and a Jewish edition where the same word was rendered "young woman" or transliterated as "la alma," (Margolis, 1917: 62), so there could have been Jewish and Christian editions of King James. But a Judaized version of a Christian translation would not have satisfied Leeser. To his mind, Jews were the guardians of Scripture, bearers of a long interpretive tradition of their own. They had no reason to defer, as subordinates, to a translation authorized by, as he put it, "a deceased king of England who certainly was no prophet" (1856: v). Nor did he agree that the Authorized Version created the standard from which all subsequent revisions derived. He rather staked Jews' claims on the Bible in the original; that was their source of legitimacy. By publishing a translation "made by one of themselves," he placed Jews on an equal footing with Protestants. To the extent that his translation could claim to be a better approximation of the original, he could even insist that Jews were more than equals.

Leeser was not alone in seeking independent legitimacy through a Bible translation. His Philadelphia contemporary, Bishop Francis P. Kenrick, was making a new Catholic translation of the Bible at roughly the same time (1849–1860), though whether the two men knew each other is not clear. Kenrick's translation principles, of course, differed from Leeser's, since the Catholic translator, though informed by the Hebrew, "did not always feel at liberty to render closely where it would imply a departure from the Vulgate" (Fogarty: 171). But the two translators shared a common desire: to translate the Bible into an English version that was both visibly different from, and arguably better than, the Authorized (Protestant) Version that the majority of Americans held dear.

The translation that Leeser finally produced in 1853, after fifteen years of work, derived from the original Hebrew, and depended, according to the preface, only on traditional Jewish commentators and "the studies of modern German Israelites" (including that of the German Reform leader, Ludwig Philipson). Leeser avoided making use of Christian or English language scholarship, boasting with only slight exaggeration that "not an English book has been consulted except Bagster's Bible" (even this exception was deleted in a later preface.) Although he was more familiar with Christian works than he admitted, he wanted to stress that his was a *Jewish* translation. When he was done, he pridefully pointed to the many differences which distinguished his version from the authorized one. His only concession to the King James was to follow its old English style, which, he felt, "for simplicity cannot be surpassed," and to conform to many of its spellings (Sussman, 1985).

Leeser strove to render the Hebrew text into English "as literally as possible," even at the expense of stylistic beauty (1856: vi). This immediately set his translation apart from the flowery King James, and simultaneously ensured that it would face criticism on literary grounds, criticism that was frequently deserved. Leeser provoked Israel Abrahams's scorn (1920: 254–59) by abandoning the standard translation of Ps 23:2: "He maketh me to lie down in green pastures," for the awkward, if slightly more literal "in pastures of tender grass he causeth me to lie down." "The heavens relate the glory of God; and the expanse telleth of the work of his hands" (Ps 19:1) rang similarly awkward, especially when contrasted with "the heavens declare the glory of God; and the firmament sheweth his handiwork," the King James reading. Leeser did carry over the standard and to his mind literal "until Shiloh come" for his translation of the controversial passage in Gen 49:10, which Christians have interpreted as foreshadowing Jesus. (The new Jewish Publication Society translation, by contrast, reads "So that tribute shall come to him," following the Midrash.) Rather than deviating from the plain meaning as he saw it, he appended a long explanatory footnote, which concludes by asserting that "the pious and intelligent reader will have enough to satisfy all doubts."

Matitiahu Tsevat (1958) has pointed out that in his quest for literalism "Leeser wanted the impossible." Translation by its very nature involves interpretation. Furthermore, all Bible translators are heir to interpretive traditions which, consciously or not, shape their scriptural understanding. Calls for "literalism," or movements "back to the Bible," Tsevat shows, really seek to cloak with legitimacy efforts aimed at replacing one mode of interpretation with another.

In Leeser's case, literalism usually meant resorting to rabbinic exegesis. Thus, in Exod 21:6, dealing with the laws for servants, the

King James translation reads straightforwardly "his master shall bore his ear through with an awl; and he shall serve him for ever." Leeser, influenced by rabbinic interpretation of Lev 25:10 and, likely as not a raging American debate over the relationship between the biblical form of slavery and the Southern one,[1] translated the last clause "and he shall serve him till the jubilee"—which, of course, is not what the verse literally says. It must be admitted that this is an unusual instance. It was more often the case that Leeser encased his interpolations in parentheses. Instead of having Samuel "lying down in the temple of the Lord," for example, he more demurely had him sleep "in (the hall of) the temple of the Lord" (1 Sam 3:3)—a bow to decorum that the commentators endorsed, but that literalists assuredly would not.

Isaac Leeser labored initially under the assumption that Jews alone would be interested in his translation. In 1845, when his Hebrew-English edition of the Pentateuch appeared, he presented the volume only to his "Jewish friends," explaining that "I speak of my Jewish friends in particular, for however much a revised translation may be desired by all believers in the word of God, there is no probability that the gentiles will encourage any publication of this nature emanating from a Jewish writer" (1845: iii). Leeser, however, was mistaken. By the time his full Bible with notes appeared in 1853, he himself realized that those "who are of a different persuasion" might indeed find the work valuable "as exhibiting . . . the progress of biblical criticism among ancient and modern Israelites" (iv). When Rev. Charles Hodge, a leading Presbyterian theologian at Princeton Theological Seminary, recommended his (Leeser's) translation in the *Princeton Review*, and called for "a work on a similar plan from a competent Christian scholar," Leeser happily reprinted the review in the *Occident* (1854: 360), the Jewish monthly that he founded and edited.

Christian interest in Leeser's work reflects yet another aspect of the Jewish-Christian relationship that deserves attention. More than it is generally recognized, American Protestants in the nineteenth century sought out and respected Jewish expositions of the Hebrew Scriptures. The roots of this interest, of course, lay in Europe, where Christian scholars had overtly or covertly been studying the Bible with Jews for centuries. They knew, as did their nineteenth-century successors, that Jewish religious leaders understood Hebrew, read the Bible in the original, and studied traditional Jewish commentators— or at least claimed to. But beyond this, especially in America, many Protestants saw Jews as lineal descendants of the biblical figures they read and heard about. According to the Richmond *Constitutional Whig* in 1829:

> When we see one of these people, and remember that we have been told by good authority, that he is an exact copy of the Jew who worshipped in the Second Temple two thousand years ago—that his physiognomy and religious opinions—that the usages and customs of his tribe are still the same, we feel that profound respect which antiquity inspires. (Ezekiel and Lichtenstein: 56)

Protestants who adhered to this view naturally assumed that Jews preserved special knowledge of the biblical world that others did not share. Acting on that basis, they often turned to Jews when Hebrew or Old Testament questions arose.

Two early American Jews, Jonathan (Jonas) Horwitz and Solomon Jackson received non-Jewish encouragement when they sought to publish Hebrew texts of the Bible—a much needed task considering that in 1812, by Horwitz's estimate, fewer than a dozen Hebrew Bibles were available for purchase in the whole United States. Horwitz, a scholarly European immigrant who brought Hebrew type with him when he came to Philadelphia, collected recommendations from twelve Christian clergymen and numerous subscriptions for his work, but eventually transferred his rights to the edition to Thomas Dobson who completed the task based on the text of van der Hooght's Hebrew Bible that Horwitz had prepared. The Dobson Bible (1814) is the first independently produced edition of the Hebrew Bible in the United States (Vaxer; Wolf and Whiteman: 308–311; Fein: 75–76).

Jackson, better known as editor of *The Jew*, an antimissionary periodical and the first Jewish magazine in America, planned an even more ambitious undertaking: a Hebrew-English linear Bible. His earlier vituperative attacks on leading Protestants notwithstanding, three clergymen, including the Episcopal Bishop of New York, John Henry Hobart, joined six leading Jews in recommending him and urging support for his work. One of the clergymen specifically praised the fact that the "author and editor belong to the *literal* family of Abraham," suggesting that this improved the proposed volume's credibility (Jackson). Apparently, the recommendation did not help, for the book never appeared.

Americans also looked to Jews from time to time to defend the Bible against "infidels." *Letters of Certain Jews to Monsieur Voltaire* (1795), a French work defending both Jews and the integrity of Scripture, appeared in two American editions, as did England's David Levi's *A Defence of the Old Testament in a Series of Letters Addressed to Thomas Paine* (1797). Thomas Jefferson, who read Levi's earlier

Letters to Dr. Priestly, noted in 1816 that Levi "avails himself all his advantage over his adversaries by his superior knowledge of the Hebrew, speaking in the very language of divine communication, while they can only fumble on with conflicting and disputed translations" (Lipscomb: 469–70; Abrahams and Miles). Three decades later, when the Bible was "threatened" by new discoveries in geology, Jonathan Horwitz, who since the appearance of the Dobson Bible had become a medical doctor, published *A Defence of the Cosmogony of Moses* (1839), a "vindication" of the Bible "from the attacks of geologists," based on a close reading of the Hebrew text (which, he lamented, was so little known), a cursory reading of geological theory, and a firm conviction that "not the slightest foundation is to be seen in the Holy Record for any interpretation lengthening the age of the world beyond 6,000 years" (29). Later still, Rabbi Isaac Mayer Wise, the leading figure in American Reform Judaism, attempted to defend tradition against what he called the theory of "homo-brutalism," as expounded by Charles Darwin (1876:47–69).

More commonly, Americans looked to Jews to teach them the language of the Bible: Hebrew and Hebrew grammar. Many of the Hebrew grammars used by Americans were composed by Jews or Jewish converts to Christianity, and numerous Jews taught Hebrew to Christian students (Chomsky; Fellman). Isaac Nordheimer, the most notable early American Hebrew grammarian, wrote the highly original *Critical Grammar of the Hebrew Language* (1838–1841) and was the first Jew to teach Hebrew at New York University (Pool; Neill). Joshua Seixas, son of the famous Shearith Israel minister and also the author of a Hebrew grammar (1833, 1834), taught Hebrew at various colleges in Ohio. His best known student was Joseph Smith, the Mormon prophet, who held Seixas in high regard (Davis, 1970: 347–54). Jews continued to be associated with Hebrew and Hebrew studies later on in the century, in a few cases at the university level.

The fact that these Jews were exceptional—most American Jews could not understand Hebrew—detracted not at all from the image of all Jews as biblical experts. McGuffey's *Eclectic Third Reader* taught school children to "consider the Jews as the keepers of the Old Testament. It was their own sacred volume, which contained the most extraordinary predictions concerning the infidelity of their nation, and the rise, progress, and extensive prevalence of Christianity" (Westerhoff: 139). Seeing Jews in this light, Christians periodically called on Jews to offer biblical views on questions of the day. Jewish leaders presented widely publicized testimony regarding "The Biblical view of Slavery" (the question divided Jews as much as it did non-

Jews), the biblical view of temperance, the biblical view of capital punishment, and even on the biblical view of baptism (Kalisch: 37). Biblical magazines, particularly late nineteenth-century ones like *The Old Testament Student*, welcomed Jewish participation. Jewish lectures and books on biblical subjects received respectful Christian attention. Even those who considered Jews misguided and doomed recognized that Jews preserved important traditions and could be valuable assets in the battle against infidelity. Not surprisingly, therefore, Leeser's Jewish Bible translation met with considerable approbation.

The Rise of Jewish Bible Scholarship in the United States

The decades following the publication of Isaac Leeser's translation saw the first flickering of Jewish biblical scholarship on American shores. Harry Orlinsky, in his valuable survey (1974), highlights the pioneering efforts in this area of Isidor Kalisch, Adolph Huebsch, Isaac Mayer Wise, Michael Heilprin, and Benjamin Szold. All of these men were trained in Europe, all but Heilprin were active rabbis, and all immigrated with the great wave of central European Jews that swelled America's Jewish population from less than 15,000 in 1840 to about 250,000 just forty years later. A desire to strengthen the hands of the faithful against missionaries and biblical critics motivated some of these men, notably Kalisch in his *Wegweiser für rationelle Forschungen in den biblischen Schriften* (1853), and Wise in his *Pronaos to Holy Writ* (Kalisch, 1891: 14–18; Wise, 1954: 180; Sandmel). Others, especially Michael Heilprin, best known as an editor for *Appleton's Cyclopaedia*, "accepted, not grudgingly, but with enthusiasm and delight, those views of the Old Testament which have been defended by Graf and Kuenen and Wellhausen and Reuss" (Pollak: 9). Indeed, Heilprin's articles about biblical criticism in the *Nation* helped familiarize Americans with what these European scholars were doing, and his magnum opus, *The Historical Poetry of the Ancient Hebrews Translated and Critically Examined* (1879–1880), carried critical scholarship forward and won considerable academic acclaim.

The lonely efforts of these scholarly pioneers contrast with the widespread neglect of biblical studies on the part of the mass of American Jews. Heavily engaged as most were in mercantile pursuits, they found little time for any kind of study; critical scholarship was certainly beyond them. Immigrants did sometimes send their intellectually gifted youngsters back to Germany for advanced degrees, a practice that continued down to World War I. Once there, however, few American Jews took the opportunity to gain mastery in biblical scholarship—and for good reasons.

First of all, they found the subject of the Bible heavily freighted with Christian theology, if not anti-Judaism, and particularly with the dogma of the Hebrew Scriptures as *praeparatio* for the New Testament. Second, they learned that the Jewish renaissance movement known as *Das Wissenschaft des Judentums* generally excluded biblical studies from its purview. It concentrated instead on rabbinic literature, which had been sorely neglected and stood in dire need of redemption for scientific research. Leopold Zunz, programmatic founder of the Wissenschaft movement, was content to leave biblical scholarship in Christian hands. Many American Jews followed suit, believing that the Bible was, as Max Margolis put it, "a non-Jewish subject" (Gordis: 2). Finally, American Jews knew that biblical studies held open to them almost no promise of gainful employment. Positions in biblical studies at major American universities remained generally the preserve of Protestants, many of them ministers. Jews—witness the case of Arnold Ehrlich or Israel Eitan—found themselves excluded, even if their contributions did win recognition elsewhere. This may help explain why no Jews numbered among the founders of the Society of Biblical Literature (SBL), and only a mere handful (notably the father and son teams of Rabbi Marcus Jastrow and Prof. Morris Jastrow and Rabbi Gustav Gottheil and Prof. Richard J. H Gottheil) took out membership during its first decade, even though the regulations of the society explicitly specified that conditions of membership were to disregard what it termed "ecclesiastical affiliation." By the semicentennial meeting, the roster of members included at least forty-three Jews, of whom, it would seem, seventeen bore the title "Rabbi," and twenty were professional Jewish scholars. Whether the proportionately large number of rabbis may be taken as indicative of broader intellectual horizons and deeper scholarly interests on the part of the Jewish clergy of two generations ago than is the case with their modern successors or whether it means that a relatively large number of would-be Jewish biblical scholars turned to the rabbinate as the outlet for their thwarted aspirations in an era of complete lack of opportunity for academic employment is hard to say. What is worthy of more than the mere passing mention possible here, is that a half-century ago Jewish scholars in Talmudics and the traditional branches of medieval learning maintained an abiding and serious interest in biblical studies, something apparently made all but impossible today due to the unprecedented explosion of scholarship and research, pursued with ever-increasing degrees of specialization. We refer to the presence on the 1930 membership rolls of such illustrious names as Cyrus Adler, Salo Baron, Israel Davidson, Alexander Marx, Ralph Marcus, Chaim Tchernowitz, Harry Wolfson and Solomon Zeitlin (*Journal of Biblical Literature*, ii, xvii, xx, lii).

Theoretically, of course, Jews and Christians could join together on a scientific basis to study the Bible. Rabbi Bernhard Felsenthal made this clear in 1884 when, in an article in *The Old Testament Student*, he declared that "a Bible scholar should free his mind from all misleading preconceptions, from all sectarian bias;—truth, nothing but the truth, should be his aim." In fact, however, this proved easier said than done. William Rainey Harper, although agreeing with Felsenthal's "*principle* . . . that, whether Jews or Christian, we are to seek the truth" nevertheless reminded the rabbi that "Our paths diverge. Our conceptions of the Old Testament must, of necessity, be largely molded by what we find in the New."

American Jewish scholars found themselves more easily welcomed as fellows in the broader realm of Semitic studies, a field which was from a theological point of view far safer than biblical studies, yet did nevertheless still bear on the biblical text and history. Cyrus Adler (1926), in his cursory survey of "The Beginnings of Semitic Studies in America," mentions several very early American Jewish contributions to the subject, most of them dealing with language and grammar, as well as the valuable if amateurish pre-Civil War work of Mendes I. Cohen who brought to America a large collection of Egyptian antiquities, later deposited at Johns Hopkins University. More rigorous works of scholarship began to appear only in the last quarter of the nineteenth century, when, as part of a larger movement to upgrade American higher education, Semitics programs were initiated, first at the graduate level at Johns Hopkins, and later at other major universities. At Hopkins, under the direction of Paul Haupt, brought over from Göttingen in 1883, such Jewish students of Semitics as Cyrus Adler, William Rosenau, and Aaron Ember embarked on their first serious scholarly endeavors. At the same time, Maurice Bloomfield, already a professor at Hopkins, was beginning his pioneering studies of Sanskrit, which also held important implications for students of Semitics. Other Jewish Semitists of this period included Richard J. H. Gottheil, who became chairman of the Semitics Department at Columbia University; Morris Jastrow, who became Professor of Semitic Studies at the University of Pennsylvania; and Max L. Margolis, of whom more below, who from 1909 until his death occupied the chair in biblical philology at Dropsie College. Gottheil, Jastrow, and Margolis all served terms as president of the Society of Biblical Literature: Gottheil as its first Jewish president, in 1903, and the other two, respectively, in 1916 and 1923.

That so many Jews found a home in Semitic studies is not accidental. Jews, particularly the great Jewish philanthropist Jacob Schiff, supported Semitic studies with liberal endowments in the belief that Jews were, in Schiff's words, "the modern representatives of the Semitic people." To combat "social prejudice and ostracism" against Jews, Schiff felt that "opportunities should be created for a more thorough study and a better knowledge of Semitic history and civilization, so that the world shall better understand and acknowledge the debt it owes to the Semitic people" (Adler, 1929: 21). To this end, Schiff supported archeological acquisitions and excavations in the Near East, built the Harvard Semitics Museum, and founded the Semitic and Hebrew departments of the New York Public Library and the Library of Congress. Other Jews supported Semitic studies at Yale and the University of Chicago (Chiel; Feuer: 433). Although for the time being biblical studies remained a separate domain, outside the realm of Semitic studies, in fact, albeit through the backdoor and under the guise of a more acceptable rubric, the groundwork for Jewish Bible scholarship in America had been laid. A new era was about to begin.

The First Jewish Publication Society Translation

As biblical and Semitic studies developed in Jewish scholarly circles, popular pressure mounted within the American Jewish community for a new Bible translation to replace Isaac Leeser's. The late nineteenth century witnessed a great upsurge of general interest in the study of the Bible. In Jewish circles, as also in Christian ones, the demand for Bibles that embodied "the Jewish point of view" reached unprecedented levels. A Jewish cultural revival took place—a fact that the onrush of East European Jewish immigration during this period usually overshadows—and during one stunning decade the Jewish Publication Society, the American Jewish Historical Society, the National Council of Jewish Women, and the Jewish Chautauqua Society all came into being, while at the same time preparations began for publication of the *Jewish Encyclopedia*. Except for the American Jewish Historical Society every one of the above had as one of its aims the furthering of biblical scholarship or the encouraging of Bible study by the laity. "There has been, during the past ten years, a great awakening among our people," Daniel P. Hays correctly noted in

1901. He considered the change "a realization that the Jew has not become great by his material achievements, but by his contribution toward the higher ideals of life and by his endeavors toward the uplifting of the race" (*American Jewish Year Book*, 1902: 216).

Christian interest in Jewish work on the Bible also reached new heights during this period. Rabbis, notably Emil G. Hirsch, Bernhard Felsenthal, and Gustav Gottheil received invitations to teach the Bible to Christian audiences, while Rabbi Moses Gries in Cleveland reported having "many requests from non-Jews who wish to secure a translation accepted by Jewish scholars" (*JPS Annual Reports*, 1897: 24).

In the face of all this popular interest in Jewish biblical exegesis, the Leeser Bible, although it had become the standard Anglo-Jewish Bible, nevertheless proved totally inadequate. First of all, it was too expensive. The smallest edition cost one dollar, much more than the equivalent Protestant edition, and more also than many people were apparently willing to pay. Over and over Jews called for "a cheap edition of the English Bible." The Central Conference of American Rabbis, in 1909, thought that a fifty-cent Bible was all that the market could bear (*CCAR Year Book*, 1895: 25; 1909: 155).

Even had the price been right, however, the Leeser Bible would still have proved unsatisfactory. Its English style was embarrassing and in some cases unintelligible. Its "literal" approach to the Bible along with Isaac Leeser's professed belief "in the Scriptures as they have been handed down to us, as also in the truth and authenticity of prophecies and their ultimate literal fulfillment" (1856: v) found fewer and fewer adherents. It was also antiquated; biblical scholarship had advanced enormously since Leeser's day, permitting new translations of formerly obscure passages. Most important of all, a new Protestant translation of the Bible had appeared, the (Anglican) English Revised Version (1885), which was produced by some of the greatest Christian scholars of the day, and from the point of view of biblical studies was relatively up-to-date. Leeser's translation paled by comparison.

It did not follow, however, that a whole new Jewish translation had to be produced from scratch. As had been true with the King James, so too with the English Revised Version Jews could simply have issued a "Jewish revised version," repairing offensive renderings (the ERV continued such christological King James readings as "virgin" for Isa 7:14), and putting the biblical books into a traditional Jewish order and format. The Jewish Religious Education Board in London made the task of composing a Jewish revision easier by publishing sixteen pages of corrections titled *Appendix to the Revised Version* (1896). In 1907, the Central Conference of American Rabbis (CCAR) resolved to carry out the project:

> Be it resolved, that in view of the immediate need of a cheap edition of the English Bible in the best available translation, the C.C.A.R. enter into negotiations with the publishers of the Revised version for an issue of the Old Testament exclusively (*CCAR Year Book*, 1907: 35).

Negotiations proceeded, and before long, Oxford University Press agreed to issue a special edition of its translation, complete with a sixteen-page appendix prepared by the CCAR, containing "corrections and emendations of the text necessary from the Jewish standpoint" (*CCAR Year Book*, 1908: 149).

Rabbi Samuel Schulman of Temple Beth El in New York, rejoiced at the "implied recognition of a Jewish body by the Christian world, in so important a matter as changes in a widespread version of the Bible." But at the last minute, the CCAR backed out of the undertaking. Instead, it accepted an invitation from the Jewish Publication Society to cooperate in "issuing an English translation of the Bible under Jewish auspices" (JPS Publication Committee Minutes, 5 April 1908). Whatever benefits cooperation with Oxford University Press might have promised faded before the renewed possibility of a translation produced by Jews independently.

The Jewish Publication Society (JPS) had been talking about a new Jewish Bible translation since 1892. Three years later, in the very midst of the heady revival already described, it proudly announced that a new translation was underway. Specialization and division of labor, concepts much discussed at the time, seem to have left their impact on the JPS, for it decided to produce its translation as a series of independent volumes, each one by a different person—mostly rabbis with European training. Marcus Jastrow, who had immigrated to America in 1866 and become one of American Jewry's leading luminaries (author of a Hebrew-Aramaic-English dictionary that is still in print) was appointed general editor. He was aided by Kaufmann Kohler and Frederick de Sola Mendes: both rabbis, both trained abroad. Rhapsodic reports of progress—descriptions of editors "busily pursuing the work of revising and editing the books of the Bible as they came to them from the hands of the translators"—had to be tempered annually by tedious reminders that "the work is necessarily slow, and . . . a considerable time must elapse before the entire Bible can be ready for publication" (*JPS Annual Reports*, 1899: 17). By the time Jastrow died in 1903, only Kaufmann Kohler's translation of Psalms, revised by the editors, had actually been published. Although work on a few other books had proceeded, a new translation of the whole Bible seemed more distant than ever.

Solomon Schechter, freshly arrived from Cambridge University and viewed in his day as America's preeminent Judaic scholar, replaced Jastrow as translation chairman, but he soon wearied of the task. The endlessly complex and hopelessly disorganized manner in which the translation was being pursued and a chronic scarcity of funds led him to submit his resignation in mid-1907. But just as the project seemed in danger of collapse, the CCAR overture to Oxford University Press became public. At first, Judge Mayer Sulzberger (1843-1923), chairman of the JPS Publication Committee and a lay scholar in his own right (Davis, 1965: 362–65), considered the CCAR scheme a good one, and wrote to Rabbi David Philipson that "it might be well for the Publication Society to consider the question of joining the Central Conference in its project of disseminating the Revised Version as widely as possible." A few months of reflection, however, convinced him that "official recognition" by Jews of the English Revised Version could be inappropriate (Philipson Papers). Since Philipson was coming around to the same view, Cyrus Adler, long the power behind the throne at JPS, stepped in and hammered out an agreement that both the JPS and the CCAR accepted.

Both sides agreed on "the desirability of issuing an English version of the Bible under Jewish auspices," and both sides agreed on the need to produce the new Bible as quickly as possible ("two years would be an outside limit"). Secretly, both sides also agreed that the only way to accomplish this feat was "that the text of the Revised Version be used as the basis, and that the revision of it . . . be primarily of such a nature that it will remove all un-Jewish and anti-Jewish phrases, expressions, renderings and usages" (JPS Publication Committee Minutes, 5 April 1908). The new Bible, in short, would conform to the latest Protestant fashion but would still be distinctive enough to bear a separate Jewish label.

Although it is likely that nobody noticed the fact at the time, the discussions between Adler, Sulzberger, and Philipson evidenced the growing Americanization of Jewish scholarship in the New World. All three of the men were products of the American educational system (Sulzberger, though born abroad, immigrated with his parents as a young boy) and had obtained the bulk of their Jewish knowledge in the United States. Perhaps it is not surprising that the man selected to be the new editor-in-chief of the Bible translation was also, at least in part, American trained: Max L. Margolis. Born in Russia, Margolis immigrated to America from Berlin in 1889 at the age of twenty-three, and two years later under Richard Gottheil received the first Ph.D. in oriental studies ever awarded by Columbia University. His subject was "an attempt to improve the damaged text of the Talmud through reference to variant readings in Rashi's Commentary on the Talmud, demonstrated through the tractate Erubhin," and Margolis wrote the thesis in Latin. But given the difficulty of obtaining rabbinic sources in the United States, he then shifted his focus to Semitics, and quickly gained scholarly recognition. The depth and breadth of his learning, coupled with his fine command of the English language, made him the ideal person to head up the translation effort (Gordis; Orlinsky, 1974: 305–10).

As editor-in-chief, Margolis singlehandedly prepared all of the first drafts of the Bible translation "with the aid of previous versions and with constant consultation of Jewish authorities." More than anyone originally expected, he also proceeded to deviate from the English Revised Version, sometimes on scholarly, not just religious, grounds. Only when he was done did he submit his drafts to an editorial committee consisting of six scholars, perfectly balanced so as to span both the Jewish academic world (two each from the Jewish Theological Seminary, Hebrew Union College, and Dropsie College) and the spectrum of Jewish observance. Cyrus Adler, well known for his administrative capabilities, chaired the translation committee, thereby ensuring that the work progressed and that the deliberations remained at least relatively peaceful.

Viewed retrospectively, the Bible translation committee, aside from Margolis himself, represented much less than the best that Jewish Bible scholarship in America had to offer. Morris Jastrow, Casper Levias, William Rosenau, Moses Buttenwieser, Julian Morgenstern, Jacob Hoschander, and, the most talented of all, Arnold Bogumil Ehrlich (Kabokoff), although recognized by their peers as qualified biblical and Semitic scholars, were conspicuously absent (several had contributed to the abortive 1895 JPS translation effort). Scholarly rabbis representing the CCAR (Samuel Schulman, David Philipson, and Hebrew Union College President Kaufmann Kohler), and wide-ranging Jewish scholars (Solomon Schechter, Joseph Jacobs, and Cyrus Adler) representing the JPS were deemed more suitable for the task. Religious politics, personality factors, facility in the English language, and, above all, the desire to move ahead expeditiously without becoming bogged down in scholarly fine points may explain this decision; evidence is lacking. Still, and despite all good intensions, unforeseen, highly delicate problems continually cropped up.

To cite just one example, at the very end of the translation process, a fierce and quite revealing dispute broke out over how best to render Isa 9:5 (9:6 in Christian texts). The King James translation exuded Christology:

> For unto us a child is born, unto us a son, is given: and the government shall be upon his shoulder: and his name shall be called Wonderful, Counsellor, The Mighty God, The Everlasting Father, The Prince of Peace.

The English Revised Version followed suit, with only minor modifications in style. Jewish translators properly insisted that nothing in Isaiah's original referred to the future (Leeser's text read "government is placed on his shoulders and his name is called . . ."), but they had trouble with the translation of "*šar šālôm.*" Leeser employed the phrase "prince of peace," using the lower case to avoid (presumably) misinterpretation. Samuel Schulman of the JPS translation committee urged his colleagues to follow the same practice, since "it calls attention to the fact, that we wish to avoid any possible Christological interpretation of the phrase." Max L. Margolis and Cyrus Adler, by contrast, insisted that using the lower case would imply that the "prince of peace" was a human being, "exactly the thing we wished to avoid." Strongly worded letters flew back and forth. The final translation, clearly influenced more by the desire to instruct Christians and defend Jews than by considerations of scholarship, banished "prince of peace" altogether:

> For a child is born unto us,
> A son is given unto us;
> And the government is upon his shoulder;
> And his name is called
> [a] Pele-joez-el-gibbor-Abi-ad-sar-shalom
> That is, Wonderful in counsel is God the Mighty, the
> everlasting father, the Ruler of peace.[2]

Many similar compromises had to be hammered out by the committee before it could, as a group, pronounce itself satisfied.

Seven years after it was promised, The Holy Scriptures finally appeared in print in 1917. The event received considerable publicity and this was fitting, since the Bible would sell more copies than any other JPS volume: over one million to date. The impact of the new Bible, however, went much further. As Abraham Neuman put it retrospectively:

> It was a Bible translation to which American Jews could point with pride
> as the creation of the Jewish consciousness on a par with similar products
> of the Catholic and Protestant churches. It was a peace-offering to the
> Jewish and the non-Jewish world. To the Jews it presented a Bible which
> combined the spirit of Jewish tradition with the results of biblical schol-
> arship, ancient, mediaeval and modern. To non-Jews it opened the
> gateway of Jewish tradition in the interpretation of the Word of God.
> (156)

Neuman's comment encapsulates the major reasons why Jews felt
that the enormous expenditure of time, energy, and money that the
Bible translation represented had in the end been thoroughly justified. Having a Bible they could proudly call their own, the product of
their community's scholars, in some cases native born and native
trained, American Jews felt better both about themselves and about
their relations with non-Jewish neighbors. The new Bible translation
served, in a sense, like a rite of passage. With its completion, Jews
looked forward hopefully toward a coming new era.

With respect to non-Jews, the community proved with its new
Bible that it could successfully compete. The fact that Jews actually
formed only three percent of the population made no difference. They
acted as if they held complete parity with Protestants and Catholics.
The others had long had official English Bibles; now Jews had an
"official" Bible too. It took only a few more decades for this myth of
the "triple melting pot"—Protestant-Catholic-Jew, all three equivalent—to gain acceptance on a broad level, a development of enormous importance in American and American Jewish history
(Herberg).

The new Bible translation also allowed Jews to compete with
Christians on the level of religious scholarship. The scholarly trap-
pings of the English Revised Version had formerly given its
christological renderings an air of authority, which Leeser's "old fashioned" Bible could not pierce. In the formidable scholarship behind
the new Jewish version, however, the English Revised Version met its
match. Indeed, the Jewish translators, by boasting in their preface
that they "took into account the existing English versions," as well as
"the standard commentaries, ancient and modern, the translations
already made for the Jewish Publication Society of America, the
divergent renderings from the Revised Version prepared for the Jews
of England, the marginal notes of the Revised Version, . . . the
changes of the American Committee of Revisers, . . . the ancient
versions," "Talmudic and midrashic allusions, . . . all available Jewish
commentators, [and] all the important non-Jewish commentators,"
implied that their translation was even better than the Christian

version. This triumphalist magniloquence was somewhat tempered by the pluralistic expression of gratitude, also found in the preface, "for the work of our non-Jewish predecessors, such as the Authorized Version with its admirable diction, which can never be surpassed, as well as for the Revised Version with its ample learning." But it still remained distant indeed from the near syncretism propounded by those who had earlier advocated that a modified version of the authorized Anglican revision be given a Jewish imprimatur.

Beyond competition lay the matter of internal Jewish pride. Solomon Schechter had long insisted that the Jew needs "his own Bible, not one mortgaged by the King James version" (*American Jewish Year Book*, 1914: 173). Though he was dead by the time that the JPS Bible appeared, its preface echoed his sentiments: "The Jew cannot afford to have his Bible translation prepared for him by others. He cannot have it as a gift, even as he cannot borrow his soul from others" (vii). More clearly than before, Jews stressed here their belief in a special, deeply spiritual Jewish relationship with the *Tanakh*, one that set Jewish and Christian readers of the Bible apart from one another. Since, as we have seen, American Christians had long before accepted the notion that the Old Testament was the Jews' "own sacred volume," for Jews to defend their separateness on this basis was thoroughly acceptable. Separateness, of course, did not imply strict exclusiveness. Indeed, the new Bible translation's preface specifically hoped that "the non-Jewish world" would "welcome" the translation. Instead, the Jewish Publication Society's Bible translation, like Leeser's before it, reflected the ambivalent nature of Jewish-Christian relations in America, the countervailing forces that on the one hand pushed Jews and Christians together and on the other hand kept them separate and distinct.

As a symbol, the new Bible also went further. It boldly announced the American Jewish community's emergence on the world stage as a center of Jewish life and creativity. "The historical necessity for translation was repeated with all the great changes in Israel's career," the new Bible's preface significantly declared. Then, with growing exuberance, it proclaimed that "the greatest change in the life of Israel during the last two generations" had taken place in the New World:

> We have grown under providence both in numbers and in importance, so that we constitute now the greatest section of Israel living in a single country outside of Russia. We are only following in the footsteps of our greatest predecessors when, with the growth of our numbers, we have applied ourselves to the sacred task of preparing a new translation of the Bible into the English language, which, unless all signs fail, is to become the current speech of the majority of the children of Israel (vi).

The "sacred task" alluded to, akin to the biblical injunction that a king write for himself a copy of the law (Deut 17:18), signified legitimacy, seeming confirmation of American Jewry's momentous destiny. Along with the publication of *Jewish Encyclopedia* completed in 1906, the founding of the American Jewish Committee in the same year, and other developments in the years immediately before and after World War I, the new Bible translation reflected American Jewry's changing self-image, its growing cultural independence, its quest for preeminence. The community had arrived and was seeking the recognition that it thought it deserved.

The New Jewish Publication Society Translation

The years that followed the publication of the JPS translation confirmed the prescience of those who had predicted that a new era in American Jewish scholarship was aborning. The development of great Jewish libraries in the United States, the availability of positions in Jewish studies at American Jewish institutions of higher learning, particularly Hebrew Union College, the Jewish Theological Seminary, Dropsie College, Yeshiva University, the Jewish Institute of Religion, and Hebrew Theological College, and the mass migration of Jewish scholars from Europe to America's shores, particularly in the 1930s, adumbrated America's emergence as *the* center of Jewish scholarship in the diaspora even before the destruction of European centers of Jewish scholarship in World War II. After Hitler had wreaked his terrible toll, the only question remaining was how well American Jewry would measure up.

In terms of biblical scholarship, the answer was quite well. As early as 1930, Jews comprised some nine percent of SBL members (by contrast, they formed three and one-half percent of the population), and as indicated above, these were about evenly divided between professional Jewish scholars and scholarly-inclined rabbis. To be sure, few of these scholars actually held positions in biblical studies. Most were either Semitists or scholars of later periods of Jewish life, who nevertheless maintained an abiding and serious interest in biblical studies. Still, biblical studies had acquired a greatly elevated status among American Jews, far outstripping Talmud and rabbinics, which had held pride of place among traditional Jews in Europe. Indeed, the first full set of the Talmud was not printed in America until 1944 (Eidelberg), and not a single native-born professor of Talmud could be found in this country until recently. By comparison, Bible scholarship fared well.

At least three factors account for this interest in biblical studies among American Jews. First, Reform Judaism laid heavy stress on the Bible, particularly the prophetic writings, which were held up as ethical exemplars to contemporary Jews and non-Jews alike. Having declared themselves independent of rabbinic legislation, Reform Jews sought legitimacy in the Bible, frequently using it in proof-text fashion against conversionists on the one hand and traditional Jews on the other. This, of course, sometimes made for tendentious scholarship, but it did at least direct greater Jewish attention to the Bible than had hitherto been the case (Plaut: 224–31; Agus: 282–33).

The Zionist movement was the second factor that lay behind the revival of biblical studies among American Jews. Although Zionists tended to stress different chapters from the Bible than did Reform Jews, they too turned to the Bible for inspiration and ideological justification. The Bible legitimated the Jewish claim to a homeland. Biblical archaeology linked the Jewish past and the Jewish present. Spoken Hebrew, revived by the Zionist movement, was modeled on biblical Hebrew, not rabbinic Hebrew. Secular Zionists may have disdained works of Jewish law and scorned theology, but they respected the Bible. They also respected biblical scholars.

Finally, the interfaith movement led to greater Jewish attention to the Bible. As it emerged in the post-World War I era, the interfaith movement stressed elements common to Jews and Christians, particularly the Hebrew Bible. Not only did the Bible serve to legitimate efforts aimed at promoting "better understanding," it also frequently provided the central themes for dialogue groups and clergy institutes. Bible study led Jews and Christians to better appreciate the roots of what was termed "Judeo-Christian civilization." Indirectly, it also stimulated Jews to deepen their own knowledge of what the Bible was all about (Sussman).

Notwithstanding American Jews' growing interest in the Bible, Jewish Bible scholarship still remained largely the preserve of those born and trained abroad. There were already some important exceptions to this rule, among them Julian Morgenstern, Sheldon Blank, H. L. Ginsberg, and Harry M. Orlinsky (the last two were born in Canada, and all but Orlinsky received their advanced degrees abroad), but as late as 1948 only six of twenty-five prominent American Jewish scholars in the field of Bible, as enumerated by Ralph Marcus, could actually be termed both native-born and native-trained—the last time this would be true. The growth of academic opportunities in the postwar period, coupled with the coming-of-age of American-born children of immigrants soon resulted in a preponderance of locally produced scholars. Of thirty-one Jewish contributors to the *Interpreter's Dictionary of the Bible* (1962), for example, all but four were Americans. In the *Encyclopaedia Judaica*, published in Jerusalem in 1972, the divisional editor, associate divisional editor, and half of the departmental editors in Bible were all American Jews, and the other half was Israelis—an accurate reflection of the two mutually interacting centers of Jewish Bible scholarship in the world today.

This latter point deserves more notice than it is usually given. There exists today a huge and ever-increasing body of high caliber scholarly literature in the Hebrew language produced by Israeli-trained scholars, mainly native born, who think and express themselves naturally in Hebrew, and whose researches appear in a variety of Hebrew scholarly journals, in the various annuals of the five universities, in the multivolumed *Encyclopaedia Biblica Hebraica*, in a large number of doctoral dissertations, and in the numerous volumes turned out annually by Israeli publishing houses. The Israelis are in daily contact with the land, its geography, topography, and geology, its climatic conditions, the nature of its soil, its flora and fauna, its natural resources. Archaeology of the biblical period is a national Israeli pastime. Inevitably, all this must leave, and it surely does, its impress on the direction and coloration of biblical scholarship in Israel. The history of the Hebrew language, the history of the land (especially geopolitical conditions), biblical history, military history, the realia of biblical life, the literary artistry of the narrative, masoretic studies—all these topics are fruitfully pursued with a vigor and a passion that is characteristic of those exploring their own civilization on their and its native soil.

American Jewish scholars take it for granted that a knowledge of modern Hebrew is today as essential a tool of scholarship as is the ability to handle French and German. They are in continuous communication with their Israeli colleagues on social, intellectual, and scholarly levels. They send their students to study in Israel. There is frequent intercontinental travel in both directions. There is no doubt about the powerful impact that Israeli biblical scholarship will increasingly have on its American Jewish counterpart. The point may be illustrated by random reference to one aspect of research that is a specifically and typically Jewish contribution to the field, namely, the study of the biblical cult.

That nineteenth-century German Protestant theological presuppositions colored the study of this subject and predetermined the parameters and approach of research everywhere is hardly deniable.

Since Yehezkel Kaufmann reopened the topic, Menahem Haran in Israel and Baruch Levine and Jacob Milgrom in the United States have powerfully challenged the prevailing theories and reconstructions. They have shown how the sacrificial system, the laws of purity and impurity, and the notions of sin and atonement must all be understood within a broad framework of religious ideas, inside a structure of biblical theology and law. They have demonstrated that the pure and the impure are complementary to the moral and the immoral and are not in opposition to them, and they have been progressively uncovering the ethical supports upon which the sacrificial system was raised. Furthermore, very constructive use has been made of rabbinic sources in the exploration of these themes. In short, Jewish scholars would emphasize that biblical theology is not just story and prophecy but is equally law and cult.

Another development that needs to be recounted is that Jewish Bible scholarship in America is no longer restricted to those who teach at Jewish-sponsored institutions of higher learning. A large percentage of those presently engaged in Jewish studies generally, and biblical studies in particular, now teach at secular institutions—a function of the proliferation of Jewish studies during the 1960s and 1970s. Over ninety North American colleges and universities currently offer undergraduate concentrations in Jewish studies and almost fifty sponsor programs of graduate study. The Association for Jewish Studies, the professional organization devoted to the advancement of the academic standing and scope of Judaic studies, boasts one thousand members (1982), including emeriti, associate members, and students. Many of these members specialize in the Bible, as evidenced both by the large number of sessions devoted to biblical subjects at the association's annual meetings and by a survey of the fourteen largest graduate programs in Jewish studies in North America (1980), which found that "Bible and Ancient near East" was the most popular of all fields of specialization for Ph.D. candidates. Harry M. Orlinsky (1974: 331), who has monitored the state of the field for many years, summarized succinctly the situation as he found it in the early seventies, and his words hold equally true a decade later: "Jewish biblical scholarship . . . is currently flourishing in America-Canada as never before."

The Jewish Publication Society's new translation of the Bible, completed in 1982, stands as one of the great achievements of modern American Jewish Bible scholarship.[3] Appearing as it did in the very midst of the Jewish cultural efflorescence already described, a burgeoning Jewish religious revival (Sarna, 1982), and heightened nationwide interest in the Bible and its teachings, it seemed a most natural development, one almost to have been expected. In fact, however, the Bible translation was planned long before any of these developments were envisaged.

Although the full history of the New Jewish Publication Society's translation cannot be recounted here, we need look no further than Harry Orlinsky's famous 1953 address at the annual meeting of the Jewish Publication Society—"Wanted: A New English Translation of the Bible" (Orlinsky, 1974: 349–62)—to see that the original call for a new Jewish translation of Scripture stemmed from many of the same motivations that had precipitated earlier undertakings. For one thing, the 1917 translation had become, in Orlinsky's words, "no longer as intelligible as it should be." Old-fashioned King James English had lost the last of its appeal; what was needed, Orlinsky said, was a "simplified and modernized" style and vocabulary, "without undue loss of majesty and dignity." In addition, Orlinsky pointed to "the increased knowledge which archaeology and refined methodology have made available." New discoveries had cleared up old mysteries; the 1917 translation no longer reflected the best scholarship available. Finally, and perhaps what was most important, a new Protestant translation had appeared, the Revised Standard Version (1952), and a new Catholic translation (published as the New American Bible) had been announced. Just as the 1885 English Revised Version stimulated Jews to prove that they could do as well or better, so too did these new revisions. The new Protestant Bible still contained Christological elements (a capital "S" in "spirit," for example), and it still remained Christian in origin. "The Jew," Orlinsky said, echoing Max Margolis before him, "cannot afford to have his Bible translation prepared for him by others" (361).

In retrospect, Orlinsky has admitted (1970: 10) that there was "strong sentiment among several important members of the Jewish Publication Society's Board of Trustees" for the society to issue only a "modest revision of . . . the Revised Standard Version of 1952" (1970: 10). It was predictable, however, that those sentiments went un-heeded. Most American Jews, in the 1950s as before, used the Bible to demonstrate their apartness, their insistence on a Jewish identity separate from Protestants and Catholics. Consequently, in 1955, after years of discussion, the Jewish Publication Society finally set up a committee of seven—three scholars, three rabbis (one representing each of the major wings of American Judaism), and the editor of the JPS translation, Solomon Grayzel—and mandated it to translate the Bible afresh from a Jewish point of view.

The composition of the new translation committee is instructive. Two of its three scholars, Harry Orlinsky (editor-in-chief for the Pentateuch) and H. L. Ginsberg, were born in North America, and the third, Ephraim A. Speiser, immigrated to the United States in his teens. Orlinsky and Ginsberg, who taught respectively at Hebrew Union College-Jewish Institute of Religion and the Jewish Theological Seminary, both in New York, held chairs in Bible. Speiser, who taught at the University of Pennsylvania, was Professor of Semitic Languages and Literatures. All three of the rabbis on the committee (Max Arzt, Bernard Bamberger, and Harry Freedman) trained in the United States. Grayzel, an accomplished historian, immigrated to the United States at the age of twelve and received all his degrees in this country. The contrast with the earlier translation committee, which had a much larger number of immigrants and only one biblical scholar, Margolis himself, is striking indeed.

The mechanics of producing the Torah translation also were quite different from what they had been in Margolis's day. Harry Orlinsky has described the process in a recent interview (1982: 39–40):

> (W)e would work one day, usually a Thursday, usually in my office at the Jewish Institute of Religion in Manhattan. . . . I prepared the draft of the entire *Chumash*. I hardly ever would prepare more than two or three chapters ahead of the committee so that I would be able to benefit from the decisions that the committee members reached. Unlike the Revised Standard Version, I would prepare a draft of a chapter or part of a chapter with a tremendous amount of commentary culled from the readings and translations from sources going back to the ancient Near East, the Septuagint, Targum, Vulgate, Syriac translation, Talmud, the medieval commentators, medieval grammarians, Sa'adia's translation, the rationalist Protestant translation of the 16th century, the Catholic, and of course, the modern translations. So that, for example, when I handed in the draft of the first five verses of Genesis, the first day of creation—and believe me I worked much harder than God did, the first day anyway—I had a half a page of the text and about 12 or 13 pages of all kinds of notes for my other six colleagues to consult. So that they didn't have to, unless they wanted to, go and examine these things. I would send that off to the JPS where it would be run off and sent out to my colleagues. They, in turn, would react, verse by verse or word by word, with counter suggestions. They would type that up and send that into JPS where, again, it would be run off and sent out, so that when we got together to do Genesis, and then all the way through, we would have the draft, we would have the comments of each of the committee members, as many as had reacted. We had it all before us, and we could all study it before we came. On the other hand, however, once we got together, the argument and the discussion pro and con would go far beyond what anybody had on any sheet of paper. We were very stimulated by the oral arguments back and forth. Not infrequently what came out as our final draft was something that none of us had envisaged to begin with. It was

often quite different. Maybe not always necessarily better, but different. More than once, I was convinced that my draft was not as good as I had thought originally—but my committee colleagues would disagree with me and outvote me in favor of my draft. Not infrequently, it was the other way around. No one is every fully satisfied with a translation because no one ever gets all his ideas accepted. It is a compromise translation.

Two principles underlay every facet of this translation process. First, the translators insisted on basing their work strictly on the original Hebrew Masoretic text. Although they consulted other versions, translations, and commentaries, they refused to see themselves as "revisers" of any previous translation, not even the previous Jewish one. In this they openly distinguished their effort from that of the Revised Standard Version, which *was* a revision in name and in fact.

Second, the translators insisted on rendering their text into English idiomatically, rather than mechanically and literally. Convinced that word-for-word translation did violence to the spirit of the Hebrew original, the translators permitted themselves wider latitude than their English language predecessors ever had. They spoke of their fidelity to the deeper meaning of the biblical text, in contradistinction to the surface meaning, which they in some cases felt free to ignore.

In 1962 the new translation of the Torah appeared, after seven years of unstinting labor. (A revised version appeared in 1967, and to date over 350,000 copies have been sold.) The preface paid ritualistic tribute to "the work of previous translators," and praised earlier scholars. But having done that, the editors insisted that this translation—*The Torah: A New Translation of the Holy Scriptures According to the Masoretic Text*—was not only different but better. In an article in the *Journal of Biblical Literature,* for example, Harry Orlinsky argued that the new translation's rendering of the initial verses in Genesis was the first "correct rendering": "We are now, finally, in a position to understand exactly what the writer of the first three verses of the Bible meant to convey to his readers" (1974: 402).

Orlinsky also boasted, both in his article and in his published *Notes on the New Translation of the Torah,* that the new translation's policy on textual criticism ("translate the Hebrew text directly, and offer in a footnote the proposed emendation and its translation") was "best," and that its manner of translating Hebrew particles improved upon all that preceded it. To his mind, the New Jewish Version marked "a complete break with the past history of Bible translation." He compared it to Spinoza's philosophical revolution in that it "set out to discard" a 2,200 year tradition "of literal, mechanical translation," in order to capture the text's original meaning. Speaking in the name of the entire translation committee, he hoped that this "break with the past" would "set a new pattern which authorized Protestant and Catholic translations of the future will tend to follow" (1970: 12–14).

The trailblazing image that Orlinsky's comments conjured up found no parallel in earlier American Jewish versions. Expressions of pride and distinctiveness, claims of superiority, evocations of destiny, and hopes for Christian approval had, as we have seen, all been heard before, but in no previous translation had American Jews so triumphantly expressed the belief that Protestants and Catholics might follow their lead. That, as Orlinsky himself realized reflected American Jewry's heightened self-confidence, its "verve, growing maturity, and optimism," "its new status . . . unprecedented in the two and one-half millennia of Jewish Diaspora life" (1970: 11, 14). Whereas the 1917 translation announced American Jews' cultural emergence, the new translation displayed heady awareness of their cultural influence and impact, their capacity as innovators and leaders on the national and religious scenes. The Prophets translation, published in 1978 by the same committee with H. L. Ginsberg as senior editor, though E. A. Speiser was no longer alive, carried forward this mood of self-confidence in its very language. It then went further, boldly proposing in footnotes a host of possible emendations designed to render texts judged to be corrupt more intelligible than they had ever been before.

Having monitored the pace of the Bible translation for a full decade, the trustees of the Jewish Publication Society realized, in 1965, that the undertaking would be both more arduous and more time-consuming than anyone had originally envisaged. Determined that the translation should nevertheless appear within "a reasonable time," they decided to create a new committee, charged with the task of translating the third division of the Bible, known as the Kethubim (the Writings), with the exception of the five Megilloth, which had already been translated by the original committee.

In 1966, the new committee, younger by a full generation than the earlier one, and overwhelmingly American trained, came into being. Like the earlier committee, it consisted of three scholars (Moshe Greenberg, Jonas C. Greenfield, and Nahum M. Sarna), three rabbis, one representing each major wing of American Judaism (Saul Leeman, Martin Rozenberg, and David Shapiro), and the editor of the Jewish Publication Society, later better-known as a bestselling novelist, Chaim Potok. It is revealing that all of the scholars selected taught at secular universities, a fact that reflected both the growing acceptance of Jewish studies as a legitimate academic discipline and the increased willingness on the part of universities to permit biblical studies to be taught by Jews. It is also revealing that two of the three scholars on the committee (Greenberg and Greenfield) eventually assumed positions at the Hebrew University in Jerusalem. This illustrates the point made above that American Jewish Bible scholarship has in the last three decades been in close touch with its Israeli counterpart on social, intellectual, and scholarly levels. The fact that the new committee met in Jerusalem on numerous occasions both symbolized and reinforced this spirit of harmony.

In its procedures, the Kethubim translation committee generally adhered to the practices established for the translation of the Torah and Prophets. Each professional scholar undertook the preparation of an annotated draft, which was circulated to all concerned, and everyone then had an opportunity to criticize the rendering and to offer detailed suggestions at the regular, periodic gatherings of the committee. In its style, however, the new committee struck a decidedly more cautious and conservative stance. Unlike the older committee, it stressed (in the preface) the inherent difficulties in translating the Hebrew, and the "as yet imperfect understanding of the language of the Bible." It refused to hazard emendations, and its favorite footnote read "meaning of Heb. uncertain." Instead of exuding confidence, it admitted right from the beginning that its translation had "not conveyed the fullness of the Hebrew, with its ambiguities, its overtones, and the richness that it carries from centuries of use." It made no triumphalistic claims.

From a broader perspective, the scholarly caution expressed in the translation of the Writings may be more in harmony with the new mood that overtook Americans generally in the 1970s and 1980s, a mood at once both more hesitant and less self-confident. Americans seemed less self-assured in 1982, when the translation of the Writings appeared, than two decades earlier, at the time of the publication of the Torah. The translation of the Writings seems to have reflected this fact, even if those involved may not have realized it.

In light of past experience this should not prove surprising. As we have seen, a Bible translation is much more than just a scholarly effort to render a sacred text into a form easier for all to understand. Since it is created by human beings, a translation is also a child of history, a product of its times. It cannot escape the impact of contemporary concerns.[4]

NOTES

/1/   Leeser, like Rabbi Morris Raphall, believed that the Bible sanctioned slavery but mandated better treatment of the slave than was practiced in the South (*Occident*, 1861: 267–68, 274; Korn, 1970: 15–55; D. Davis, 1975: 523–56).

/2/   The New Jewish Publication Society translation reads, "For a child has been born to us, /A son has been given us. /And authority has settled on his shoulders. /He has been named/"The Mighty God is planning grace; /The Eternal Father, a peaceable ruler."

/3/   The Yehoash translation of the Bible into Yiddish, by Solomon Bloomgarden, first published in 1937, is a tribute to Yiddish scholarship in the United States, but stands outside the scope of this essay; see Orlinsky (1974: 418–22).

/4/   Part of the research for this essay was supported by the American Council of Learned Societies and the Memorial Foundation for Jewish Culture.

WORKS CONSULTED

Abrahams, Harold J. and Miles, Wynham D.
1961   "The Priestley-Levi Debate." *Transactions of the Unitarian Historical Society in London* 12:1–19.

Abrahams, Israel
1920   *By-Paths in Hebraic Bookland*. Philadelphia: Jewish Publication Society.

Adler, Cyrus
1914   "The Bible Translation." *American Jewish Year Book* 15:101–21.
1926   "The Beginnings of Semitic Studies in America." *Oriental Studies Dedicated to Paul Haupt*, eds. Cyrus Adler and Aaron Ember (317–28). Baltimore: Johns Hopkins Press.
1941   *I Have Considered the Days*. Philadelphia: Jewish Publication Society.

Altmann, Alexander
1973   *Moses Mendelssohn*. Philadelphia: Jewish Publication Society.

American Jewish Year Book
1899–1920   Philadelphia: Jewish Publication Society.

Agus, Jacob M.
1978   *Jewish Identity in an Age of Ideologies*. New York: Frederick Ungar.

Baumgarten, A. I.
                     "Justinian and the Jews." *Rabbi Joseph H. Lookstein Memorial Volume*, ed., Leo Landman (37). New York: 1980.

Billigheimer, S.
1968   "On Jewish Translations of the Bible in Germany." *Abr-Nahrain* 7:1–34.

Central Conference of American Rabbis
1895–1917   *Year Books*.

Chiel, Arthur A.
1978   "The Kohut Collection at Yale." *Jews in New Haven*, ed., Jonathan D. Sarna (80–94). New Haven: Jewish Historical Society of New Haven.

Chomsky, William
1958   "Hebrew Grammar and Textbook Writing in Early Nineteenth-

Century America." *Essays in American Jewish History*, (123–
45). Cincinnati: American Jewish Archives.

Davis, David Brion
1975   *The Problem of Slavery in the Age of Revolution*. Ithaca, NY:
                Cornell University Press.

Davis, Moshe
1965   *The Emergency of Conservative Judaism*. Philadelphia: Jewish
                Publication Society.
1970   *Beit Yisrael Be-Amerikah*. Jerusalem: Jewish Theological Semi-
                nary.

Eidelberg, Shlomo
1978   "The Story of the Shulsinger Press and Its Publications."
                Kovetz Massad, ed., Meir Havatzelet (44–56). New York: Mas-
                sad Camps.

Elbogen, Ismar
1943   "American Jewish Scholarship: A Survey." *American Jewish
                Year Book* 45:47–65.

Englander, Henry
1918   "Isaac Leeser." *Central Conference of American Rabbis Year-
                book* 28:213–52.

Ezekiel, Herbert T. and Lichtenstein, Gaston
1917   *The History of the Jews of Richmond from 1769 to 1917*.
                Richmond: Ezekiel.

Fein, Isaac M.
1917   *The Making of an American Jewish Community*. Philadelphia:
                Jewish Publication Society.

Fellman, Jack
                "Notes Concerning Two Nineteenth-Century Hebrew Text-
                books." *American Jewish Archives* 32:73–77.

Felsenthal, Bernhard
1884   "Bible Interpretation; How and How Not." *The Old Testament
                Student* 4:114–19.

Feuer, Lewis S.
1982   "The Stages in the Social History of Jewish Professors in Amer-
                ican Colleges and Universities." *American Jewish History*
                71:432–65.

Fogarty, Gerald P.
1982   "The Quest for a Catholic Vernacular Bible in America." *The
                Bible in America*, eds., Nathan A. Hatch and Mark A. Noll
                (163–80). New York: Oxford.

Gordis, Robert, ed.
1952   *Max Leopold Margolis: Scholar and Teacher*. Philadelphia:
                Dropsie College.

Grossman, Lawrence
1980   "Isaac Leeser's Mentor: Rabbi Abraham Sutro, 1784–1869."
                Rabbi Joseph H. Lookstein Memorial Volume, ed., Leo Land-
                man (151–62). New York: Ktav.

Harper, William R.
1884   "The Jewish Attitude." *The Old Testament Student* 4:187.

Hatch, Nathan O. and Noll, Mark A., eds.
1982   *The Bible in America*. New York: Oxford.
Herberg, Will
1955   *Protestant-Catholic-Jew*. Garden City, NY: Doubleday.
Horwitz, Jonathan
1812   *Prospectus*. Philadelphia (copy in Hebrew, Cincinnati: Union College Library).
1839.   *A Defence of the Cosmogony of Moses*. Baltimore: Matchett.
Jackson, Solomon
1826   *Prospectus*. New York (Lyons Collection, Scrapbook I, American Jewish Historical Society, Waltham, MA).
Jewish Publication Society
n.d.   Papers. Philadelphia: Philadelphia Jewish Archives.
1888–1899   *Reports of the Jewish Publication Society*. Philadelphia: Jewish Publication Society.
Jick, Leon A.
1976   *The Americanization of the Synagogue*. Hanover, NH: Brandeis University Press.
Journal of Biblical Literature
1931
Kabakoff, Jacob
1984   "New Light on Arnold Bogomil Ehrlich." *American Jewish Archives* 36: 202–224.
Kalisch, Isidor
1928   *Studies in Ancient and Modern Judaism*. New York: George Dobsevage.
Karff, Samuel E., ed.
1976   *Hebrew Union College-Jewish Institute of Religion at One Hundred Years*. Cincinnati: Hebrew Union College Press.
Korn, Bertram W.
1967   "Isaac Leeser: Centennial Reflections." *American Jewish Archives* 19:127–41.
1970   *American Jewry and the Civil War*. Philadelphia: Atheneum.
Kraut, Benny
1983   "Judaism Triumphant: Isaac Mayer Wise on Unitarianism and Liberal Christianity." *AJS Review* 7.
Leeser, Isaac
1853   *The Twenty-Four Books of the Holy Scriptures*. Philadelphia: L. Johnson.
1856   *The Twenty-Four Books of the Holy Scriptures*. Philadelphia: C. Sherman.
1867   *Discourses on the Jewish Religion*, vol. 5. Philadelphia: Sherman.
1868   *Discourses on the Jewish Religion*, vol. 10. Philadelphia: Sherman.
Lipscomb, Andrew A., ed.
1904   *The Writings of Thomas Jefferson*, vol. 14. Washington, DC.

Marcus, Ralph
1948   "American Jewish Scholarship Today." *Chicago Jewish Forum*
                       6/4 (Summer):264–68.

Margolis, Max L.
1917   *The Story of Bible Translations*. Philadelphia: Jewish Publica-
                       tion Society.
1918   "The New English Translation of the Bible." *American Jewish
                       Year Book* 19:161–93.

Marx, Alexander
1947   *Essays in Jewish Biography*. Philadelphia: Jewish Publication
                       Society.

Neill, H.
1874   "Reminiscences of I. Nordheimer." *New Englander and Yale
                       Review* 33:506–12.

Neuman, Abraham A.
1942   *Cyrus Adler*. New York: American Jewish Committee.

Newman, Selig
1839   *Emendations of the Authorized Version of the Old Testament*.
                       London.

Occident
1844–1864

Orlinsky, Harry M.
1965   "Old Testament Studies." *Religion*, ed., Paul Ramsey 51–109.
                       Englewood Cliffs, NJ: Prentice Hall.
1970   *Notes on the New Translation of the Torah*. Philadelphia: Jew-
                       ish Publication Society.
1974   *Essays in Biblical Culture and Bible Translation*. New York:
                       Ktav.
1982   "Telling It Like It Was." *Moment* 8/1 (December):37–44.

Philipson, David
n.d.   Papers. Cincinnati: American Jewish Archives.
1941   "Cyrus Adler and the Bible Translation." *American Jewish Year
                       Book* 42:693–97.

Plaut, W. Gunther
1965   *The Growth of Reform Judaism*. New York: World Union for
                       Progressive Judaism.

Pollak, Gustav
1912   *Michael Heilprin and His Sons*. New York: Dodd, Mead.

Pool, David de Sola
1934   "Nordheimer, Isaac." *Dictionary of American Biography*,
                       13:547–48.

Sandmel, Samuel
1976   "Isaac Mayer Wise's *Pronaos to Holy Writ*." *A Bicentennial
                       Festschrift for Jacob Rader Marcus*, ed., Bertram W. Korn
                       (517–27). New York: Ktav.

Sarna, Jonathan D.
1982   "The Great American Jewish Awakening." *Midstream* 28/8 (Oc-
                       tober):30–34.

Sarna, Nahum M.
    1974   "Bible: Old Testament, Canon, Texts and Versions." *En-cyclopaedia Brittanica, Macropaedia*, 2:881–92. Chicago:

Saunders, Ernest W.
    1982   *Searching the Scriptures*. Chico, CA: Scholars Press.

Sussman, Lance J.
    1982   "'Toward Better Understanding': The Rise of the Interfaith Movement in America and the Role of Rabbi Isaac Landman." *American Jewish Archives* 34:35–51.
    1985   "Another Look at Isaac Leeser and the First Jewish Translation of the Bible in the United States." *Modern Judaism* 51:159–190.

Tsevat, Matitiahu
    1958   "A Retrospective View of Isaac Leeser's Biblical Work." *Essays in American Jewish History* (295–313). Cincinnati: American Jewish Archives.

Vaxer, M.
    1940   "The First Hebrew Bible Printed in America." *Jewish Journal of Bibliography* 1:20–26.

Weinberg, Werner
    1982   "Moses Mendelssohn's 'Biur' 200 Years Later." *Jewish Book Annual* 40:97–104.

Westerhoff, John H.
    1978   *McGuffey and His Readers*. Nashville:

Whiteman, Maxwell
    1959   "Isaac Leeser and the Jews of Philadelphia." *Publications of the American Jewish Historical Society* 48:207–44.

Wise, Isaac M.
    1876   *The Cosmic God*. Cincinnati: American Israelite.
    1891   *Pronaos to Holy Writ*. Cincinnati: Robert Clarke.
    1954   "The World of My Books." Translated and edited by Albert H. Friedlander. *American Jewish Archives* 6:107–48.

Wolf, Edwin 2nd and Whiteman, Maxwell
    1956   *The History of the Jews of Philadelphia from Colonial Times to the Age of Jackson*. Philadelphia: Jewish Publication Society.

V

American Catholic Translations of the Bible

Gerald P. Fogarty, S.J.

On 30 January 1789, John Carroll, the superior of the American Mission of the Catholic Church and the soon to be first Bishop of Baltimore, wrote Matthew Carey, a Catholic publisher in Philadelphia, about publishing an American edition of the Douay Bible. It was the first such venture for the tiny American Catholic community—Carroll estimated the Catholic population in 1785 as twenty-five thousand out of a total American population of 3,500,000. From the colonial period, moreover, because of the small size of the Catholic community and the penal laws against Catholics' publishing, American Catholics had to depend on Bibles imported from England. Carroll encouraged Carey in his proposed edition of the Douay Bible, "by which," he said, "I presume you mean the Douay Bible, agreeable to the last corrections made in it by the late Bishop Challoner. I still retain the same desire of seeing it in the hands of our people, instead of those translations, which they purchase in stores & from Booksellers in the Country . . ." (Hanley: 1: 348).

Carroll's concern to provide the American Catholic faithful with an authoritative translation of the Bible remained a pressing issue for his episcopal successors for more than the next century. A Catholic translation had to meet the norms set by Rome not only for orthodoxy but also for theological and liturgical use. The issue of determining which was the authentic version of Scripture and the attitude toward translations into the vernacular languages had been problematic during the Middle Ages, but it reached critical proportions with the advent of printing, the influence of humanism, and the Reformation. The Council of Trent in 1546 declared to be canonical the books of Scripture contained in the old Latin Vulgate. It thus accepted those deuterocanonical books of the Old Testament found only in the Septuagint and rejected by the Reformers. The council further decreed that "the old vulgate edition, which has been proven by its long use of so many centuries in the church, is to be held as authentic in public readings, lectures, preaching, and expositions, and that no one should on any pretext whatsoever dare or presume to reject it." No one was to interpret the Scripture in a sense contrary to that held by the church, and all editions of the Vulgate or sections of it could not be published without episcopal approval (Denzinger and Schönmetzer 1506–7).

It is important to note that Trent was legislating for the Latin Church and that, in declaring the Vulgate to be authentic, it was not saying anything about Scripture in the original languages. Nor did the council fathers, who were divided on the issue, directly address the issue of translations into the vernacular. The matter of vernacular translations was left to postconciliar legislation. On 24 March 1564, Pius IV published rules pertaining to the newly established *Index librorum prohibitorum*. In regard to vernacular translations, the pope warned against those which "are indiscriminately circulated" and declared that "in this matter the judgment of the bishop or inquisitor must be sought, who on the advice of the pastor or the confessor may permit the reading of a Bible translated into the vernacular by Catholic authors" (McNally: 226).

Neither Trent nor the postconciliar legislation had specified that vernacular translations were to be made from the Vulgate, but this became the prevailing practice—and later law—because of the use of the Vulgate in theological discourse, sermons, and the liturgy. In 1582, English Catholics in exile published a translation of the New Testament from the Vulgate in Rheims. During the years 1606–1610, the translation of the Old Testament from the Clementine edition of the Vulgate was completed and the entire Bible published at Douay College—or "Doway," as Carroll and other Englishmen preferred to spell and pronounce it (Pope: 249–97). The Douay version became the standard Bible for English-speaking Catholics, but it had itself gone through a series of revisions, the most recent being that of Bishop Richard Challoner, vicar apostolic of the London District. Challoner's first revision of the New Testament appeared in 1749 and the fifth in 1772. His first revision of the Old Testament was published in 1750 and his second in 1763 (Pope: 355–71). It was Challoner's version with his annotations to which Carroll was referring in his encouragement that Carey publish the "Doway Bible."

In 1790, Carey published the first Catholic Bible in the United States, based on Challoner's second edition of the entire Bible of 1763–1764 (Parsons: 89). In 1805, he published another version, based this time on the Dublin "fifth edition," a slight revision of Challoner published under the auspices of Archbishop John Troy of Dublin (Parsons: 90). But the project was expensive and Carroll frequently referred to the difficulty of obtaining sufficient subscribers—he noted on one occasion that Maryland Catholics were too accustomed to receiving free books from the clergy (Hanley 1: 355; Hennesey: 93). The problem of providing an authorized Catholic version of the Bible for the faithful, however, continued to plague Carroll, who had been elevated to archbishop of Baltimore in 1808. Two years later, he met with the suffragan bishops of the newly created dioceses and with them decreed that "*the Douay* Bible is to be literally followed and copied, whenever any part of the Holy Scripture is inserted in any prayer-book, or book of devotion & no private or other translation is to be made use of in those books" (Hanley 3: 133). The Catholic community was still too small and its scholarly potential still too underdeveloped to undertake an original translation of its own.

In addition to the publication of various editions of the Douay Bible, there were also various American publications of Catholic translations of the Bible into French, Spanish, Portuguese, and German (Parsons: 90, 92–94), a reflection of the growing ethnic pluralism of the American Catholic church as it began to receive huge waves of immigrants. American Catholicism became foreign not only in its spiritual loyalty to Rome but also in its composition. This gave rise to nativism; and the Catholic prohibition of private interpretation of Scripture and of using unauthorized translations, such as the King James Version, was misrepresented as a Catholic prohibition of private reading of the Bible. The Catholic response to these charges was not always judicious. One Catholic priest collected all the King James Bibles distributed to his parishioners and publicly burned them (Fogarty: 164–675).

Anti-Catholicism shaped the deliberations of the American bishops about the Bible when they assembled in 1829 for the First Provincial Council of Baltimore, whose legislation bound the entire American Catholic Church. In their pastoral letter, the bishops warned the laity

> . . . against the indiscriminate use of unauthorized versions, for unfortunately many of those which are placed within your reach are extremely erroneous and defective. The Douay translation of the Vulgate of the Old Testament, together with the Remish translation of the New Testament are our best English versions; but as some printers have undertaken in these States, by their own authority, without our sanction, to print and publish editions which have not been submitted to our examination, we cannot hold ourselves responsible for the correctness of such copies (Nolan, 1971: 28).

In addition to warning the faithful against unauthorized translations of the Bible, the council decreed that the "bishops see to it that, according to the most proven exemplar designated by them, all editions of the Douay version of both the New and Old Testament be made in the future as free as possible from error." Before the conciliar decrees could bind the American church, they had to receive the approbation of the Sacred Congregation of Propaganda in Rome, the missionary congregation of the Roman Curia to which the American church was then subject. Propaganda inserted in the decree that all editions of the Douay version be accompanied "with notes drawn from the holy fathers of the Church, or from learned Catholics" (*Acta et decreta Sacrorum* 3: 28). The insertion had been taken from Pius IV's 1564 norms for the Index pertaining to vernacular Bibles as amended in 1757 (*Collectanea:* 593). The desire of the American bishops to have a proven exemplar of the Douay Bible with annotations was not immediately fulfilled. Over a decade passed before Francis P. Kenrick undertook the task. He had been present at the council as a theologian to the bishop of Bardstown, Kentucky, and became coadjutor bishop of Philadelphia in 1830. He began his work on the revision while he was bishop of Philadelphia (1842–1851) and completed it as archbishop of Baltimore (1851–1863).

Kenrick had originally begun a revision of Genesis with the assistance of his brother, Peter Richard Kenrick, vicar general of the Diocese of Philadelphia, before the latter became the coadjutor bishop of St. Louis in 1841. Two years later, Francis chided his brother for ceasing their collaboration, for "if . . . you are not willing to undertake the work, the faithful will be left without it." Francis was also becoming sensitive to the historical difficulties of Genesis—a fact which may have accounted for his not publishing his revision until 1860. At this point in 1843, he felt the theory proposed by J. G. Eichhorn for the composition of the Pentateuch "appeals to me as having merit." Eichhorn had suggested that in composing the Pentateuch Moses had used preexisting written sources (Kenrick-Frenaye: 174). The theory was hardly an advanced one in the developing world of historical criticism, but at least Kenrick was open to considering new developments. He continued to seek his brother's advice—in correspondence, which, as befitted two Catholic prelates, was formal and in Latin—but the main work of the revision was Francis's alone.

It is somewhat paradoxical—and tragic—that even as Kenrick was working on his revision, he was also embroiled in controversy over the Bible in Philadelphia. In 1843, he succeeded in gaining the permission of the school board that Catholic children in public schools would not be required to read the King James Version. He was then accused of attempting to remove the Bible from the schools altogether. In May

1844, nativists clashed with Catholics and burned two Catholic churches. In July, rioting again broke out and at least thirteen men were killed (Billington: 221–30). Though nativism gave Kenrick an added incentive to provide a readable Catholic translation of the Bible, it did not seem to color his irenic treatment of the King James Version in his notes.

Kenrick's version appeared in six volumes between 1849 and 1862. He first published the Gospels. In the preface, he noted his indebtedness to the translation from the Greek made by John Lingard, an English Catholic priest, and acknowledged his familiarity with the critical work done on the Greek text by J. J. Griesbach and J. M. Scholz in Germany and George Campbell and S. T. Bloomfield in Britain (27, 29). His notes indicated where the Greek text or the King James Version differed from the Vulgate. But at times, his notes also disclosed his preoccupation with preserving Catholic doctrine. Thus, while his note on Matt 1:3–23 would receive praise in certain Catholic circles as late as 1952 (Pope: 462), Catholic scholars could hardly agree that "the Hebrew term strictly means a virgin. . . ." (n. 38).

The version received mixed reviews. In the *Dublin Review*, Nicholas Wiseman, who became a cardinal and first archbishop of Westminster in 1850, praised Kenrick for vindicating the Vulgate and for his English style and notes. Orestes Brownson, the philosopher-convert to Catholicism, commented that "if the learned doctors and scholars so numerous among us, would each be half as industrious in some department . . . as the learned Bishop of Philadelphia is in the several departments he cultivates, we should soon rise to literary independence, and be able to collect an English library not un-adapted to the wants and tastes of a cultivated Catholic family" (Nolan, 1948: 394).

Not all the reactions were positive. Kenrick had rendered the Vulgate reading *poenitentiam agite* (Matt 3:2) as "repent" and then explained in a note that he was trying to bring out the notion of the need for a change of heart rather than the exercise of the virtue of penance. Bishop Ignatius Reynolds of Charleston, as Francis told Peter, "finds fault seriously with my new version of the Bible; and in particular blames my use of the expression in some instances 'to repent,' instead of the accepted term, 'to do penance.'" Reynolds wanted Kenrick to abandon the planned revision, although he was "not unfavorable to the design for a corrected [English] version, to be made by the cooperation of three Bishops, one in England, one in Ireland, and one in this country." Francis Kenrick could only "marvel at the vehemence" with which Reynolds attacked what he called "the 'Repent' Version" (Kenrick-Frenaye: 395). Reynolds had, of course, raised only a minor point, but this was the type of criticism which would plague new American Catholic—and Protestant—versions of the English Bible for the next century.

Despite this one episcopal voice raised in opposition, Kenrick continued his work of revision. In 1851, he published the Acts of the Apostles, the Epistles, and the Apocalypse. For the rendering of Acts, he acknowledged the assistance of Father Augustine Hewitt, a convert to Catholicism, then a Redemptorist, and later one of the first Paulists (Nolan, 1948: 395). In 1857, Kenrick produced the Psalms, Wisdom, and Canticles.

By 1850, new metropolitan provinces had been established in the United States. One of the dioceses elevated to an archdiocese was that of St. Louis, whose archbishop was Peter R. Kenrick. In 1858, the bishops of the Province of Baltimore held their ninth council, an assembly whose legislation would bind only the Province of Baltimore and not the entire American church. During a special session from which Archbishop Francis Kenrick was absent, the senior suffragan, Bishop Michael O'Connor of Pittsburgh, presided. The bishops praised Kenrick's revision and proposed that, when completed, it be accepted for common usage in the United States. They had, however, heard that the English bishops had entrusted a new translation to John Henry Newman. They, therefore, suggested that Kenrick and Newman collaborate so "that, from the combined study and labor of each man, a single version would be prepared, which could be brought into use in both England and these states." Bishops John McGill of Richmond, Patrick Lynch of Charleston, and Augustine Verot of Florida, were deputed to seek the cooperation of the English hierarchy in the venture (*Acta et decreta Sacrorum* 3: 174). Thus, the bishops—for reasons far different than Reynolds had earlier proposed—were suggesting a common Catholic translation of the Bible for use in English-speaking nations.

The information the Americans had was correct. In 1855, at the second synod of Westminster, the English bishops had resolved to entrust a new translation of the Vulgate to Newman. Only after two years, however, did Cardinal Wiseman officially notify Newman of the decision; the bishops had made no provision for expenses for the project and had only stipulated that Newman was to own the copyright. Newman was, therefore, in a quandary when Bishop Lynch informed him of the decision of the American bishops about a joint venture with Kenrick. He replied to Lynch that Kenrick was "a

man so immeasurably superior to me, in station, in services to the
Church, in theological knowledge, in reputation, in qualifications for
the work, and in careful preparation for it, (who moreover has actually
given to the world complete and ready for the use of the faithful, so
great a portion of it); but on the other hand I am pledged to the
Bishops of England by duty, by gratitude, and by my word" (from a
letter to Lynch, 7 December 1858; Newman: 531–34). As it turned
out, the English bishops made no response to the Americans for a
Kenrick-Newman collaborative effort and Newman never completed
his own translation. Newman would, however, have further comments
on Kenrick's work in particular and on the problems of translating the
Vulgate in general.

In the meantime, Kenrick was proceeding with his work on the
Pentateuch. In October 1859, he wrote Peter that Brownson wanted
him to make greater use of the King James Version, but this he felt he
could not do "since the Holy See holds the [Latin] Vulgate to be the
norm for translations into the vernacular." Though there were discre-
pancies between the Vulgate and the King James Version, based on
the original languages, Francis feared he would be thought too "daring" if he followed the latter too closely. In his mind, the translator of
the Pentateuch in the King James Version had "turned the text with
much freedom . . ., [but] if I set forth all the peculiarities of the text
as they are, and follow closely the way of the Protestant translations, it
will appear that I am betraying the cause which I have undertaken to
vindicate, that is, the integrity of the Vulgate." Kenrick, then, although attempting to provide a good English Catholic translation of
the Bible, still had an apologetic purpose, perhaps shaped by his
battle with the Philadelphia nativists. On the other hand, he did seem
to confide in his brother that he did have some reservations about the
Vulgate. In a disclosure, surprising in view of Brownson's earlier
antipathy for Newman's theological method, he reported that
"Brownson believes that Newman ought to do the work, with hardly
any consideration of the Vulgate" (Kenrick-Frenaye: 430).

In 1860, Kenrick published his version of the Pentateuch. Although he had written to his brother in 1843 about his fascination with
Eichhorn's theory, he now shifted his opinion at least in public. In the
second edition of his *Theologia Dogmatica*, published in 1858, he
held strongly to the position that Moses was the actual author of the
Pentateuch (1: 20–21). In his preface to his version of the Pentateuch,
however, he was still conservative, but more nuanced. Whereas the
suppositions of the "rationalistic School," he said, could be reconciled
with "the authority, or even the inspiration of the work," he main-

tained the validity of the Jewish and early Christian testimony to the
Mosaic authorship. In his opinion, "Eichhorn and others who regard
it as a compilation, are forced to admit many things which it requires
great ingenuity to reconcile with their theory" (Kenrick, 1860: vii–
viii). Conservative though Kenrick may have been toward emerging
higher criticism, he did, nevertheless, alert his readers that there
were divergent views on the composition of the sacred books.

In what pertained more directly to the problems of translation,
Kenrick exhibited the awareness of the difficulties which would con-
front later translators. First of all, he still wished to vindicate the
Vulgate. He noted that A. Geddes, a Scottish Catholic critic, had said
that the principal difficulty with the Protestant translation was that
"the chief study of the English translators was to give a strictly literal
version, at the expense of every other consideration, whilst the author
of the Vulgate endeavored to render his originals equivalently into
such Latin as was current in his age."

In expanding on Geddes's observations about the superiority of
the Vulgate to the Protestant translations, Kenrick gave his own views
about the relationship between the Vulgate and the Hebrew. He
praised the King James Version's "literary excellence, especially as
regards its close adherence to the text," but he admitted that "in
revising the Douay translation I have constantly had in view the
Hebrew original, which, however, I did not always feel at liberty to
render closely, when it would imply a departure from the Vulgate,
since this is the standard of all vernacular translations for general use,
according to the settled usage of the Holy See."

Although he defended the Vulgate, Kenrick also acknowledged
that at times it had rendered the Hebrew "somewhat freely." In those
cases, he thought "it desirable that the English translation should
approach as nearly as possible to the original." He was comfortable in
adopting the King James Version's spelling of proper names and had
"otherwise deferred to usage, although of Protestant origin, feeling
that, in things indifferent, conformity is desirable, and that every
approach to uniformity in the rendering of the inspired word, without
sacrifice of principle, or violation of disciplinary rules, is a gain to the
common cause of Christianity." Here seemed to be a man able
carefully to distinguish between nativism and Protestant Christianity.
He knew, however, that "to many I may appear bold, in the emendations which I have suggested; but as my work is in the nature of a
literary essay, for examination by my venerable colleagues, I hope I
shall escape the censure of temerity. To the judgment of the Chief
Bishop it is most unreservedly submitted" (Kenrick, 1860: ix–x).

Similar to what he had done with the New Testament, Kenrick indicated in his notes where the Vulgate deviated from the Hebrew and where the King James Version conformed to it.

From Kenrick's prefaces and introductions to each book, it is obvious that he was interested in providing more than a translation of the Vulgate or a revision of the Douay Bible. He also wanted to place Scripture in the context of nineteenth-century developments in both scriptural criticism and science. In his introduction to Genesis, for example, he argued that in some instances modern science might force the alteration of the literal interpretation of the scriptural account of creation. He wished, however, to avoid the extremes of too great a fascination with science or a slavish adherence to the letter. He reminded his readers that not only had the ancients not known the "science of geology," but the fathers of the church had also differed in their understanding of "the Mosaic narrative . . . as implying the creation of the world in six days." This "diversity of views [among the Fathers] . . . shows that on this point the tradition of the Church was not absolute and dogmatical, so that if, with the progress of science, it become manifest, that a vast succession of ages can alone account for the structure of the earth . . . such indefinite periods may be admitted, without departing in any respect from the authoritative teaching of antiquity" (Kenrick, 1860: 17018). In short, then, Kenrick did not believe that Genesis necessarily presented a historical account of creation. His brother, however, would like to have seen his introduction expanded and thought the treatment of geology "presents some hesitation" (AAB: P. Kenrick to F. Kenrick, 7 March 1860).[1]

Later in 1860, Kenrick completed his revision with the publication of the historical books of the Old Testament. Peter congratulated him but counselled against a new publication of the entire version. The archbishop of St. Louis would have preferred to see a totally new translation either from the Vulgate or from the original languages, for, in his opinion, the Douay text had already been sufficiently revised, "but the Douay version itself has already ceased to be pleasing" (AAB: P. Kenrick to F. Kenrick, 8 September 1860). Peter Kenrick's remark was one of the first expressions in the American church of dissatisfaction with the Douay Bible and may well have accounted for his later opposition to having his brother's version adopted as the official American Catholic Bible.

Francis Kenrick never published an edition of the entire Bible, but in 1862, he did put out the complete New Testament, with some minor changes in the notes. Newman had never seen the version, but, he told John Acton, "from what I have heard said, I suppose he will have done a good work, in breaking down many narrow traditions as to translation. He has been accused of going too near the Protestant version, and has defended himself." Newman, however, had some additional observations on the difficulties of translating the Vulgate. Kenrick's "translation will at least be a platform," he said, "and in that light an important gain necessarily, considering his position, his theological knowledge, etc., etc." But he thought there was "another platform" and asked Acton for any information he might have on what German critics may have done in terms of "a dissertation on the Latin of the Vulgate, and a history of the change of the Latin tongue, in point both of structure and style, between Cicero and (say) St. Augustine." For Newman, this was "a necessary preliminary to a *translation* from the Vulgate" (from a letter to Acton, 31 August 1862; Newman:265). Although he did not challenge the use of the Vulgate, he did realize the necessity of understanding the words of the text in the sense in which they had been used at the time of Jerome's work.

In retrospect, Kenrick's revision of the Douay Bible was a project far too ambitious for one man and for one trained, not in ancient languages, but in theology. Nevertheless, although he remained conservative in his translation, he did manifest a certain openness to biblical criticism, which was then only in its infancy in the Catholic world. Even Newman, at that time, objected not to the use of the Vulgate or to what he had heard of Kenrick's work, but only to the manner in which the English bishops had handled his possible collaboration.

Kenrick's revision failed to become the official American Catholic version. He died in 1863 and in 1866, the American bishops assembled for the Second Plenary Council of Baltimore. Archbishop John Baptist Purcell of Cincinnati reported that the committee for choosing an English version of the Bible recommended that Kenrick's version be adopted. Peter Kenrick, always an enigmatic man, "vehemently opposed" the suggestion. After considerable discussion, the bishops voted to delete the proposed legislation on an English Bible (*Acta et decreta Sacrorum* 3: 357). Peter may have still, as he had in 1860, simply objected to the Douay Bible in any form.

When the decrees were sent to Rome for approval, the Congregation of Propaganda may have been a bit confused, for Francis Kenrick had sent the volumes of his version to the congregation (Kenrick, 1862: vi–vii). Moreover, the congregation had also seen and approved the decrees of the Ninth Provincial Council of Baltimore in 1858, which contained the proposal for adopting Kenrick's version. On 24 January 1868, Cardinal Alessandro Barnabo, prefect of propaganda, wrote Archbishop Martin John Spalding of Baltimore, who had presided over the council of 1866. The congregation, he said, approved the suppression of the decree pertaining to an English Bible, but was still concerned about "the grave danger to Catholics in the United States of having in their hands Bibles corrupted by heretics." Recalling the vote of the Baltimore council of 1858, the cardinal recommended that Spalding gather theologians and biblical scholars to compare the various versions of the Douay Bible and "other English versions, if any exist besides the Douay," and to produce an emended text which could be submitted to a future plenary council for common use throughout the country (*Acta et decreta Sacrorum* 3: 380).

Barnabo's letter would late provide an impetus for the Confraternity edition of 1941. It also formed the basis for discussion of an English Bible at the Third Plenary Council of Baltimore in 1884. Several of the bishops praised Kenrick's "version," but Peter Kenrick objected, as he had in 1866, this time stating that his brother had not produced "a version properly speaking, but rather a new edition of the Douay version" (*Acta et Decreta Concilii* lxvi–lxvii). As at the previous council, the bishops failed to adopt a standard version of the Catholic Bible. In their pastoral letter, however, they urged every family to have "a correct version" of the Bible and, "among other versions," they recommended "the Douay, . . . which was suitably annotated by the learned Bishop Challoner, by Canon Haydock, and especially the late Archbishop Kenrick" (Nolan, 1971: 177–78). Despite this relative acclaim, Kenrick's version was virtually forgotten in American Catholic circles.

Until the 1930s, American Catholics seemed generally content with various editions of the Douay-Challoner-Rheims version. In 1899, a Bible was published in Baltimore with a preface by Cardinal James Gibbons, archbishop of Baltimore. The text used was eclectically chosen from Challoner's three revisions of the New Testament, but with no reference to Kenrick (Pope: 482–83). In 1935, Father James A. Carey, professor of scripture at St. Joseph's Seminary, Dunwoodie, New York, published an updating of the Challoner text, which was revised only in terms of making punctuation, some grammatical points, and other items more intelligible to an American reader. This was the last revision of the Douay Bible prior to the new undertaking of the Confraternity edition (Pope: 489–91).

The hesitancy of American Catholics to attempt a new translation of the Bible was probably due to the anti-Modernist atmosphere that built up in the 1890s and became more stifling after 1907. There was,

however, one effort to provide a new American translation of the New
Testament. Francis Aloysius, O.P., a convert to Catholicism and former Paulist, published a translation of the Gospels from the Latin in
1898. He then began a translation of the Gospels from the Greek,
which he published in 1901, with a preface by Cardinal Gibbons. He
had completed his translation of the other books of the New Testament from the Greek shortly before his death in 1913. Though Pope
states that the bishops, at their annual meeting in 1935, urged that
the Spencer edition be published, there is no evidence for this in the
minutes of that meeting. In 1937, however, Spencer's work, revised
by Charles J. Callan, O.P., and John A. McHugh, O.P., was published
in New York. It was to go through five reprintings between 1940 and
1946 (Pope: 498). Its appearance coincided with and complicated the
decision of the Confraternity of Christian Doctrine (CCD), under the
direction of the American hierarchy, to produce a new translation
from the Vulgate. This translation project also led to the formation of
the Catholic Biblical Association (CBA).

The guiding light of the new project and of the CBA was Bishop
Edwin Vincent O'Hara, then bishop of Great Falls, Montana, later
bishop of Kansas City, and chairman of the bishops' committee, the
Confraternity of Christian Doctrine. Recognizing the long-standing
inadequacy of the Challoner-Rheims translation of the New Testament, he summoned a select group of Scripture professors to meet at
the Sulpician Seminary (later Theological College) in Washington,
D.C., on 18 January 1936. He hoped to involve in the translation
project a cross section of both religious and secular priests. The
thirteen priests who attended the first meeting determined that the
basis for their work would be the Clementine Vulgate. But they were
ambiguous as to the extent of their task. "The Editorial Board," they
voted, "can decide later whether it is to be known as a revision of the
Rheims or a new translation." Each book was assigned to a different
reviser, who was to have recourse to placing in footnotes variants from
the Greek text. The completed work was to be submitted to an
editorial board, chaired by Edward Arbez, S.S., of the Sulpician
Seminary, as editor, with Romain Butin, S.M., of the Catholic University of America, as associate editor, and William L. Newton of St.
Mary's Seminary, Cleveland, as secretary. Charles J. Callan, O.P., was
entrusted with the final English editing (SAB: Arbez, minutes, 18
January 1936).

Not everyone was in accord with the decision to make a new
translation of the Vulgate. Callan, who had revised the Spencer
translation from the Greek, strongly suggested to O'Hara that it be

adopted as the American text (ADKC: 116 [Callan to O'Hara, 8 February 1936]). This was the first in a series of challenges to the Confraternity edition issued by the Dominican editor of the *Homiletic and Pastoral Review (HPR)*. Moreover, in England, Catholic scholars, under the auspices of the hierarchy, had been working on a translation of the Bible from the original languages since 1913. The Westminster Version of the New Testament, under the editorship of Cuthbert Lattey, S.J., had been published in 1935, and the translators then began to work on the Old Testament. In 1934, however, the Dutch bishops had asked the Pontifical Biblical Commission whether it was permitted to read in churches the pericopes of the liturgical texts, translated not from the Vulgate but from the original languages. The Commission responded that the text to be "publicly read" was to be translated "from the text approved by the Church for the sacred liturgy," that is, the Vulgate. Because of the close association between vernacular translations of the Bible and the Latin version used in the Church's public worship, then, the Americans felt compelled to use the Vulgate as the basis for their translation. Even in England, the Westminster Version could not be used in the vernacular proclamation of the liturgical texts.

Though the Americans were committed to making their translation from the Vulgate, opposition to it came from a surprising quarter, Father A. E. Breen, a professor at the Milwaukee archdiocesan seminary. Earlier in the century, Breen had taught at St. Bernard's Seminary in Rochester and had accused one of his colleagues, Edward J. Hanna, of heresy. It was a major scene in the relatively minor role that the American Catholic church played in the modernist controversy (DeVito: 269–72). By 1936, he had changed his stance, at least in regard to the text of Scripture. He protested to William Newton, secretary of the CCD project, that "the Rheims NT can not be adequately revised. The only thing that would be effective is to make a version such as the Revisers of Oxford have made. Rome will not permit this. The Gasquet revision [the revision of the Vulgate entrusted by Pius X to the Benedictines, under the direction of Cardinal Aidan Gasquet, O.S.B.] will put back the real revision of the Vulgate another thousand years" (CBA: Breen to Newton, 28 August 1936).

On 19 April 1936, O'Hara met with the editorial board to finalize the norms for the revision. At the same time, they made a decision which had far-reaching significance not only for the translation of the scriptures but also for the development of American Catholic biblical scholarship. At the January meeting, Romain Butin had proposed the formation of an association of Catholic biblical scholars. At the April meeting, O'Hara and the editors decided to issue an invitation to all professors of scripture to attend a meeting in New York on 3 October 1936 in conjunction with the national convention of the CCD. This New York meeting resulted in the formation of the Catholic Biblical Association (CBA) and in the decision to establish the *Catholic Biblical Quarterly (CBQ)*. Of more direct pertinence to the project of translation, however, was the report that about one quarter of the New Testament was then translated. Butin reminded his audience that, while there should be "close adherence to the vulgate," there should also be "more attention . . . given the Greek . . . in clarifying the Latin" (SAB: Arbez, meeting, 3 October 1936). In retrospect, it is obvious that the translators had little scholarly grasp of the complexity involved in their work—they still hoped that their task would be complete by the summer of 1937.

By the spring of 1938, the manuscript of the first revision of the Confraternity New Testament was in the hands of the editors, who then turned to the Old Testament. That summer, William Newton, secretary of the editorial board, visited Rome and England to stir up interest in the newly founded CBA and to sound out officials on what text should be used for the translation of the Old Testament. In Rome, he met first with J. B. Frey, secretary of the Biblical Commission. Since the American hierarchy made no formal request of the commission, however, Frey recommended that Newton consult members of the commission individually. He then interviewed Augustin Bea, S.J., rector of the Biblical Institute; A. Vaccari, a professor at the institute; Ernesto Ruffini, secretary of the Congregation of Seminaries; and J. M. Vosté, subsequently secretary of the Biblical Commission. From his survey of these officials, Newton reported that opinion was divided on whether to use the Vulgate or the original languages. If the original languages were used, however, the work would have to "remain in 'campo scientifico.'" If the bishops wished, they could request "a formal decision" on the matter from the commission, but that could take several years and delay the American translation (ADKC: 348, Newton to O'Hara, 11 June 1938).

In England, Newton met Canon J. M. T. Barton, English consultor of the Biblical Commission, and Cuthbert Lattey. Both agreed to serve as advisers to the editorial board of the new translation but recommended that it be made from the original languages. Behind this recommendation, however, lay the desire to enlist American collaboration with the Westminster project. It was at this point, moreover, that the English hierarchy, probably in an effort to conform with the Biblical Commission's response of 1934, commissioned

Ronald Knox to do a new translation of the Bible from the Vulgate. Subsequent efforts to gain Knox's cooperation with the American project were unsuccessful (ADKC: 348, "England and the revision," n.d.).

Newton had received conflicting advice in regard to using the original languages as the basic text for translation. More than four years later, his recollections of the attitude in Rome was different from what he reported back at the time. Early in 1944, he said that the members of the Biblical Commission, whom he had consulted, had stated that the translation of the Old Testament could be made from the Vulgate, rather than the original languages, "if the bishops insisted," but then only after comparing the Latin with the original text (ADKC: 108, Newton memo, 13 February 1943 *(sic)*. Although it is now difficult to determine how Roman officials felt toward translations from the original languages, it is clear that they agreed that the text of the Vulgate was defective. Until a critical text of the Vulgate was available, the Clementine text would have to be used with great caution and with careful comparison with the original languages. In October 1938, the editorial board of the Confraternity edition adopted the policy of using "a criticized Vulgate" as the basic text not only for the translation of the Old Testament, then just beginning, but also for further revision of the translation of the New Testament (ADKC: 348, Newton, "Revision of the Challoner-Rheims NT," n.d.). The American translators were learning that their task was more complicated than they had originally thought. The project, ambiguous from the beginning, had now definitively shifted from revision to translation.

In the meantime, the editorial board had already made a decision related to the new policy of translation. In August 1938, Newton's own translation of John was privately printed and distributed to all the American and Canadian bishops, each member of the CBA, and every English-speaking Catholic biblicist. The translation was based on the Vulgate but greater attention was given to the Greek text. In sending out his work, Newton quoted Cardinal Barnabo's letter to Archbishop Spalding in 1868, calling for a definitive edition of the Douay Bible. It was "in the spirit of this instruction," said Newton, that the Episcopal Committee of the CCD had undertaken the new revision (SAB: Newton to Arbez, 26 August 1938). The purpose of the distribution of the new text was to evoke the constructive criticism of as many people as possible before making further revisions. The editors, however, had not submitted the text first to Charles Callan, who was to put it in final English form. The text and its distribution brought out into the open many of the tensions seething beneath the surface of the project from its inception. :

By January 1939, the editorial board had received numerous comments on the text, most of them favorable. Then, that summer, Thomas J. Kennedy published an article in *HPR* charging that the new translation was heretical. He found nine mistranslations in the first eighteen verses, but he was particularly disturbed by the rendering of John 1:15 as: "he who is to come after me, has been made above me, because he was before me." For Kennedy, this rendition was "strongly tinged with Arianism" (73). O'Hara, who had become bishop of Kansas City, immediately wrote Callan, the editor of the *HPR*, chastising him for making public the text, intended only for private circulation among Scripture scholars, and for publishing an article, charging that text with heresy (ADKC: 116, O'Hara to Callan, 31 July 1939). Edward Cerney, S.S., professor of Scripture at St. Mary's Seminary in Baltimore, then published a strong defense of Newton's preliminary text in the *CBQ*.

Despite the tensions surrounding the revision/translation, the Confraternity edition of the New Testament was published in the spring of 1941. O'Hara enlisted the aid of the Holy Name Society in distributing it throughout the United States and procured a letter from the Biblical Commission praising the work. This letter, dated 6 March 1941, and signed by Cardinal Eugene Tisserant, president of the commission, was printed in the front of the edition. A lectionary for the Sunday masses was also published. The translation, however, received little scholarly notice in non-Catholic circles.

Members of the CBA were well aware of the limitations of the translation. In November 1941, the association met in Philadelphia. In his presidential address, Edward J. Byrne, professor of Scripture at St. Bernard's Seminary in Rochester, spoke of the difficulties of using the Vulgate text and thought it would "be regrettable if the Confraternity Edition were to be used by our seminarians as an adequate foundations for the laying of the foundations of our faith." No translation, he concluded, could "adequately fill the place of a critical text based on the study of the best Greek manuscripts, of the Versions, and of the Patristic quotations" (7–8). American Catholic biblical scholars, then, were reserved in their attitude toward the Confraternity edition, but there were also strong critics both inside and outside the Catholic church.

On 17 April 1942, Cardinal Tisserant wrote O'Hara that the Biblical Commission had compared the Confraternity edition with the Challoner version and had discovered "certain stylistic divergences . . . which seemed less favorable to the new text." The CCD, he continued, had formally requested the commission's intervention and he, therefore, thought it his duty, "for the benefit of the new Catholic version, as well as for the name of the Biblical Commission, to recommend a serious revision, which should be entrusted to the representative of the Pontifical Biblical Commission in America, the Very Reverend Consultor Father Charles J. Callan, O.P."

O'Hara lost no time in gathering the opinion of the other members of the Episcopal Committee of the CCD, in particular that of the Dominican archbishop of Cincinnati, John T. McNicholas. Regarded as the leading theologian among the bishops, McNicholas candidly replied that "Father Callan is capable of using the Pontifical Commission for selfish reasons, for an approval which he is likely to interpret as singling him out as the most outstanding Biblical scholar in the United States, and for publicity reasons which he is apt to turn to his own advantage." The archbishop proposed that the Episcopal Committee make a strong but respectful representation to Tisserant, which he himself would draft (ADKC: 117 [McNicholas to O'Hara, 16 May 1942]). In the meantime, O'Hara went to see Archbishop Amleto Cicognani, apostolic delegate to the United States. The delegate read over the proposed letter, recommended some changes, and offered to send it to Rome with a covering letter of his own.

The bishops wrote their letter to Tisserant on 27 June 1942. They called to the cardinal's attention that the CCD had not requested the intervention of the Biblical Commission, but that Callan, for his own purposes, had sought that intervention. They could not accept Tisserant's evaluation of the Challoner version, which both Cardinal Wiseman and Cardinal Newman had so strongly criticized for style. Whereas they were well aware of the need for further revision, the bishops could not take the "responsibility" of entrusting this to Callan, whom neither the bishops nor Scripture scholars regarded as an "eminent Biblical scholar." Finally, the bishops had never regarded Tisserant's letter of 6 March 1941, "as an approval [of the translation] of the New Testament," but only as an encouragement of the Holy Name Society, which distributed the text. To avoid all confusion, subsequent editions of the New Testament would omit the letter (ADKC: 117, O'Hara, McNicholas, and Murray to Tisserant, 27 June 1942).

Communications between Rome and the United States were slow during wartime and Tisserant did not respond until 14 October. He acknowledged that it was "the unquestioned privilege of the Episcopal Hierarchy to procure for the faithful committed to their care

suitable translations in the vernacular of the Sacred Scriptures."
Callan's "recommendation . . . made by the Biblical Commission," he
continued, "was intended simply as a suggestion submitted to the
Episcopal Committee, which we cordially thank for the frankness of
its statement in his regard." Tisserant's own reference to the Challoner version was to be construed "in the sense of considering it as a
standard for the observance of grammatical rules, rather than for the
value of its style" (ADKC: 117, Tisserant to O'Hara, 14 October 1942).
This was neither the first nor the last time that Roman officials issued
as a clarification what in fact was a retraction. On the same day
Tisserant wrote the bishops, J. M. Vosté, O.P., then the secretary of
the Biblical Commission, wrote Callan. It was pointless for Callan to
undertake a revision, said Vosté, if he lacked the "good will" of the
bishops, who had to "take their responsibility before their people and
the world." The secretary's own recommendation was that his fellow
dominican "not . . . move [sic] war against the Bishops" (ADKC: 117,
Vosté to Callan, 14 October 1942). This, however, did not end Callan's
attacks on the translation.

The exchange between the Episcopal Committee and the Biblical
Commission was a critical turning point in the development of American Catholic biblical scholarship. To provide a good American English translation of the Bible, it was imperative that the work be in the
hands of men trained in biblical studies and the original languages.
Callan represented the tendency toward Romanization of the American church, which had begun in the early part of the century. The
episcopal support of indigenous American Scripture scholarship was a
move away from that Romanization and toward the collegiality and
legitimate national traditions recognized by the Second Vatican Council.

Roman and American conservatives were not the only critics of
the new translation. Early in 1943, there were also complaints that
the translation was anti-Semitic. At issue was the Confraternity edition's rendering of Rev 2:9 as: "and thou art slandered by those who
say they are Jews and are not, but are a synagogue of Satan." A note
explained that "the Jews are the *synagogue of Satan*. The true synagogue is the Christian Church." Though both Arbez and Newton
initially thought the sense of the note was clear in the context, they
finally agreed that a change should be made in future editions
(ADKC: 349, Newton to O'Hara, 5 and 24 April 1943).

From within the American Catholic church, however, criticism
continued to be leveled against the translation, just at the moment
when the CBA was about to turn to the totally new project of translat-

ing the Bible from the original languages. In August 1943, the Biblical Commission issued a clarification of its response of 1934. It stated that translations for the use of the faithful could be made from the original languages, but that the pericopes of the texts used in the liturgy were to be translated from the Vulgate. The *HPR* published this new document, but the editors, Callan and John A. McHugh, O.P., concentrated on the latter portion of the response and stated unequivocally that the translations of the liturgical pericopes must strictly conform to the Vulgate. Paradoxically, this new response occasioned not only a renewed attack on the Confraternity edition but also the decision of the CCD to translate the Old Testament from the original languages.

The attacks came from a now familiar source, the *HPR*. In March 1944, the journal published a communication from a reader who signed himself "Amator Evangelii," who challenged that the new pulpit lectionary, containing the liturgical pericopes according to the Confraternity edition, did not conform with the Biblical Commission's recent decision. "Amator" cited two passages, which, he argued, were not accurate translations of the Vulgate. The CCD edition had translated Phil 2:6 as: "Christ Jesus, . . . though he was by nature God, did not consider being equal to God a thing to be clung to." Amator believed this endangered the Christian doctrine that the Father and the Son are equal. The new translation had also rendered John 2:4 as: "What wouldst thou have me do, woman?" Amator thought this not only disrespectful to the Virgin Mary, but also violated the clear theological meaning of the text as a "most explicit confirmation by Our Saviour of their [the young married couple's] confidence in the efficacy of Our Lady's intercession" (1944a).

It was no secret to anyone that Amator was either Callan himself or someone inspired by him. Joseph L. Lilly, C.M., general secretary of the CBA, immediately consulted O'Hara and then wrote a rejoinder to the *HPR*. The CCD edition had the approval of the American bishops, as required by the Biblical Commission's decree, he noted, and moreover, the Challoner-Rheims text itself had not been a slavishly literal translation of the Vulgate. But the *HPR* was hardly the proper vehicle for a learned dialogue. Printed right after Lilly's letter was a response from Amator, who charged that, among other things, the CCD edition had "imposed *on everyone* . . . its purely private and personal surmise" about the meaning of the passages in question (1944b: 619).

Michael J. Gruenthaner, S.J., the editor of the *CBQ*, then published a strong defense of the CCD translation in the *American*

Ecclesiastical Review (AER), which, like the *HPR*, had a wide circulation among priests. After refuting Amator's arguments about grammar and theology, he concluded: "We hope that Amator Evangelii will gird himself like a man and make the *amende honorable* to Fr. Lilly, the theological censors, and the bishops whom he has insulted with so little cause and so grievously. We regret that the editors of the *Homiletic and Pastoral Review* were beguiled into accepting these communications of *Amator Evangelii*" (415). This was, of course, a direct attack on Callan and McHugh, who had been trying to undermine the CCD project from its inception. Bishop O'Hara ordered Gruenthaner's article reprinted and distributed to every bishop and priest in the United States. Even this did not definitively silence Amator, who published one more letter in the *HPR* (1944c), but his criticism had little ultimate effect.

Amator's criticism, in retrospect, might be seen as a minor incident. It did, however, indicate not only the continuing resistance of certain Catholics to changing the familiar language of their older translation but also the close association between vernacular Bibles and the liturgy. During the next twenty years, American Catholics accepted the Confraternity translation as the traditional one by hearing it read at all their Sunday masses. But biblical studies were undergoing rapid change, the most dramatic sign of which came in September 1943, when Pius XII issued his encyclical, *Divino Afflante Spiritu*. He called for Catholic scholars to use higher criticism in their work and stated that, in holding the Vulgate to be authentic, the council of Trent had forebade neither the study of the Bible in nor translations of it from the original languages.

While the encyclical provided the *magna charta* for Catholic biblical scholarship, it was not it, but the Biblical Commission's response the previous August—the same one which occasioned Amator Evangelii's criticism—which prompted the Confraternity to abandon its translation of the Old Testament from the Vulgate. In this change of policy, it is difficult to determine now whether O'Hara or Newton actually took the initiative. Newton and others had, from the beginning, preferred translating the Old Testament from the original languages. The editorial board, nevertheless, decided to base its translation on the Vulgate and by late 1941, the work was about one third complete (*CBQ*, 1941: 182). By early February 1944, the text of *Divino Afflante Spiritu* had still not arrived in the United States, but Newton wrote O'Hara that the Biblical Commission's response provided strong argument for a translation from the original languages

(ADKC: 350, Newton to O'Hara, 1 February 1944). He subsequently recalled his consultation with Roman officials in 1938 and stated that no bishop could object that a translation from the Hebrew would confuse the faithful, who did not read the Old Testament in any case (ADKC: 108, Newton to O'Hara, 13 February 1943 *(sic)*).

O'Hara needed little encouragement. After circularizing the other members of the Editorial Committee, he wrote Archbishops McNicholas and Cicognani. To McNicholas, he said that the response of the Biblical Commission, "if not directive, seems strongly to advise that the translation be from the original languages." Since the translation of the Old Testament had already begun, however, it was imperative that the bishops on the confraternity committee make a decision as soon as possible (ADKC: 280, O'Hara to McNicholas, 21 February 1944). With Cicognani, he used a similar argument (ADKC: 280, O'Hara to Cicognani, 21 February 1944). By March, O'Hara had gained the approval of the confraternity committee to begin the translation of the Old Testament anew from the Hebrew. The sole exception was the Psalms, a Latin critical edition of which was then being completed in Rome (ADKC: 350, O'Hara to Newton, 1 March 1944). In April, O'Hara appointed Newton chairman of a committee to investigate a new translation of the New Testament from the Greek (ADKC: 350, O'Hara to Newton, 24 April 1944). Granted that the war was then occupying most of the energy of Americans, O'Hara had lost no time in having the CCD translation project keep apace of the new instructions from Rome.

When the CBA held its annual meeting at St. Mary's College, Notre Dame, Indiana, on 22 August 1944, it received added encouragement for its new translation. Cicognani wrote O'Hara praising the work. After citing *Divino Afflante Spiritu*, the apostolic delegate stated that the new translation was conformable "to the recommendations of His Holiness" and should "elicit the interest, sympathetic understanding, and aid, as far as possible, of both clergy and laity." He recognized "the difficulty of this noble work," which entailed gaining an "adequate knowledge of the events and of the language and manner in which they are narrated." "Perfection cannot be demanded," he said, "and no translation can ever hope to win the unreserved approval of every scholar." He concluded his letter by quoting Pius's encyclical, which urged that these new scholarly efforts "should be judged not only with equity and justice, but also with the greatest charity; all moreover should abhor that intemperate zeal which imagines that whatever is new should for that very reason be opposed or suspected." Cicognani's letter may well have been intended to silence the criticism of the *HPR*, for it was printed at the front of the October issue of the *CBQ*.

The work of the CBA gradually began to take on a more scholarly cast. Yet, the translators still had much to learn about the nature of translation. By the meeting of the CBA in 1945, the draft of twenty-six books had been submitted to the editors and Arbez expressed the hope of circulating a preliminary version of Genesis within a year (*CBQ*, 1945: 116). Not until 25 August 1948, however, was the translation of Genesis published. By that time thirty-nine of the forty-six books of the Old Testament had also been translated (*CBQ*, 1948: 5). In 1950, the Psalms and the Canticles, used in the breviary or divine office of the church, were published. Between 1952 and 1961, three volumes of a projected four-volume translation of the Old Testament appeared—volume 1, *Genesis to Ruth* (1952); volume 3, *The Sapiential Books: Job to Sirach* (1955); and Volume 4, *The Prophetic Books: Isaiah to Malachi* (1961).

In the meantime, a translation of the New Testament from the Greek had been completed by 1948. The joint work of James A. Kleist, S.J., and Joseph L. Lilly, C.M., with some assistance from Dominic J. Unger, O.F.M.Cap., it failed to gain approval of the episcopal censors. Angry at the rejection of his translation, Kleist resigned from the committee of revisers (ADKC: 115, Kleist to O'Hara, 1 October 1948). Kleist died a short time later and in the following summer, O'Hara ceded the CCD's copyright of the manuscript to Paul Reinert, S.J., president of St. Louis University, who had arranged to have the entire translation published (ADKC: 115, O'Hara to Reinert, 23 June 1949). The "Kleist-Lilly" translation appeared in 1954, but stylistically it was never well received (*CBQ*, 1954: 445).

By the opening of the Second Vatican Council in 1962, there were in print only three volumes of the translation of the Old Testament and the 1941 Confraternity edition of the New Testament. The late 1950s and early 1960s were years of turmoil for Catholic biblical scholars both in the United States and Canada and throughout the world, as conservative forces within Catholicism sought to put the brakes on the scholarship initiated by *Divino Afflante Spiritu*. Though not directly related to the problems of translation as such, this turmoil seems to have slowed down the American work. Considerations of Catholic dogma, for instance, led the hierarchy to demand that Isa 7:14 be translated as "the virgin shall be with child" (*CBQ*, 1960: 433).

Once the council got under way, however, it gave a renewed impetus not only to scriptural studies but also to ecumenism and the liturgy.

By the summer of 1964, the editors of the Old Testament reported that the translation of the historical books was about halfway complete. They and the editors of the New Testament were cooperating with the bishops' committee on the liturgy, newly revised at the council, to complete the translations of the readings in the liturgical lectionary, which would be used when the vernacular liturgy was introduced on the first Sunday of Advent (*CBQ*, 1964: 170).

This interim translation presented a number of problems. Some difficulties arose from the people's unfamiliarity with a translation from the Greek. For example, the CCD edition had rendered Luke 24:6 as "He is not here, but has risen." The new translation read: "He is not here; he has been raised up." For some Catholics, the translation seemed to diminish Christ's divinity. Other difficulties were occasioned by an effort to render the meaning of the text in too colloquial a form of American English. Thus, in Luke 15:8, the woman was described as having lost "a dime." This may have been a better rendition of *drachma*, but hardly seemed sufficient cause for the woman to awaken her friends and neighbors when she found it.

In light of the criticisms received, the editors continued their revision of the liturgical texts. When the CBA met in 1965, however, it made a more important decision. Vatican II had called for ecumenical cooperation in the translation of the Bible. The CBA, therefore, assigned the untranslated scriptural books to Protestant scholars. For the Old Testament, David Noel Freedman agreed to revise the translation of Genesis, the first book of the Old Testament published by the CBA; Frank Cross and James A. Sanders translated the books of Samuel and books of Kings, respectively. For the New Testament, John Knox was assigned the Pastoral Epistles and W. D. Davies the Epistle to the Hebrews (*CBQ*, 1965: 409–140). Many of the older distinctions between a "Catholic" and "Protestant" Bible had begun to blur. The difficulties that John Carroll and Francis Kenrick had with the Protestant Bible had ceased to apply. What did apply was whether the scholarship was good or bad. Catholics and Protestants were beginning to use the same translations. In 1966, for instance, Cardinal Richard Cushing of Boston gave his imprimatur to an unaltered Revised Standard Version, an event which, incidentally, some saw as lessening enthusiasm for the CCD translation still in progress.

In 1969, volume 2, *Samuel to Maccabees*, appeared. Finally, in 1970, the New American Bible was published, the first American

Catholic translation of the entire Bible from the original languages, except for the Book of Psalms. In fact, it was the first single-volume American Catholic translation from any language. Its publication coincided with the introduction of the final revisions of the liturgy with its extended scriptural readings—three readings for each Sunday (one taken from the Old Testament), placed on a three-year cycle.

It had been a long road from the day in 1937 when Bishop O'Hara gathered a group of biblical scholars to discuss placing in the hands of American Catholics a readable translation of the Vulgate. That gathering led to the formation of the CBA, which provided a group of scholars ready to respond to the new norms for Catholic biblical scholarship presented in *Divino Afflante Spiritu*. As the CBA developed, it became increasingly attuned not only to advanced scholarship in general but also to textual criticism, a prerequisite for an adequate translation.

Yet, there is not universal satisfaction in Catholic circles for the New American Bible. As Archbishop Cicognani, reflecting Pius XII, had written in 1944, the work of translation is also a work of interpretation and, therefore, "no translation can ever hope to win the unreserved approval of every scholar." Some scholars, for instance, object that the final English form of the new translation is too free. Others point out that the translators completed their work too hastily in order to have the text ready for the new liturgy. In view of these and other criticisms, the CBA has undertaken a virtually new translation. In 1987, the new translation of the New Testament was published.

NOTES

/1/   Archival abbreviations used:
AAB = Archives of the Archdiocese of Baltimore
ADKC = Archives of the Diocese of Kansas City
CBA = Archives of the Catholic Biblical Association
SAB = Sulpician Archives, Baltimore

WORKS CONSULTED

Acta et Decreta Concilii Plenarii Baltimorensis Tertii . . .
      1886   Baltimore: John Murphy & Co.

Acta et decreta Sacrorum Conciliorum Recentiorum: Collectio Lacensis.
      1875   7 vols.; Freiburg im Breisgau: Herder.

Amator Evangelii
      1944a   "Communication." *Homiletic and Pastoral Review* 44: 449–51.

1944b	"Communication." *Homiletic and Pastoral Review* 44: 617–19.
1944c	"Communication." *Homiletic and Pastoral Review* 44: 807–12.

Biblical Commission
1934	"Decretum." *Acta apostolicae sedis* 26: 315.
1943	"Responsum." *Acta apostolicae sedis* 35: 270–71.

Billington, Ray Allen
1964	*The Protestant Crusade: A Study of the Origins of American Nativism.* Chicago: Quadrangle.

Byrne, Edward J.
1942	"President's Address." *CBQ* 4: 5–8.

Callan, Charles J. and John A. McHugh
1944	"Roman Documents: On the Use and Authority of Vernacular Versions of Sacred Scripture." *Homiletic and Pastoral Review* 44:381–82.

Catholic Biblical Quarterly
1941	"Meeting of the Catholic Biblical Association, Nov. 15–16, 1941." 4: 175–85.
1945	"Meeting of the Catholic Biblical Association, Aug. 22–23, 1945." 8:114–20.
1948	"Meeting of the Catholic Biblical Association, Aug. 24–26, 1948." 11: 1–8.
1954	"Meeting of the Catholic Biblical Association, Aug. 24–25, 1954." 16: 444–48.
1960	"Meeting of the Catholic Biblical Association, Aug. 30–31, 1960." 22: 430–38.
1964	"Meeting of the Catholic Biblical Association, Sept. 1–3, 1964." 26: 468–74.
1965	"Meeting of the Catholic Biblical Association, Aug. 31–Sept. 2, 1965." 27: 407–14.

Cerny, Edward A., S.S.
1939	"Problems of Bible Revision: The Translation of St. John 1:15." *CBQ* 1: 363–68.

Collectanea S. Congregationis de Propaganda Fide seu Decreta Instructiones Rescripta pro Apostolics Missionibus.
1907	Vol. 1; Rome: Typographia Polyglotta S.C. de Propaganda Fide.

Confraternity of Christian Doctrine
1941	*The New Testament of Our Lord and Savior Jesus Christ.* Paterson, NJ: St. Anthony Guild Press.
1970	New American Bible. New York: Catholic Book Publishing.

DeVito, Michael J.
1977	*The New York Review (1905–1908).* New York: United States Catholic Historical Society.

Denzinger, Henry, and Adolf Schönmetzer, S.J.
1963	*Enchiridion Symbolorum.* 32d ed.; Freiburg im Breisgau: Herder.

Fogarty, Gerald P.
1982	"The Quest for a Catholic Vernacular Bible in America." *The*

Bible in America, Nathan O. Hatch and Mark A. Noll., eds.
New York: Oxford University Press.

Gruenthaner, Michael J., S.J.
1944   "An Unfounded Charge of Heresy." *AER* 110: 407–15.

Hanley, Thomas O., ed.
1976   *The John Carroll Papers*. 3 vols. Notre Dame: Notre Dame
                University.

Hennesey, James, S.J.
1981   *American Catholics*. New York: Oxford University Press.

Kennedy, Thomas J.
1939   "A Much-Debated Text in St. John's Gospel." *Homiletic and
                Pastoral Review* 39: 1164–78.

Kenrick, Francis Patrick
1849   *The Four Gospels*. New York: Dunigan.
1851   *The Acts of the Apostles, the Epistles of St. Paul, the Catholic
                Epistles and the Apocalypse*. New York: Dunigan.
1858   *Theologia Dogmatica*, 2d ed. Baltimore: John Murphy
1860   *The Pentateuch*. Baltimore: Kelly, Hedian & Piet.
1862   *The New Testament*. Baltimore: Kelly, Hedian & Piet.

Kenrick-Frenaye
1920   *The Kenrick–Frenaye Correspondence: Letters Chiefly of
                Francis Patrick Kenrick and Marc Antony Frenaye: 1830–1862*.
                Transl., Frederick E. Tourscher. Philadelphia: Philadelphia Ar-
                chives.

Lilly, Joseph L., C.M.
1944   "Communications." *Homiletic and Pastoral Review* 44: 615–16.

McNally, R. E., S.J.
1966   "The Council of Trent and Vernacular Bibles." *Theological
                Studies* 27: 204–27.

Newman, John Henry
1961   *Letters and Diaries*. London: T. Nelson.

Newton, William L.
1937   "Principles Governing the Revision of the New Testament."
                *Proceedings of the Catholic Biblical Association: First General
                Meeting, St. Louis, MO, October 9 and 10, 1937*. St. Meinrad,
                IN: Abbey Press.

Nolan, Hugh J.
1948   *The Most Reverend Francis Patrick Kenrick: Third Bishop of
                Philadelphia: 1830–1851*. Philadelphia: American Catholic His-
                torical Society.
1971   *Pastoral Letters of the American Hierarchy, 1792–1970*. Hunt-
                ington, IN: Our Sunday Visitor.

Parsons, Wilfrid, S.J.
1937   "First American Editions of Catholic Bibles." *Historical Rec-
                ords and Studies* 27: 89–98.

Pope, Hugh, O.P.
1952   *English Versions of the Bible*. St. Louis: B. Herder.

Skehan, Patrick W.
     1960   "The Translation into the Vernacular." *Guide to the Bible: An
                     Introduction to the Study of Holy Scripture.* A. Robert and A.
                     Tricot, eds. 2d ed.; trans., Edward B. Arbez and Martin R. P.
                     McGuire. Paris: Declee.

VI
Thomas Jefferson's Bible
F. Forrester Church

Thomas Jefferson's Bible, *The Life and Morals of Jesus of Nazareth*, was first published by the government in 1904. Fourteen years earlier, the Committee on Library had suggested that it be printed should the Congress see fit to purchase Jefferson's manuscript papers and correspondence, which it did not. In 1895, however, the purchase was approved, and arrangements were made to have the work included both as a part of the government's Federal Edition of Jefferson's works, and also independently of that in a special printing for the Congress. In his introduction, Cyrus Adler cites the following concurrent resolution adopted by the first session of the Fifty-seventh Congress: "[Be it resolved] that there be printed and bound, by photolithographic process, with an introduction of not to exceed twenty-five pages, to be prepared by Dr. Cyrus Adler, Librarian of the Smithsonian Institution, for the use of Congress, 9,000 copies of Thomas Jefferson's Morals of Jesus of Nazareth, as the same appears in the National Museum; 3,000 copies for the use of the Senate and 6,000 copies for the use of the House" (19).

In 1957 my father, Frank Church, was elected to the Senate. As had been the custom since 1904, he was presented with a copy of Jefferson's Bible. He gave the book to me. After reading it once, I went through again, marking all the appropriate citations in the margin. I then transferred the contents back into a New Testament, using a yellow market to cover the passages Jefferson had extracted. Years later, after a bit of exploration, I discovered that relatively little is known about Jefferson's Bible, or the circumstances attending its inception.

A list of the passages included by Jefferson in *The Life and Morals of Jesus of Nazareth* was first published by Henry S. Randall in 1858 as a part of the thirtieth appendix to his three-volume biography, *The Life and Times of Thomas Jefferson*. Randall did not address himself to the problem of Jefferson's Bible, except to describe its appearance, "a handsome octavo, bound in Morocco," and to wonder that the collection was unknown to Jefferson's grandchildren until after his death (3:

655). Randall's appendix retains its importance, however, due to the inclusion of Jefferson's first synopsis, "The Philosophy of Jesus of Nazareth" (3: 654). Considerably different from the later *Life* both in selection and arrangement, "The Philosophy" evinces an earlier and less judgmental attitude toward the evangelists' verisimilitude.

The questions remain. When did Thomas Jefferson create his own version of the Gospels? When did he revise it? And, in each instance, what led him to do so? First, a little background.

A Gentleman's Library

On 17 July 1771, Jefferson was petitioned by a Mr. Robert Skipwith to propose to him a library befitting the dignity of a Virginia gentleman (Boyd, 1: 74–75). Skipwith was prepared to invest some twenty-five or thirty pounds. He wished to have his volumes bound in gold. Jefferson promptly drew up a catalogue of books, plainly bound, costing no less than one hundred and seven pounds, and suggested, by way of invitation, that Skipwith abandon the scheme, and come to his home, "the new Rowanty, from which you may reach your hand to a library formed on a more extensive plan" (Boyd, 1: 76).

When Jefferson offered the same opportunity to Congress in proposing to sell his library to replace that which had been destroyed by fire when the British took Washington in 1812, Congressman Cyrus King of Massachusetts was offended. From the floor of the House he exclaimed: "It might be inferred, from the character of the man who collected it, and France, where the collection was made, that the library contained irreligious and immoral books, works of the French philosophers, who caused and influenced the volcano of the French Revolution. The bill would put $23,999 into Jefferson's pocket for about 6,000 books, good, bad, and indifferent, old, new, and worthless, in languages which many cannot read and most ought not" (Bestor: 2).

More telling than Mr. King's invective is the scheme of classification as formulated in the catalogue that Jefferson had submitted to Congress on approval. Fashioned from the framework upon which Francis Bacon in 1605 had constructed his essay, *The Advancement of Learning*, it affords one the opportunity of gauging certain further "advancements" occasioned by the intervening centuries. Following Bacon, Jefferson classified his books with reference to the processes of mind employed on them: *Memory*, which is applied to factual data, such as "History"; *reason*, or according to Bacon, *understanding*, which is applied to theoretical investigations, such as "Philosophy";

and *imagination,* which is applied to innocent pleasures, such as "Fine Arts." Once having appropriated Bacon's three divisions of learning, however, Jefferson proceeded to adapt them to conform with modern canons of epistemology. Under "Philosophy," of the two primary subdivisions, "From Reason" and "Revealed," only the former remains, no longer identified as such, but assumed to be guiding the "Moral" and "Mathematical" pursuits into which it has been divided. "Mathematics" had been a subsection of "Metaphysics/Speculative," twice removed from the rank to which Jefferson assigned it; "Natural Religion," which had stood in its place, having first been transformed by Jefferson into "Law of Nature and Nations," now served to fill the lacuna left by "Mathematics" on the lowest rank (Bestor).

One could go on. It need only be pointed out that "Religion" was subtended to "Jurisprudence," a category of "Philosophy/Moral," where its awkwardness suggests that Jefferson had been reluctant to ascribe it to an autonomous, if more appropriate, status; and that "Ecclesiastical History" was demoted from a partner to a function of "Civil History," its more speculative subdivisions, such as "History of Providence," having been eliminated entirely. To substantiate any conclusions one might draw from such schemes of subordination, one needs only look to Jefferson's breakdown of authors and titles under the various headings. As his library catalogue reflects in the main those principles of relegation illustrated by the list of books he had proposed to Skipwith, turning to this one may gain a clear notion of his criteria. To Skipwith, under "Religion" and shouldering Sterne's sermons, he commended: Xenophon on Socrates, Epictetus, Antoninus, Seneca, Cicero, and of the moderns, Lord Kame's *Natural Religion,* Bolingbroke and Hume. Classified under ancient history, together with Bayle's *Dictionary* and Plutarch's *Lives,* are Caesar, Livy, Sallust, Josephus, Tacitus, and the Bible (Boyd, 1: 76–81).

Jefferson's "Syllabus"

As a young man, Jefferson had recorded the following sentiment of Bolingbroke's into his commonplace book.

> It is not true that Christ revealed an entire body of ethics, proved to be the law of nature from principals of reason, and reaching all the duties of life. . . . Were all the precepts of this kind, that are scattered about in the whole new testament, collected, like the short sentences of ancient sages in the memorials we have of them, and put together in the very words of the sacred writers, they would compose a very short as well as unconnected system of ethics. A system thus collected from the writings

of ancient heathen moralists, of Tully, of Seneca, of Epictetus, and others, would be more full, more entire, more coherent, and more clearly deduced from unquestionable principles of knowledge" (Chinard: 50)

If Jefferson were convinced of this in his youth, by 1803 he had come to reconsider and adjust his opinion on the subject. Although admitting, in a letter to Joseph Priestly, that the teachings of Jesus were incomplete and had suffered badly at the hands of those who had edited them, Jefferson asserted that the fragments remaining showed a master workman, whose "system of morality was the most benevolent and sublime . . . ever taught, and consequently more perfect than those of any of the ancient philosophers" (Lipscomb, 10: 325). One must look to the years falling between for evidence that may help to explain Jefferson's change of heart.

In the evenings of 1798–1799, when Jefferson was Vice President, he had occasion to engage Dr. Benjamin Rush in a series of "delightful conversations . . . which served as an anodyne to the afflictions of the crisis through which our country was then laboring" (Ford, 9: 453). The Christian religion was sometimes their topic, and in the course of one discussion Jefferson promised Rush, an outspoken Universalist, that one day he would give him his view of it. In September of 1800 he wrote Rush to assure him that he had not forgotten his promise. "On the contrary," Jefferson explained, "it is because I have reflected on it, that I find much more time necessary for it than I can at present dispose of." For the moment he could only say, "I have a view of the subject which ought to displease neither the rational Christian nor Deist, and would reconcile many to a character they have too hastily rejected. I do not know that it would reconcile the *genus irritabile vatum* who are all in arms against me. Their hostility is on too interesting ground to be softened" (Ford, 9: 148).

Jefferson was then a candidate for the presidency. It was natural that his thoughts, in turning to religion, should fix on certain sectaries, the more vocal of whom were reviling him as an infidel too impious to be president. "The returning good sense of our country threatens abortion to their hopes," Jefferson wrote to Rush. "[T]hey believe that any portion of power confided to me, will be exerted in opposition to their schemes. And they believe rightly; for I have sworn upon the altar of God, eternal hostility against every form of tyranny over the mind of man" (Ford, 9: 149).

The following spring, a triumphant Jefferson ascribed to his victory legendary proportions. "It was the Lilliputians upon Gulliver," he wrote. "Our countrymen have recovered from the alarm into which art and industry had thrown them; science and honesty are replaced on their high ground; and you, my dear Sir, as their great apostle, are on its pinnacle" (Ford, 9: 217). This "great apostle" was none other than Dr. Priestley himself, prominent scientist and Unitarian theologian.

Men like Benjamin Rush and Joseph Priestley helped to reestablish Christianity as a viable option for "reasonable" and "enlightened" republicans such as Thomas Jefferson. J. B. Bury, in developing his special theme, cited Priestley's doctrine of historical progress as a "solvent of theological beliefs" heralding Comte's Religion of Humanity (111). Rush, whose principal contribution to American thought was made in chemistry and medicine, also provided an ardent champion of theological openness. Urging the Universalists, of whom he was a member, to eschew sectarian association and include persons of every Christian society into their fellowship, he sought the establishment of an ecumenical body which would serve the interests of many in a shared and single cause. Like Priestley, Rush too believed that "All truths are related, or rather there is but one truth," as he wrote to the Reverend Jeremy Belknap in 1791. "Republicanism is a part of the truth of Christianity. It derives power from its true source. It teaches us to view our rulers in their true light. It abolishes the false glare which surrounds kingly government, and tends to promote the true happiness of all its members as well as of the whole world, for peace with everybody is the true interest of all republics" (Cassara: 92).

If Rush, a political ally and trusted friend, had prompted Jefferson to consider incorporating a constructive Christian philosophy into this thought, Priestley augmented the means by which he might do it. By consulting the annals of history, Priestley had determined that much of Christian doctrine was either defiant of or superfluous to the Christian message. Thereby, the Gospel not only was obscured, but distanced from the lives of many persons who neither had the time nor the means to investigate it properly.

It was to be four years before Jefferson would find the time to fulfill his promise to Rush. "The more I considered it, the more it expanded beyond the measure of either my time or information," Jefferson explained (Ford, 9: 457). Just as he was about to return to Washington from an early spring visit to Monticello, however, he received in the mail from Priestley his short treatise, *Socrates and Jesus Compared*. Otherwise unoccupied for the return trip, he had occasion to peruse it. Finding the contents to a great extent supportive of his own tentative conclusions, alluding to his promise to Rush,

Jefferson sketched the form that the fulfillment of that promise might take.

> I should proceed to a view of the life, character, and doctrines of Jesus, who sensible of the incorrectness of [his forbears'] ideas of the Deity, and of morality, endeavored to bring them to the principles of a pure deism, and juster notions of the attributes of God, to reform their moral doctrines to the standard of reason, justice, and philanthropy, and to inculcate the belief of a future state. This view would purposely omit the question of his divinity, and even his inspiration. To do him justice, it would be necessary to remark the disadvantages his doctrines had to encounter, not having been committed to writing by himself, but by the most unlettered of men, by memory, long after they had heard them from him, when much was forgotten, much misunderstood, and presented in every paradoxical shape. Yet such are the fragments remaining as to show a master workman, and that his system of morality was the most benevolent and sublime probably that has been ever taught, and consequently more perfect than those of any of the ancient philosophers. His character and doctrines have received still greater injury from those who pretend to be his special disciples, and who have disfigured and sophisticated his actions and precepts, from views of personal interest, so as to induce the unthinking part of mankind to throw off the whole system in disgust, and to pass sentence as an imposter on the most innocent, the most benevolent, and the most eloquent and sublime character that ever has been exhibited to man (Lipscomb, 10:374–75).

Jefferson drew up his "Syllabus of an estimate of the merit of the Doctrines of Jesus, compared with those of others," sometime during the two weeks following his letter to Priestley. An enlargement upon the outline there suggested, he sent it to Benjamin Rush in fulfillment of their long-standing agreement. Four years had passed, during which, Jefferson claimed, "At the short intervals . . . when I could justifiably abstract my mind from public affairs, the subject has been under my contemplation." As he had before to Priestley, Jefferson went on to explain how, in time, his conception of the task had outdistanced his ability to accomplish it. In lieu of something more substantial, the "Syllabus" was sent to Rush, "as the only discharge of my promise I can probably ever execute" (Ford, 10: 457). Divided into three sections, "Philosophers," "Jews," and "Jesus," Jefferson articulated his thesis more explicitly than he had in the letter to Priestley. Of Jesus, he wrote:

> 1. Like Socrates & Epictetus, he wrote nothing himself.
> 2. But he had not, like them, a Xenophon or and Arrian to write for him. On the contrary, all the learned of his country, entrenched in its power and riches, were opposed to him, lest his labors should undermine their advantages; and the committing to writing his life and doctrines fell on the most unlettered and ignorant men; who wrote, too, from memory, and not till long after the transactions had passed.

3. According to the ordinary fate of those who attempt to enlighten and reform mankind, he fell an early victim to the jealousy and combination of the altar and the throne, at about 33 years of age, his reason having not yet attained the maximum of its energy, nor the course of his preaching, which was but of 3 years at most, presented occasions for developing a complete set of morals.

4. Hence the doctrines which he really delivered were defective as a whole, and fragments only if what he did deliver have come to us mutilated, misstated, and often unintelligible.

5. They have been still more disfigured by the corruptions of schismatising followers, who have found an interest in sophisticating and perverting the simple doctrines he taught by engrafting on them the mysticisms of a Grecian sophist, frittering them into subtleties, and obscuring them with jargon, until they have caused good men to reject the whole in disgust and to view Jesus himself as an imposter. Notwithstanding these disadvantages, a system of morals is presented to us, which, if filled up in the true style and spirit of the rich fragments he left us, would be the most perfect and sublime that has ever been taught by man (Ford, 9: 461–62).

In his cover letter to Rush, Jefferson described his "Syllabus" as "the result of a life of inquiry and reflection, and very different from the anti-Christian system imputed to me by those who know nothing of my opinions. To the corruptions of Christianity I am indeed opposed; but not to the genuine precepts of Jesus himself" (Ford, 10: 457).

Jefferson had convinced himself that wherever he followed, Priestly would lead. It was for this reason that he commended his proposed study of Jesus' doctrines to Priestley's care. That December, when Priestley agreed to investigate the matter, Jefferson was delighted. "I have prevailed upon Priestley to undertake the work," Jefferson wrote to his daughter, Mary. "He says he can accomplish it in the course of a year." The only stumbling block appeared to be Priestley's health. "In truth his health is so much impaired," Jefferson admitted, "and his body become so feeble, that there is reason to fear he will not live out even the short term he has asked for it" (Boyd: 250). A month later, in renewing his support and appreciation, Jefferson wrote to Priestley, "I rejoice that you have undertaken the task of comparing the moral doctrines of Jesus with those of the ancient Philosophers. You are so much in possession of the whole subject, that you will do it easier and better than any other person living" (Ford, 10: 70). Quite probably the letter was not seen by Priestley, who died within a week of its posting.

When Jefferson wrote his last letter to Priestley, he included one further bit of advice, which he expected Priestley to take without question. "I think you cannot avoid giving, as preliminary to the comparison, a digest of his moral doctrines, extracted in his own words from the Evangelists, and leaving out everything relative to his personal history and character. It would be short and precious. With a view to do this for my own satisfaction, I had sent to Philadelphia to get two testaments Greek of the same edition, and two English, with a design to cut out the morsels of morality, and paste them on the leaves of a book, in the manner you describe as having been pursued in forming your Harmony. But I shall now get the thing done by better hands" (Ford, 10: 70).

As well as being the first intimation of Jefferson's Bible, this passage suggests a gap between Jefferson's perception of Priestley and Priestley himself. Were Priestley to have compiled such a digest, it would likely have included every saying of Jesus recorded by the evangelists, with the probable exception of duplications. What Jefferson failed to recognize was that, whereas Priestley doubted the genuineness of certain phenomena suggested by Scripture, he did so by showing them to be secondary to the original accounts of the evangelists. To Priestley, the evangelists were inspired, or rather, were accurate and thus trustworthy in all particulars; certain others who managed to graft their own speculations into the Scriptures, were not. Accounts of the virgin birth, for instance, clearly went against his grain. Given that the story was missing from Mark, the first chapters of Matthew and Luke might accordingly be dismissed as interpolations.

If Priestley exposed the corruptions of Christianity, it was to defend the purity of the scriptural witness. If he reviled the credulous for accepting on faith unreasonable manifestations of the Spirit in later times, he did it to protect the special authority of the wonderworkers whose deeds were attested in the Old and New Testaments. To Jefferson, however, the evangelists were ignorant, unlettered men. If they were guilty of a considerable amount of presumption in proposing to record Jesus' life and teachings, one would be even more presumptuous uncritically to accept their accounts. Accordingly, had Priestley lived Jefferson would have been disappointed by his fidelity to the evangelists' accounts of Jesus' teachings. But Priestley did not live, And so it was that Jefferson determined to try his hand at cutting up the Gospels.

Shortly before importuning Priestley, Jefferson had written to a Philadelphia bookseller for duplicate copies of both the English and the Greek New Testament. As identified by Cyrus Adler, the English edition was the King James translation published by Jacob Johnson in Philadelphia in 1804 (11). The Greek has been recognized by Edgar

Goodspeed as Wingrave's printing of Leusden's Greek Testament, published in London in 1794 (73). Whether or not Jefferson intended it, the Greek text came with a parallel Latin translation, done in "a very dubious kind of Latin" in Goodspeed's estimation, which proved to be the work of Benedictus Arias Montanus, the Spanish editor of the Antwerp polyglot of 1569–1572 (72). Though Jefferson had expressed an interest only in the Greek with an English translation facing, when the Bibles arrived in three versions, he appears to have determined, for the sake of symmetry, to incorporate also a French translation. A year after Priestley's death, on 31 January 1805, Jefferson ordered from Reibelt of Philadelphia two copies of "le Nouveau Testament corrige sur le Grec," which Goodspeed has shown to be identical with the Paris Ostervald edition, published in 1802 under the auspices of the British and Foreign Bible Society in London (75–76). Hence, by mid-1805 Jefferson was in possession of the makings of his four-volume *Life and Morals of Jesus of Nazareth*. The six books were to sit on his shelves unamended for at least fourteen years.

"The Philosophy of Jesus of Nazareth"

The most mysterious chapter in the story of Jefferson's Bible concerns his first actual abstraction of Jesus' words from the four Gospels. Entitled "The Philosophy of Jesus of Nazareth," this little work is first mentioned in a letter to John Adams dated 13 October 1813.

> We must reduce our volume to the simple evangelists, select, even from them, the very words only of Jesus, paring off the amphiboligisms into which they have been led, by forgetting often, or not understanding what had fallen from him, by giving their own misconceptions as his dicta, and expressing unintelligibly for others what they had not understood themselves. There will be found remaining the most sublime and benevolent code of morals which has ever been offered to man. I have performed this operation for my own use, by cutting verse by verse out of the printed book, and by arranging the matter which is evidently his, and which is as distinguishable as diamonds in a dunghill. The result is an octavo of forty-six pages, of pure and unsophisticated doctrines, such as were professed and acted on by the unlettered Apostles, the Apostolic Fathers, and the Christians of the first century (Lipscomb, 13: 289–90).

We must inquire, first, when did Jefferson perform this operation, and further, what has "The Philosophy of Jesus" to do with Jefferson's designs of 1803–1805?

As to the former question, Goodspeed, in differentiating the two redactions, notes that this one was completed in 1813, the year of its first appearance in Jefferson's correspondence (72). This assumption is easily discredited by reference to a letter written in 1816, in which Jefferson ascribed the work to the time when he was in Washington (Lipscomb, 15: 2). This establishes a *terminus ad quem* of 1808. Randall, in the appendix to his biography, gives 1803 as the date of composition, and in this is followed by others (Randall, 3: instance, 654; Gould: 203). Though this is not precluded by any explicit evidence to the contrary, on the face of it, so early a date seems most unlikely. The only other testimony from Jefferson in this regard comes from a letter to William Short, another Unitarian, in October 1819. There Jefferson simply says that he attempted the work "some twelve or fifteen years ago" (Ford, 12: 142). This would place it roughly between the winter of 1804–05 and the end of his term of office in 1808.

On the cover page, Jefferson described the contents as "an abridgment of the New Testament for the use of the Indians, unembarrassed with matters of fact or faith beyond the level of their comprehensions" (Randall, 3: 654). As this ascription of purpose is not to be reiterated, much less elaborated, in any subsequent mention of the "Philosophy," it must therefore be entertained with caution. On the other hand, it is in no way impossible that Jefferson should have sponsored such a project. In 1809 a secular plan for civilizing the Indians was to be greeted by him as "undoubtedly a great improvement on the ancient and totally ineffectual one of beginning with religious missionaries." Once the Indians had been taught to raise cattle, to reckon value, to keep accounts, and to read, only then, stated Jefferson, should the missionaries be brought in. "Our experience has shown that this must be the last step of the process," Jefferson wrote (Lord, 12: 270–71). Jefferson's ideal curriculum for the education of Indians might well have included in the "final quarter's" instruction and expurgated account of Jesus' doctrines.

There is evidence, however, to suggest that Jefferson's mind was more on himself than on the Indians when he prepared "The Philosophy of Jesus." For one thing, on none of the several instances when the book was introduced in correspondence did Jefferson describe it as a collection for the Indians. "I have performed this operation for my own use," he wrote in a letter to Adams (Lord, 13: 390). On another occasion, Jefferson spoke of the project as an extension of ideas contained in the "Syllabus" made "for my own satisfaction" (Lord, 15: 2).

In either case, Jefferson looked on the "Philosophy" as the partial fulfillment of a promise. That promise would finally be fulfilled in *The Life and Morals of Jesus of Nazareth*, a late and, by that time,

unexpected fruit of Jefferson's old age. More precisely, "The Philosophy of Jesus" was a draft of Jefferson's volume as proposed to Priestley.
It was an incomplete final draft of such a volume, awaiting only the
Greek parallels for completion. Though the book itself is lost, one can
deduce from its length, roughly half that of the *Life*, that accommoda-
tion was not made for either the Latin or the French translation. The
English had been put on half of every page, but in the *Life* each
version would receive but half of every second page, so that the four
might be shown together across the open book. Therefore, when
Jefferson decided to attempt the operation, the order from Philadelphia had not yet arrived. He must have procured two Bibles in
Washington, or taken two from his shelves, with the intention of
replacing them with the books on order. Later, when the Greek texts
arrived with facing Latin translations, it seemed a pity not to incorporate the Latin text as well. Since Jefferson had left room only for a
single additional column, his original design would be insufficient for
the enlarged edition. He therefore put it aside. Intending to incorporate the work he had already done, he redesigned the volume along
broader lines. He had the two extra English testaments. All that was
wanting was something to fill the fourth column of a double page. This
would most naturally be a French translation. Accordingly, Jefferson
wrote away to Philadelphia for two more testaments. This letter was
postmarked the thirty-first of January 1805. Hence, the "Philosophy"
was compiled after the day Jefferson received word of Priestley's
death, namely sometime in the second or third week of February
1804, and before the end of January 1805. One can narrow the
perimeters no further than this.

The Adams Correspondence

By mid-1805, when the needed testaments finally arrived from
Philadelphia, the motivation necessary to complete the work was
gone. Wanting the provocation of a correspondent, Jefferson could not
sustain his interest in the project.

Before his letter of September 1800 to Benjamin Rush, Jefferson's
published correspondence contains only one extended reference to
his religious beliefs. Following the promise to Rush, however, come a
dozen more in the space of three and a half years, each of them
alluding to the reflections evoked by that promise.

After almost ten years of silence, the subject of Jefferson's religious opinions was again brought to the fore on the occasion of
Benjamin Rush's death. Saddened by the loss of a close and beloved

friend, Jefferson was also concerned lest, in the sorting of Rush's papers, his "Syllabus" should arouse curiosity and be indiscreetly used. To Richard Rush, Benjamin's son, Jefferson wrote:

> My acquaintance with him began in 1776. It soon became intimate, and from that time a warm friendship has been maintained by a correspondence of unreserved confidence. In the course of this, each had deposited in the bosom of the other, communications which were never intended to go further. In the sacred fidelity of each to the other these were known to be safe: and above all things that they would be kept from the public eye. There may have been other letters of this character written by me to him: but two alone occur to me at present, about which I have any anxiety. These were of April 21, 1803 and January 16, 1811. The first of these was on the subject of religion, a subject on which I have ever been most scrupulously reserved. I have considered it as a matter between every man and his maker in which no other, and far less the public had a right to intermeddle. To your father alone I committed some views on this subject in the first of the letters above mentioned, led to it by previous conversations, and a promise on my part to digest and communicate them in writing (Ford, 11: 291–92).

This was written on the thirty-first of May 1813. By way of amplification to his fears, Jefferson was to learn only nine days later that his letter of March 1801 to Joseph Priestley had been printed in another's memoirs. This news was passed along by none other than John Adams.

Thus began the notable correspondence between Jefferson and Adams on the subject of religion. In reading *The Memoirs of Theophilus Lindsey,* a British Unitarian minister, Adams happened upon Jefferson's letter to Priestley of 1803, in which he described his compact with Rush and commended his proposed outline of Jesus' doctrines to Priestley's care. Assuming that Jefferson had not fulfilled his pledge to Rush, Adams wrote to him, "Your letters to Priestley have increased my grief, if that were possible, for the loss of Rush. Had he lived, I would have stimulated him to insist on your promise to him, to write him on the subject of religion. Your plan I admire." Having done what he could to redispose Jefferson to contemplate such matters, Adams closed by announcing, "I have more to say on this subject of religion" (Lipscomb, 13: 316).

Two days later Adams made good on his boast. The letter is full of credentials and the names of divines and philosophers and their books, many "whose titles you have never seen." It is as if Adams were impressing the breadth of his knowledge on Jefferson. But actually he was pledging his openness, his willingness to listen, his childlike delight in variety. It may be summed up in his statement, "I

think I can now say I have read away bigotry, if not enthusiasm"
(Lipscomb, 13: 319).

In the third letter of twice as many days, Adams stated clearly, "I
hope you will still perform your promise to Doctor Rush." Two weeks
later he reiterated that hope, including excerpts of Priestley's letter of
19 December 1803 to Lindsey, in which his work on the project
suggested to him by Jefferson is discussed. "I send you this extract for
several reasons," Adams wrote. "First, because you set him upon this
work. Secondly, because I wish you to endeavor to bring it to light and
get it printed. Thirdly, because I wish it may stimulate you to pursue
your own plan which you promised to Dr. Rush" (Lipscomb, 13: 323).

On August 22, Jefferson responded. "Since my letter of June the
27th, I am in your debt for many; all of which I have read with infinite
delight. They open a wise field for reflection, and offer subjects
enough to occupy the mind and pen indefinitely." He was particularly
pleased by Adams's approval of his outline to Priestley. "Your approbation of my outline to Dr. Priestley is a great gratification to me"
(Lipscomb, 13: 349). The case was again opened, and Jefferson's *Life
and Morals of Jesus of Nazareth* accordingly was brought one step
closer to reality.

The Life and Morals of Jesus of Nazareth

How and when *The Life and Morals of Jesus of Nazareth* finally
came into being is nowhere made explicit. The "Philosophy" was first
mentioned during the correspondence with Adams, and then again in
a letter to Jefferson's good friend Charles Thompson in January of
1816. In the spring of that same year, Francis Adrian van der Kemp, A
Dutch scholar and Unitarian minister, having been shown the "Syllabus" when visiting John Adams, wrote to Jefferson inquiring after it.
During this period, Jefferson seems to have recommitted himself to
his original task.

"If I had time," Jefferson wrote to Charles Thompson, "I would
add to my little book the Greek, Latin and French texts, in columns
side by side" (Ford 11: 498–99). That was in January of 1816. By April
of the same year, Jefferson had elected the coming winter as the time
during which he would complete his design. "It was too hastily done,"
remarked Jefferson, ". . . being the work of one or two evenings only,
while I lived at Washington, overwhelmed with other business, and it
is my intention to go over it again at more leisure. This shall be the
work of the ensuring winter" (Lipscomb, 15: 2).

Failing to find time for it that winter, Jefferson seems, once again, to have abandoned any hope of completing his design. Three years later, he wrote to William Short, "These are now idle projects for me. My business is to beguile the wearisomeness of declining life, as I endeavor to do, by the delights of classical reading and of mathematical truths, and by the consolations of a sound philosophy, equally indifferent to hope and fear" (Ford 12: 142–43).

Whatever drove him out of his idleness long enough, first to revise the "Philosopy," and further, to cut out the passages determined upon and paste them in a book, is nowhere made explicit. Nor is it evident what year he did so. Every scholar consulted gives 1819 as the probable time of its execution, but given his mood of late October that year, this is less likely than a date subsequent to that. For a more reasonable estimate, we must turn to Jefferson's additional correspondence with Short.

The chronology appears to be as follows. Upon learning of Jefferson's "Syllabus"—as was the case before with Rush, Priestley, Adams, and Vand der Kemp—on the twenty-seventh of March 1820, William Short duly requested a copy. In responding to this request, Jefferson had occasion to review the "Syllabus," and consequently to assess its inadequacy as a guide for his present thoughts. Apparently, he once again determined to undertake revising the "Philosophy," partly in order to clarify in his own mind which of the sayings extracted before from the Gospels would survive a more deliberate scrutiny. This he seems to have had well in hand by the thirteenth of April when he forwarded the "Syllabus" to Short. In the body of the covering letter, he specified the doctrines to be those of Jesus and those not necessarily his (Jesus') own. He also spoke of restoring the Scriptures to their original purity, without, however, mentioning the "Philosophy" per se, or expressing any dissatisfaction with his compilation, as had been his custom in correspondence since 1816 whenever the subject came up.

In this covering letter he wrote:

> While this syllabus is meant to place the character of Jesus in its true and high light, as no imposter Himself, but a great Reformer of the Hebrew code of religion, it is not to be understood that I am with Him in all His doctrines. I am a Materialist; he takes the side of Spiritualism. He preaches the efficacy of repentance towards forgiveness of sin; I require a counterpoise of good works to redeem it, etc., etc.. It is the innocence of His character, the purity and sublimity of His moral precepts, the eloquence of His inculcations, the beauty of the apologues in which He conveys them, that I so much admire; sometimes, indeed, needing indulgence to eastern hyperbolism. My eulogies, too, may be founded

> on a postulate which all may not be ready to grant. Among the sayings
> and discourses imputed to Him by His biographers, I find many pas-
> sages of fine imagination, correct morality, and of the most lovely benev-
> olence; and others, again, of so much ignorance, so much absurdity, so
> much untruth, charlatanism and imposture, as to pronounce it impossi-
> ble that such contradictions should have proceeded from the same
> Being. I separate, therefore, the gold from the dross; restore to Him the
> former, and leave the latter to the stupidity of some, and roguery of
> others of his disciples (Lipscomb, 15: 244–45).

Jefferson's opinions on Jesus and the evangelists had undergone a
change. The process apparently had begun with the Adams correspondence of 1813–1814. It led to his decision to revise the "Philosophy" in 1816, and culminated, most likely, during the spring of 1820
with the composition of the *Life*. This last conjecture is based upon
the second and third of Jefferson's letters to Short. As can be seen
from the passage just cited, we meet a significant change of tense in
those sentences that describe the process of extraction: "I find, . . .
separate, . . . restore, . . . leave." One senses here either present or
recent involvement in the task.

In a third letter to Short, mailed on 4 August, there is even
stronger evidence that the work has finally been done and is fresh in
mind.

> We find in the writings of [Jesus's] biographers matter of two distinct
> descriptions. First, a groundwork of vulgar ignorance, of things impossi-
> ble, of superstitions, fanaticisms and fabrications. Intermixed with
> these, again, are sublime ideas of the Supreme Being, aphorisms, and
> precepts of the purist morality and benevolence, sanctioned by a life of
> humility, innocence, and simplicity of manners, neglect of riches, ab-
> sence of worldly ambition and honors, with an eloquence and per-
> suasiveness which have not been surpassed. These could not be the
> intentions of the groveling authors who related them. They are far
> beyond the powers of their feeble minds. They show there there was a
> character, a subject of their history, whose splendid conceptions were
> above suspicion aof being interpolations from their hands. Can we be at a
> loss in separating such materials and ascribing each to its original author?
> The difference is obvious to the eye and to the understanding, and we
> may read as we run to each his part; and I will venture to affirm that he
> who, as I have done, will undertake to winnow this grain from the chaff,
> will find it not to require a moment's consideration. The parts fall
> asunder of themselves, as would those of an image of metal and clay
> (Lipscomb, 15: 258–59).

Jefferson could look back here upon a work accomplished. He was
not looking back, however, at a work hastily done some sixteen years
before, with which he was no longer pleased. The memories are fresh,
the product satisfying. In 1820, at seventy-seven years of age, Thomas
Jefferson removed the six testaments from his shelf, where they had

been sitting for a decade and a half, and proceeded to carve out a gospel for himself, whose witness he could respect and whose message he could understand.

Thomas Jefferson's interest in the Bible was restricted entirely to the biography of Jesus. Eloquent, benevolent, innocent, a victim first of the Roman state and then of the Christian Church, Jesus was the lamb whom humankind would never tire of slaughtering. In a statement of his faith, Jefferson wrote to Rush, "I am a Christian, in the only sense he wished any one to be; sincerely attached to his doctrines, in preference to all others; ascribing to himself every human excellence; and believing he never claimed any other" (Ford, 10: 457). Historian Daniel J. Boorstin notes, "The Jeffersonian had projected his own qualities and limitations into Jesus, whose career became his vivid symbol of the superfluity and perils of speculative philosophy" (157).

As with many Unitarians of like spirit who have followed him, Jefferson's was a search not so much for the historical as for the intelligible Jesus (Foote; Church). John Adams recognized it as such in 1813 when he wrote to Jefferson, "I admire your employment in selecting the philosophy and divinity of Jesus, and separating it from all mixtures. If I had eyes and nerves I would go through both Testaments and mark all that I understand" (Lipscomb, 13: 440). And that is precisely what Thomas Jefferson did, not only once but twice, with the gospels.

WORKS CONSULTED

Adler, Cyrus, ed.
    1904   *The Life and Morals of Jesus of Nazareth*, by Thomas Jefferson. Washington, DC: Government Printing Office.

Bestor, Arthur 1955 "Thomas Jefferson and the Freedom of Books." *Three Presidents and Their Books*. Urbana: University of Illinois.

Boorstin, Daniel J. 1960. *The Lost World of Thomas Jefferson*. Boston: Beacon.

Boyd, Julian P., ed.
    1950   *The Papers of Thomas Jefferson*. Princeton: Princeton.

Bury, J. B. 1913. *A History of Freedom of Thought*. Oxford: Oxford.

Cassara, Ernest 1971 *Universalism in America: A Documentary History*. Boston: Beacon.

Chinard, Gilbert, ed.
    1928   *The Literary Bible of Thomas Jefferson: His Commonplace Book of Philosophers and Poets*. Baltimore: Johns Hopkins.

Church, F. Forrester 1974 "The Gospel According to Thomas Jefferson." Unpublished Master's thesis, Harvard Divinity School.

———— 1979 "Politics and Priestcraft: Jefferson's Case Against the Clergy." *Alone Together: Studies in the History of Liberal Religion.* Peter I. Kaufman and Spencer Lavan, eds. Boston: Beacon/Skinner House.

Foote, Henry Wilder 1960 *The Religion of Thomas Jefferson.* Boston: Beacon.

Ford, Paul Leicester, ed.
1905   *The Writings of Thomas Jefferson.* New York: Putnam.

Goodspeed, Edgar J. 1947 "Thomas Jefferson and the Bible." *Harvard Theological Review* 15: 71–76.

Gould, William D. 1933 "The Religious Opinions of Thomas Jefferson." *Mississippi Valley Historical Review* 20/2: 191–208.

Lipscomb, Andrew A. and Albert Ellery Bergh, eds. 1903 *The Writings of Thomas Jefferson.* Washington: Government Printing Office.

Randall, Henry S. 1858 *The Life and Times of Thomas Jefferson.* New York: Darby and Jackson.

Bibliographic Addendum

Since the completion of this article, an important new resource for the study of Jefferson's Bible has been published: *Jefferson's Extracts from the Gospels: "The Philosophy of Jesus" and "The Life and Morals of Jesus,"* ed. Dickinson W. Adams, in The Papers of Thomas Jefferson, 2d ser., ed. Charles T. Cullen (Princeton: Princeton, 1983). In addition to a facsimile of the original "Life and Morals of Jesus," the volume contains a fine general introduction to Jefferson's religious thought and specific introductions to the two compilations. Adding to its utility, a generous selection of Jefferson's letters on religion and the Bible are contained in an appendix.

VII

The Sacred Literature of the Latter-day Saints

Kent P. Jackson

Introduction

Joseph Smith, who is acknowledged by members of the Church of Jesus Christ of Latter-day Saints (often called Mormons) as the founding prophet of their faith, once wrote: "We believe all that God has revealed, all that He does now reveal, and we believe that He will yet reveal many great and important things pertaining to the Kingdom of God" (Article of Faith 9; see Pearl of Great Price, below). These words state in a concise fashion the view of Latter-day Saints regarding canon and scriptural authority. Not only has God revealed his will in the past, they believe, but he does so now and will continue to do so in the future. Latter-day Saints hold a view of canon that is not restricted to the revelations of the past, whether they be those that they revere in common with their fellow Christians or those believed uniquely by the Saints. Their view is broader. The canon is not closed, nor will it ever be. To them, revelation from God has not ceased; it continues in the church. Future revelation is not only viewed as theoretically possible, it is expected, as changing circumstances in the world necessitate new communication from God.

Latter-day Saint theology demands adherence to sacred books which are the products of ancient times. Yet it requires equal belief in ongoing revelation from God to the leaders of the church in the present. Historically such a mixture of static and dynamic revelatory theology is uncommon. Most faiths end the prophetic phases of their history in the process of the canonization of what has come before. Yet Mormonism has realized a system of belief in which both elements are viewed as vital. The prospect of future revelation poses no threat to the canonized words of the past.

The sacred literature of Mormonism reflects this marriage of static and dynamic canon. With other Christians they view the Old and New Testaments of the Bible as the revelations of God. Yet they have other books that they view as equally authoritative. These they have acquired through a process of what they call "continuing revelation."

Beginning with Joseph Smith's purported theophany of 1820, the Latter-day Saints have believed that ongoing revelation has been one of the hallmarks of their faith. Over the years that have passed since then, the Mormon canon has expanded as new revelation has been received and published. As recently as 1978 an announcement concerning a new communication from God was added to their Scripture.

Mormons call their texts the Standard Works. These include the Bible, the Book of Mormon, and two collections of revelations to Joseph Smith and his successors: the Doctrine and Covenants and the Pearl of Great Price. These books will be the focus of this essay.

The Bible

James E. Talmage, an early twentieth-century apostle of the Latter-day Saint (LDS) church and one of its foremost theologians, wrote:

> The Church of Jesus Christ of Latter-day Saints accepts the Holy Bible as the foremost of her standard works, first among the books which have been proclaimed as her written guides in faith and doctrine. In the respect and sanctity with which the Latter-day Saints regard the Bible they are of like profession with Christian denominations in general, but differ from them in the additional acknowledgment of certain other scriptures as authentic and holy, which others are in harmony with the Bible, and serve to support and emphasize its facts and doctrines (Talmage: 236).

One of the "Articles of Faith" of the LDS church, written by Joseph Smith, states in part, "We believe the Bible to be the word of God as far as it is translated correctly" (Article of Faith 8). Even with the implied uncertainty concerning the accuracy of modern versions, the Bible stands on equal footing with the Book of Mormon and the other LDS Scriptures. Latter-day Saints have held it in high esteem since their beginning, following the precedent of their founding prophet, who proclaimed it to be a "sacred volume" (Smith, 1938: 56). Joseph Smith's original theophany came as the result of his reading of the Bible (JS-H 11-20; see Joseph Smith—History, below). In the years following the purported revelations that led to the founding of the new faith, the Mormon prophet's enthusiasm for the biblical record did not diminish. He preached from the Bible much more frequently than from the volumes of Scripture that he himself had published (Ehat and Cook: 421–25).

Brigham Young, who succeeded Joseph Smith in the leadership of the church, taught, "We have a holy reverence for and a belief in the

Bible" (Widtsoe: 124). His remarks can be viewed as expressing the feelings of Latter-day Saints generally with regard to the power of its message:

> I believe the doctrines concerning salvation contained in that book are true, and that their observance will elevate any people, nation or family that dwells on the face of the earth. The doctrines contained in the Bible will lift to a superior condition all who observe them; they will impart to them knowledge, wisdom, charity, fill them with compassion and cause them to feel after the wants of those who are in distress, or in painful or degraded circumstances. They who observe the precepts contained in the Scriptures will be just and true and virtuous and peaceable at home and abroad. Follow out the doctrines of the Bible, and men will make splendid husbands, women excellent wives, and children will be obedient; they will make families happy and the nations wealthy and happy and lifted up above the things of this life (Widtsoe: 125).

More recent LDS leaders have offered similar praise (e.g., Smith, 1956: 187–88; Kimball: 131–33).

Since the beginning of Mormonism, the King James Bible has been the version most widely used by English-speaking Latter-day Saints. As such it has attained somewhat of a de facto "official" status in English-speaking countries, though no canonical dictum designates it as such. In those areas, it is the only version used in the official writings and publications of church authorities, or in publications produced under the auspices of the church, except where a preferred rendering of a specific passage is desirable. The current leaders of the Latter-day Saints feel that the uniformity of using the KJV as a standard translation outweighs the problems caused by its archaic language. One of the members of the governing Council of Twelve Apostles, Bruce R. McConkie, has written: "Certainly the King James Version is by all odds the greatest of the completed English translations. Scholars universally acclaim it as containing as forceful, direct, and majestic prose as has ever been coined in the English tongue" (McConkie: 422). Most English-speaking Latter-day Saints prefer the beauty of the Elizabethan English in the KJV over the language of more contemporary translations, attaching an aura of sanctity to the archaic words. Most have come to feel that the language of the King James text conveys the scriptural messages with greater reverence than can be done in contemporary vocabulary. As a corollary to this, most Latter-day Saints use archaic pronouns such as "thee" or "thou," or their equivalents in other languages, when praying.

Joseph Smith had a keen awareness of the problems of language and translation. He was interested enough in foreign languages that he gained some exposure to several, though he never became proficient in any. He received some formal instruction in Hebrew (Roberts 1: 393–94) and extolled the value of knowing it as a means of understanding the Bible (Smith, 1938: 290). Though the text that he used was the King James Version, the common English Bible of his day, he often took exception with it. In 1844 he called the German translation that he had studied "the most correct that I have found, and it corresponds the nearest to the revelations that I have given the last 16 years" (Ehat and Cook: 351). His attitude regarding biblical authority is expressed succinctly in these words: "I believe the Bible as it read when it came from the pen of the original writers" (Smith, 1938: 327). As noted already, he taught that the Bible is God's word "as far as it is translated correctly" (Article of Faith 8). "Translated," in the Mormon prophet's vocabulary, means *transmitted*, which includes the entire process of bringing an ancient text from its original manuscript to its modern-language publication. Following their prophet's teaching, Latter-day Saints regard the biblical record as God's message to humankind insofar as current versions accurately represent the inspired intentions of the authors. They believe in literal revelation— that God in fact has spoken to human beings on earth, and that his messages have been recorded in the Bible by prophets, his spokespersons. In this sense, Latter-day Saints accept the Bible as revelatory and authoritative, believing that its ultimate source is God. Yet the history of its preservation leads them not only to allow for the theoretical possibility of inaccuracies in modern versions but to believe that such do in fact exist. Joseph Smith taught, "Many important points touching the salvation of men had been taken from the Bible, or lost before it was compiled" (Smith, 1938: 10); and "ignorant translators, careless transcribers, or designing and corrupt priests have committed many errors" (Smith, 1938: 327).

Mormons view their religion as a restoration of truths that God had revealed by prophets through the ages. The restoration was needed, in part, because many points of important theological understanding had been lost since the biblical authors wrote God's word. Through the processes alluded to by Joseph Smith (cited above), much of the Gospel of Jesus Christ had been lost, necessitating a complete restoration of doctrine in a pure and uncorrupted form. Mormons view Joseph Smith as a modern-day prophet called by God to serve in the restoration of primitive Christianity to the world. Doctrinal truths were restored in the Book of Mormon, which contains, according to one of Joseph Smith's revelations, "the fulness of the gospel of Jesus Christ" (Doctrine and Covenants 20:9; hereafter D&C). Over the course of approximately two decades, Joseph Smith reported that he received scores of revelations, which later were compiled in collections called the Doctrine and Covenants and the Pearl of Great Price (for both, see below). Many of those revelations have direct bearing on the biblical text, or on doctrines taught in the Bible. The net effect of the prophet's revelatory experience, according to believers, was God's restoration to the world of all of the doctrines and sacraments necessary for the salvation and eternal well-being of the human family—things that had been known by God's people in ancient Israel as well as in early Christianity but had not been preserved in either the Hebrew or Greek testaments. Thus Mormons view the revelation of new doctrine to be the restoration of things "taken from the Bible, or lost before it was compiled" (Smith, 1938: 10).

In 1979 the LDS Church issued, for the first time in its history, its own publication of the Bible. The primary purpose of the project was to make available a Bible containing study helps directed specifically to a Mormon readership (Matthews, 1982: 387–88). The King James text was used. The Bible includes headings above each chapter that reflect Latter-day Saint theology, a cross-referencing system that cites not only biblical references but references to other LDS scriptures, and a Bible dictionary that has been adapted and revised to include LDS theological concepts. The footnotes contain, in addition to cross-references, occasional alternative or preferred translations of obscure or mistranslated KJV words. At the back of the volume is a "Topical Guide," which is a subject-matter index containing about 3500 separate headings with references from all of the books in the Mormon canon (Matthews, 1982: 391). Under those headings, approximately fifty thousand passages of scripture are cited.

The new Bible publication has received attention as a substantial accomplishment in Bible publishing. For its involvement in the project, the Cambridge University Press, which did the graphic designing and set the type, was awarded England's top graphics arts award for typesetting excellence in 1980 (Mortimer: 40). The LDS Church was honored by the Laymen's National Bible Committee for the contribution that the publication makes in encouraging Bible study among its members. LDS Church leaders view the publication as one of the most significant developments in the Church in recent years. Apostle Boyd K. Packer foresees that it "will produce successive generations of faithful Christians who know the Lord Jesus Christ and are disposed to obey His will" (Packer: 53). Similar Bible publications are anticipated in other languages that are spoken by large numbers of Latter-day Saints.

The Book of Mormon

According to Mormon belief, the Book of Mormon is a companion Scripture to the Bible, with which it shares equal status. It purports to be the record of a people that lived in the Americas during parts of the first millennia B.C. and A.D. It is not, strictly speaking, a history, but a sacred chronical, recording theological discourse as well as historical events that serve the religious purposes of its authors.

The book begins with the account of an Israelite prophet named Lehi, who, according to the record, preached in Jerusalem just prior to the siege of that city by the forces of Nebuchadnezzar early in the sixth century B.C. Lehi was instructed by God to take his family and several other followers and leave Jerusalem to find a new home. Their travels, which were directed by God, eventually brought them to the Americas, where they established themselves, built cities, and created a civilization patterned somewhat after that from which they came. The Book of Mormon describes itself as the record of Lehi's people from the time they left Jerusalem until the fifth century A.D., over one thousand years later. It tells of the works of their prophets, who are depicted in a role very similar to that of the prophets of the Hebrew Bible. The history of Lehi's people, who later divided into two groups called Nephites and Lamanites after two of Lehi's sons, is one of prosperity and peace when they followed the direction of their prophets, and ruin and warfare when they disregarded it.

The theology of the Book of Mormon is one of its most distinctive characteristics. According to the record, Christianity was revealed to and preached by Lehi and the prophets who succeeded him. The book tells that even centuries before the birth of Jesus the Nephites and Lamanites knew of his future coming and were in fact Christians, at least during the periods of time in which they heeded the teachings of their prophets. Jesus was known to them by name, and many of the essential aspects of the Christian faith as taught in the New Testament were common knowledge among them. The Book of Mormon claims even further that Jesus appeared personally to Lehi's descendants after his resurrection in Jerusalem. He remained a number of days among the people, preached to them, called twelve disciples, and organized a church. The entire Lamanite and Nephite nations were converted as a result of his appearance and by the continued preaching of his disciples after he left. Thus an era of peace and unity was ushered in. The account then tells that after almost two hundred years of tranquility this early American civilization began a long road of terminal decline. By A.D. 400 the Nephite nation had been destroyed, the result of armed hostilities and internal decay.

Among the last of the prophets was one named Mormon. The book tells that Mormon was commanded by God to compile the account of his people from the time his ancestors left Palestine. He did this by editing the records that had been kept by prophets and historians since Lehi's time, including in his record only those things that he felt inspired to pass on to later generations. He inscribed the record in a book made of thin gold plates attached loosely at one end. Mormon is thus considered to be the primary author/editor of the book, which therefore bears his name. At his death his prophet son Moroni, the last prophet of the Nephite nation, continued the task and finished the book. In A.D. 421 he buried the plates so that they would be preserved until a later generation when the time would be right to make their message known to the world.

Joseph Smith claimed that this same Moroni, as a resurrected man, was sent to him as a messenger from the presence of God. In the fall of 1827 Moroni led him to the burial spot of the gold book and gave it into his care. Joseph Smith claimed that God enabled him to translate the record contained on the plates from its ancient language into English, after which Moroni returned and took the book from him (JS-H: 27–75). The Book of Mormon was published in Palmyra, New York in 1830, when Joseph Smith was twenty-four years old. The term "Mormon," by which members of the Church of Jesus Christ of Latter-day Saints are designated popularly, derives from their belief in that book. The Book of Mormon became a key part of the Latter-day Saint movement from the beginning and was then and still remains today a feature of Mormonism that distinguishes it from all other Christian traditions (Hill: 55–60, 70–89).

In order to understand the role of the Book of Mormon as a holy book in the LDS canon, we must examine the statements that the book makes concerning itself. This can be done best by examining the Title Page, which, according to Joseph Smith, was written by Moroni after he had completed the record. The Title Page, which is published at the beginning of every copy of the book, reads as follows (omitting a few phrases):

> The Book of Mormon: an account written by the hand of Mormon upon plates taken from the plates of Nephi. Wherefore, it is an abridgment of the record of the people of Nephi, and also of the Lamanites—Written to

the Lamanites, who are a remnant of the house of Israel; and also to Jew
and Gentile—Written by way of commandment, and also by the spirit of
prophecy and of revelation—Sealed by the hand of Moroni, and hid up
unto the Lord, to come forth in due time by way of the Gentile—The
interpretation thereof by the gift of God. . . . Which is to show unto the
remnant of the House of Israel what great things the Lord hath done for
their fathers; and that they are not cast off forever—And also to the
convincing of the Jew and Gentile that Jesus is the Christ, the eternal
God, manifesting himself unto all nations.

To summarize, the Title Page states that the Book of Mormon is an
ancient historical record containing divine revelation, written for a
specified modern audience; it would come forth in a miraculous way
"in due time," and its purpose is to testify "that Jesus is the Christ."
The self-identity of the book revolves around these concepts, which
are echoed throughout its pages. The major assertions will be considered here.

The most fundamental claim made by the Book of Mormon is that
it is an authentic ancient book. This is a basic belief of Latter-day
Saints, whose theology rules out any alternatives. It is believed to be a
true book, the record of ancient peoples, as described above, written
in ancient times and recovered anew in the nineteenth century. Yet it
is believed to be a book of a unique sort—a sacred record made by
inspired men under divine direction. As such its value to Mormons
goes far beyond that of an ancient history. To them it is Scripture—the
mind and will of God written and preserved for his people. Thus its
words carry God's message into the hearts of those who read it. It tells
them what God intends them to know in words that he caused to be
written.

The basic framework of the Book of Mormon is history. It is a
specific kind of history that seeks to teach theological principles from
the events of the past. It chronicles the dealings of God with people,
both individuals and nations. Its closest analogues elsewhere in sacred
literature, at least as far as the structure of the narrative is concerned,
are probably found in the Acts of the Apostles and those sections of
the Hebrew Bible that purport to record historical events, both in the
Pentateuch and in the historical books. The Book of Mormon is quite
similar to Genesis, Exodus, and Numbers, which record the sacred
history of a people that viewed itself as chosen by God. In the Book of
Mormon, as well as in those pentateuchal narratives, only the history
of a limited group of people is important. Events that transpire
elsewhere in the world are irrelevant, unless they directly involve in
some way those with whom the narrative concerns itself. In fact, in
the Book of Mormon, as in the Pentateuch and elsewhere in the

Bible, the history of God's interaction with humankind is what is important, not the history of more mundane events.

One biblical chapter that is significantly similar to much of the Book of Mormon is 2 Kings 17. There the historian recounts briefly the final events in the history of the kingdom of Israel, the three-year siege of Samaria, its capture, and the deportation of its population. Then he leads into a commentary on the circumstances that brought that calamity about:

> And this was so, because the people of Israel had sinned against the LORD their God, . . . and had feared other gods and walked in the customs of the nations whom the LORD drove out before the people of Israel. . . . And they did wicked things, provoking the LORD to anger, and they served idols. . . . Yet the LORD warned Israel and Judah by every prophet and every seer. . . . But they would not listen, but were stubborn, as their fathers had been. . . . Therefore the LORD was very angry with Israel, and removed them out of his sight; none was left but the tribe of Judah only. . . . The LORD removed Israel out of his sight, as he had spoken by all his servants the prophets. So Israel was exiled from their own land to Assyria until this day (2 Kings 17:7–8, 11–14, 18, 23 [RSV]).

This type of editorial moralizing on historical events is precisely the material of which much of the Book of Mormon is made. Consider the following example from the account of a large battle:

> Notwithstanding the great destruction which hung over my people, they did not repent of their evil doings; therefore there was blood and carnage spread throughout all the face of the land, both on the part of the Nephites and also on the part of the Lamanites; and it was one complete revolution throughout all the face of the land. . . . And it came to pass that when I, Mormon, saw their lamentation and their mourning and their sorrow before the Lord, my heart did begin to rejoice within me, knowing the mercies and the long-suffering of the Lord, therefore supposing that he would be merciful unto them that they would again become a righteous people. But behold this my joy was vain, for their sorrowing was not unto repentance, because of the goodness of God; but it was rather the sorrowing of the damned, because the Lord would not always suffer them to take happiness in sin (Mormon 2:8, 12–13).

In the Book of Mormon it is made clear that the events and the attendant commentary are recorded for the benefit of people not yet born, something that is, of course, also implied in the passages quoted above from 2 Kings 17. The moralizing is added so that the readers will understand the causes of the recorded events and be able to avoid the calamities experienced by the people in the narrative and to duplicate their successes. Note the comments by Moroni: "And this cometh unto you, O ye Gentiles, . . . that ye may repent, and not continue in your iniquities until the fulness come, that ye may not bring down the fulness of the wrath of God upon you as the inhabitants of the land have hitherto done" (Ether 2:11). The book's very purpose is to teach. Its approach to doing so is very deuteronomic, as is evidenced by the following passage, which is repeated at least a dozen times: "Inasmuch as ye shall keep the commandments of God ye shall prosper in the land; and inasmuch as ye will not keep the commandments of God ye shall be cut off from his presence" (Alma 38:1). This is a fundamental component of the Book of Mormon philosophy. Latter-day Saints view it as being at the core of its message for readers in modern times.

In addition to history, the Book of Mormon is a book of theology. Much of it consists of theological treatises, set in the context of the historical narrative. These are presented as discourses or writings of the prophets who are the main characters in the narrative. The prophetic material is not segregated from the historical material, as is the case for the most part in the Hebrew Bible. Instead, the prophetic words are found within the context of the overall history. The doctrinal writings and speeches of the prophets in the Book of Mormon are extremely important in Mormonism, constituting a primary source of Latter-day Saint theology.

The Title Page states specifically that the book was written by divine command and, "by the spirit of prophecy and of revelation." Joseph Smith always maintained that he was not responsible for the content of the book, but that it was delivered to him; his role was that of a translator. The book itself is consistent in its claim that what it contains is revelation from God, received and recorded by prophets who were God's spokesmen. Mormons believe that it is a book with a divine purpose and that those doctrines and events which are recorded in the book are there because God inspired someone to put them there. The Book of Mormon makes this claim in several places. A notable example is that of Nephi, the son of Lehi, whose record is found at the beginning of the book. Nephi states, "And after I had made these plates by way of commandment, I, Nephi, received a commandment that the ministry and the prophecies, the more plain and precious parts of them, should be written upon these plates; and that the things which were writen should be kept for the instruction of my people" (1 Nephi 19:3). In other words, God revealed to him what he should put in his record; specifically mentioned are the highlights of what he calls "the ministry and the prophecies." Later Nephi states, "Nevertheless, I do not write anything upon plates save it be that I think it be sacred" (1 Nephi 19:6).

The book maintains throughout that what is recorded in it is the revealed word of God. Yet it makes no claim to being either perfect or infallible. Moroni, in his efforts to complete his father Mormon's record, laments, "Lord, the Gentiles will mock at these things, because of our weakness in writing; for Lord thou has made us mighty in word by faith, but thou has not made us mighty in writing" (Ether 12:23). He continues, "When we write we behold our weakness, and stumble because of the placing of our words; and I fear lest the Gentiles shall mock at our words" (Ether 12:25). This same Moroni states in the last line of the Title Page, "And now, if there are faults they are mistakes of men; wherefore, condemn not the things of God." Latter-day Saints acknowledge the imperfection of the Book of Mormon, believing that anything placed in the stewardship of human hands—whether they be those of Mormon and Moroni, or of Joseph Smith and his successors—is susceptible to error. Yet they view the Book of Mormon as divine in origin, the effort of divinely commissioned and divinely inspired mortals to do the work of God.

As stated previously, Latter-day Saints believe that Joseph Smith was a prophet called by God to restore to the world the Christianity of Jesus and the apostles. That original Christianity, they believe, including the correct doctrines and the authority to act in Jesus' name, was lost from the world after the deaths of the apostles. Joseph Smith claimed that his commission was to reestablish it. Mormons believe that one of the major events in that retoration was the publication of the Book of Mormon. And, significantly, that took place at the very beginning of the movement, even prior to the formal organization of the Church of Jesus Christ of Latter-day Saints. The Book of Mormon is viewed as being a means by which the correct doctrines of Christianity were restored, as a foundation upon which the later works of restoration could rest. Joseph Smith referred to the book as "the keystone of our religion" (Smith, 1938: 194).

The Title Page tells us that the Book of Mormon was written and then hidden so that it would remain undisturbed in order to "come forth in due time by way of the Gentile," meaning Joseph Smith and his associates. These and their successors would take it to the three groups to whom the book is addressed specifically: (a) the Lamanites, that is, descendants of the Book of Mormon people, usually identified by Mormons as the native peoples of the western hemisphere, (b) the Jews, and (c) the Gentiles, meaning everyone else in the world who is neither Lamanite nor Jew. Mormon and the other writers specifically state that their words are intended for later generations. Their messages are directed not to people of their own time but to their distant descendants and others at the time in which God would cause the book to be brought to light. Among Latter-day Saints it is viewed as a voice from the past, speaking out of the dust to the readers of the present. Not uncommon is a kind of intimate personal counsel to the anticipated readers, as characterized by these words in the last chapter of the book:

> Now I, Moroni, write somewhat as seemeth me good; and I write unto my brethren, the Lamanites; . . . And I seal up these records, after I have spoken a few words by way of exhortation unto you. Behold, I would exhort you that when ye shall read these things, if it be wisdom in God that ye should read them, that ye would remember how merciful the Lord hath been unto the children of men, from the creation of Adam even down until the time that ye shall receive these things, and ponder it in your hearts. . . . Yea, come unto Christ, and be perfected in him, and deny yourselves of all ungodliness; and if ye shall deny yourselves of all ungodliness; and love God with all your might, mind and strength, then is his grace sufficient for you, that by his grace ye may be perfect in Christ (Moroni 10:1–3, 32).

Phrases such as "I will show unto you" and "thus we see," which occur regularly throughout the book, demonstrate the didactic nature of the material recorded (e.g., 1 Nephi 1:20; 16:29). The writers relate events and record sermons for the purpose of teaching principles to people in a later time, identified by Mormons specifically as the nineteenth century A.D. and later. Mormons thus view the book as their book for this day. It is a major source of their theology, providing the fundamental statements regarding many of the tenets of their faith. They find in its pages a paradigm for behavior as well. The historical narrative provides both positive and negative examples in the actions of nations and individuals. The events that are described in it serve as *types* for occurrences of the present as well as anticipated events of the future. It is believed that the book was brought to light to benefit the believers in a time when the issues of human existence would be such that the lessons learned from the past would provide the key to well-being. The faithful of today recognize in their societies and in their personal lives the cycles of history that are recorded in the Book of Mormon in which individual and collective behavior is followed by divinely dispensed blessings or curses. Thus, Latter-day Saints see in the pages of their book the personality of God as it relates to the actions of humankind.

The final fundamental assertion made on the Title Page of Book of Mormon is that the book's purpose is to convince the world that Jesus is the Christ. Throughout its pages this purpose is evident; indeed the subtitle of the book (added in 1983) reads: "Another Testament of Jesus Christ." The words of Nephi are typical of the emphasis placed by the Book of Mormon on Jesus: "For we labor diligently to write, to persuade our children, and also our brethren, to believe in Christ, and to be rconciled to God; for we know that it is by grace that we are saved, after all that we can do. . . . And we talk of Christ, we rejoice in Christ, we preach of Christ, we prophesy of Christ, and we write according to our prophecies, that our children may know to what source they may look for a remission of their sins" (2 Nephi 25:23, 26).

According to the Book of Mormon, Lehi and his children saw visions and conversed with heavenly messengers, as early as 600 B.C., whereby they learned concerning the future coming of their Messiah, Jesus. An angel revealed knowledge of Jesus to Lehi's sons Nephi and Jacob (2 Nephi 10:3; 25:29) and guided Nephi through a vision in which he saw in detail the distant ministry of Jesus and that of his apostles (2 Nephi 11:13–14:30). The ministry of Jesus is the very core of the Book of Mormon and thus also of Latter-day Saint theology. All of the Book of Mormon prophets are depicted as testifying of Jesus—those prior to his life in anticipation of him and those afterward in remembrance of him.

The Book of Mormon's emphasis on Jesus does not stop at purported predictions about his life. In that book Latter-day Saints find the fullest expression of the doctrines of their Christian faith. In it, couched in the words of the Lamanite and Nephite prophets, is found a theology of Christ that Mormons believe far excels in clarity and direction the doctrines preserved in the New Testament. One *raison d'etre* that the book gives concerning itself is that the New Testament, though endorsed in the Book of Mormon (1 Nephi 13:23–26) and believed and read by Latter-day Saints (Article of Faith 8; D&C 20:11), does not preserve sufficiently the "fullness of the gospel," to use the Mormon phrase. The Book of Mormon claims to be a second witness of Jesus alongside the New Testament. Yet it claims to have preserved many of the doctrines of God more perfectly and more fully than any other book in the world. Specific areas in which Mormons believe the book provides clearer statements of truth than does the Bible include, to list only a few: the nature of God, the nature of humankind, the purpose for human existence, the nature of revelation and sacred writings, the fall of Adam, and the atoning sacrifice of Jesus Christ. Even among the other LDS Scriptures, the Book of Mormon holds a special position. Latter-day Saints feel that no other book explains the basic principles of Christianity better. Moreover, the presentation of those principles in the Book of Mormon is simpler than that in Mormonism's other sacred books, making the book's message accessible to readers on any level of understanding or maturity. Because of this the Book of Mormon is used as the key book in teaching young Mormons their religion's essential doctrines, as it is used also by Mormon missionaries as the primary tool in their efforts to convert others to their faith.

While in his early twenties, Joseph Smith startled his small New York community and brought a great deal of ridicule upon himself and his family when he made it known that he intended to publish a record from ancient America. Most provocative, however, were his assertions concerning the manner in which the record came into his hands and the manner in which he translated it into English (Hill: 80–105).

The Mormon prophet said that on the night of 21 September 1823, a messenger from God named Moroni appeared in his room and told him of his (Joseph Smith's) calling to bring forth an ancient record that would be entrusted into his care. Joseph Smith reported that he learned from Moroni that the record contained "an account of the former inhabitants of this continent [the Americas], and the source from which they sprang. He also said that the fulness of the everlasting Gospel was contained in it, as delivered by the Savior to the ancient inhabitants" (JS-H: 34). In the Book of Mormon, Moroni was the last of the ancient American prophets and the one who completed the record and concealed it in the ground. Now he made its existence known to a modern counterpart, Joseph Smith. According to the latter, Moroni appeared to him often and instructed and trained him for his calling. Then on 22 September 1827, Joseph went to the burial spot and took possession of the plates, and the process of translation began. Joseph Smith did not claim to have any linguistic skills that would enable him to translate from an unknown ancient language. He stated instead that he made the translation through the power of God. The book was published in English on 26 March 1830, shortly before the formal organization of the Church of Jesus Christ of Latter-day Saints, which took place on the sixth of April of that year (Backman, 1983: 169–200).

That first edition of five thousand copies was published at a cost of three thousand dollars by Egbert B. Grandin of Palmyra, New York. Martin Harris, one of the early followers of Joseph Smith, underwrote the publication by pledging his farm as collateral (Stocks: 10, 40; Cook: 30–31). Grandin was not at all sympathetic to the cause of the new religion and could only be persuaded to publish the book with Harris' guarantee of payment. The printing, which was done in "Small Pica" type on a single-pull Smith hand press, was begun in August 1829 and contained 590 pages (Stocks: 39). The composition was done by John H. Gilbert, Grandin's employee. Since the original manuscript (and also the second copy from which the type was set) contained almost no punctuation or paragraphing, Gilbert added these, based on his judgment as to how they should be applied (Stocks: 10; see also Larson: 8–30).

The 1830 edition remained the only publication of the Book of Mormon until a five thousand-copy second edition was made available in 1837 in Kirtland, Ohio. By then the Latter-day Saints had developed their own printing facilities, enabling them to publish their literature without having to do so through nonbelievers. The chapter divisions and paragraphing of the second edition followed those of the first. But the text was changed considerably, reflecting careful correction of the 1830 edition against the manuscript. Over three thousand changes were made in the text (Howard: 41; see 25–69). According to Hugh G. Stocks, "The vast majority of the corrections made were either grammatical or stylistic in nature, but some were changes in wording designed to clarify meaning" (11). The 1837 edition is the most important of the early publications of the Book of Mormon, as far as the text is concerned. All subsequent editions until that of 1981 are based on it.

The last edition of the Book of Mormon published during Joseph Smith's lifetime was the 1840 third edition, published in Nauvoo, Illinois, but printed in Cincinnati, Ohio. This edition contains the text of the second edition with a few changes made by Joseph Smith, including some corrections based on the original manuscript. Two thousand copies were printed (Stocks: 61).

Only a few months after the publication of the third edition, the first British edition of the Book of Mormon was published in Liverpool, England (1841). Slightly more than four thousand copies were produced at a price of £210. This British edition used the text of the second American edition (Stocks: 66–75). The second British edition appeared in Liverpool in 1849 (five thousand copies); the third appeared in 1852 and was reprinted in five additional impressions over the following two decades. The third British edition, containing important format changes and some lesser textual changes as well, is significant for subsequent publications.

An 1854 impression (totaling five thousand copies) of the third British edition was shipped entirely to Utah for the use of Mormons in the United States. By the 1850s the Saints were numerous and well-established in Britain but poor in the territory of Utah, to which they had moved following their expulsion from Illinois. This placed the third British edition in the position of being the "standard" English

Book of Mormon for the entire LDS Church, which position it retained until 1879. Some time around 1870, the stereotype plates of the third British edition were brought to Salt Lake City. From these, impressions were made in 1871, 1874, 1876, and 1877 (Stocks: 99–105).

The year 1879 brought an entirely new edition of the Book of Mormon, published under the direction of Orson Pratt, a member of the Council of Twelve Apostles. Pratt had worked for two years to produce the new edition, which is most notable for its revised physical format. Since 1830, the chapter and paragraph divisions, which had been established by typesetter John H. Gilbert, had remained for the most part unchanged in later editions. The 1879 edition contained a totally new chapter system, with much smaller chapters than had been found in the previous editions. Verses were added in the new edition and numbered sequentially within each chapter. Both in its chapter divisions and its verse divisions, the 1879 Book of Mormon's format resembles that of the Bible. One can assume that such was Pratt's goal in making the revisions as he did. Also added for the first time were footnotes and cross-references to other passages.

In 1920, the LDS church published an edition of the English Book of Mormon that was to stay in use unchanged for the next 61 years. Under the direction of Apostle James E. Talmage, all previous editions were examined to produce the most accurate text possible. Unfortunately, Joseph Smith's original manuscript and its copy from which the type of the first edition was set were no longer available to Mormon scholars. The 1920 edition followed the overall format of the 1879 edition, but new cross-references and a new index were added. Until 1981 the 1920 edition was used unchanged in all English printings. Though a variety of bindings, illustrations, and other physical features was used during those years, the text remained that of 1920. Even different settings of the type were line-by-line equivalents of the 1920 text.

In 1981, following several years of research, a new edition of the Book of Mormon was published as part of a large project that included new editions of all of the LDS Scriptures. The resulting Book of Mormon is clearly the most significant reworking of the text since 1837. Latter-day Saint scholars involved in the project had access to all previous editions, but, more significantly, they also had access to manuscripts that had not been used in any of the editions since that of 1840. Of the original manuscript dictated by Joseph Smith in 1829, only about twenty-five percent remains today. The type of the first edition was set from a copy of that original, which still exists in its entirety. The 1981 revision draws from the manuscripts and includes corrections made by Joseph Smith in the 1837 and 1840 editions, which were published during his lifetime. The chapter and verse divisions have remained unchanged since 1879. Robert J. Matthews, who was a member of the committee that researched the text for the 1981 edition, has stated:

> Many of the variations in the text of the Book of Mormon consist of unintentional departures of the typesetter of the first edition from the handwritten manuscript, while others are transcription errors by Oliver Cowdery [Joseph Smith's scribe] as he made the printer's copy. Furthermore, studies show that some typographical errors have persisted in every edition of the Book of Mormon, and other variations have occurred in some, but not all, of the many printed editions. . . . The 1981 edition . . . has at least 265 corrections of which about 100 are substantial enough to affect the meaning (1982:396).

Also significant are completely new explanatory chapter headings, cross references in footnotes, and an extended index (see Matthews, 1982: 393–401).

Since its original publication in 1830, over twenty-five million copies of the Book of Mormon have been printed in the English language. Of those, over fifteen million have been produced in a variety of soft-cover formats.

English is not the only language in which the Book of Mormon has appeared. To date, all or parts of it have been translated into over seventy languages. Almost ten million non-English books have been printed, somewhat less than half of which are Spanish. Currently, about one and one-half million copies in all languages are printed each year.

The Doctrine and Covenants

The two books examined so far, the Bible and the Book of Mormon, are held in Mormon theology to contain the revelations of God to prophets of past ages. As Joseph Smith proclaimed himself to be a prophet of equal status with those of antiquity, it is not surprising that he should claim to have received revelations from God as well. He did in fact record many proclamations, which Mormons believe are the word of God delivered through the mouth of his latter-day spokesman. These are collected in a volume called, in full, the Doctrine and Covenants of the Church of Jesus Christ of Latter-day Saints. In the "Explanatory Introduction" found at the beginning of the 1981 edition, the following words outline the Latter-day Saint view of this volume of modern revelation:

The Doctrine and Covenants is a collection of divine revelations and inspired declarations given for the establishment and regulation of the kingdom of God on earth in the last days. Although most of the sections are directed to members of the Church of Jesus Christ of Latter-day Saints, the messages, warnings, and exhortations are for the benefit of all mankind, and contain an invitation to all people everywhere to hear the voice of the Lord Jesus Christ, speaking to them for their temporal well-being and their everlasting salvation. . . . In the revelations the doctrines of the gospel are set forth with explanations about such fundamental matters as the nature of the Godhead, the origin of man, the reality of Satan, the purpose of mortality, the necessity for obedience, the need for repentance, the workings of the Holy Spirit, the ordinances and performances that pertain to salvation, the destiny of the earth, the future conditions of man after the resurrection and the judgment, the eternity of the marriage relationship, and the eternal nature of the family. Likewise the gradual unfolding of the administrative structure of the Church is shown with the calling of bishops, the First Presidency, the council of the Twelve [Apostles], and the Seventy, and the establishment of other presiding offices and quorums. Finally, the testimony that is given of Jesus Christ—his divinity, his majesty, his perfection, his love, and his redeeming power—makes this book of great value to the human family and of more worth than the riches of the whole earth.

The Doctrine and Covenants consists of 138 "sections" and two "Official Declarations." All but two of the sections are revelations or official statements that came during the ministry of Joseph Smith. One section (D&C 136) is considered to be a revelation to Brigham Young, the successor to Joseph Smith in the leadership of the church (1844–1877), and another (D&C 138) is attributed to Joseph F. Smith, a nephew of the founding prophet who was president of the church, 1901–1918. Official Declaration 1 is an authoritative proclamation by Wilford Woodruff, president of the church 1889–1898, and Official Declaration 2 is an authoritative proclamation by Spencer W. Kimball, president of the church 1973–1985. Like all who have followed Joseph Smith in the presidency of the church, these four men are viewed by Latter-day Saints as prophets, and their canonized statements are therefore considered to be the revelations of the mind of God (D&C 68:4).

According to Latter-day Saint belief, the revelatory experiences of Joseph Smith began when he was fourteen years old in the spring of 1820, when God and Jesus Christ appeared to him in a wooded area near his home in Palmyra, New York, in response to his inquiry concerning which church he should join. Their message to him, he reported, was that he should join no church, for none of the churches of his day enjoyed divine approval (JS-H: 1–20; see also Hill: 41-54). His commission would be to receive the revelations whereby Jesus would restore to humankind his true church and the gospel that had been taught in its purity in the days of Jesus and his apostles but was subsequently lost from the earth. The Doctrine and Covenants contains many of those revelations.

The earliest-dated section of the Doctrine and Covenants comes from three years after Joseph Smith's first vision, but the bulk of the revelations date from 1828 to 1833, which was the period of greatest activity in the establishment of the church and its doctrines. The first effort to collect the revelations took place in 1831, the second year of the church's existence. Prior to that time, copies of revelations had circulated independently or in unofficial collections. In November of that year, a conference of members convened, at which plans were made to publish the revelations that Joseph Smith had made known up to that time (Roberts 1: 267–68). More than sixty were collected and specified for publication in a book called the *Book of Commandments*. When about two-thirds of the book had been typeset and printed, a mob of anti-Mormons attacked the printing office and destroyed the press and its soon-to-be-published book (Allen and Leonard: 68–69). Some of the scattered sheets were later placed together, and a few dozen copies of the *Book of Commandments* were bound, containing only those revelations that had been printed at the time the press was destroyed (see Lyon: 30).

In 1834 plans were made once again for the publication of Joseph Smith's revelations. When the book was published in the summer of 1835, it contained 102 sections. This edition was the first to use the title Doctrine and Covenants, the name by which all subsequent editions have been known (Lyon: 32). It was published in Kirtland, Ohio. Later editions of the Doctrine and Covenants were made in the 1840s in Nauvoo, Illinois, where most of the Latter-day Saints had settled following their explusion from their homes in Missouri. By 1844 the collection included 111 sections. During the same period and in the following decades, reprints came off the press in Liverpool, England, to serve the needs of the large number of British Mormons. It was not until 1876, however, that a new edition was published containing additional sections. This edition, published in Salt Lake City, brought the total to 136 (Lyon: 32-33), where it remained until the edition of 1981. It also divided the sections into verses for the first time.

In 1921 the Doctrine of Covenants was published in a new physical format. An introduction was added at the beginning of the book; the text was arranged in double-column pages; introductory notes were added at the beginning of each section; and the footnote and cross-referencing system introduced in 1879 was expanded (Lyon: 33–

34). More recently, a completely revised edition was published by the Church in 1981. It contains a new "Explanatory Introduction," written to introduce the reader to the book and its purposes. This includes some information concerning the need for the (1981) revised edition of the revelations. Above each section are new headings that explain the historical circumstances that led to the revelations, and brief descriptions of their content (Matthews, 1982: 401–17). The 1981 edition also contains completely new footnotes and cross-references, and maps showing the places mentioned in the book.

The most important change in the 1981 edition is the addition of new scriptural material to the text. Two sections were added to the collection of revelations: an 1836 revelation of Joseph Smith that had never been included previously (D&C 137), and a 1918 revelation by Joseph F. Smith (D&C 138). Also added was Official Declaration 2, a 1978 proclamation by Spencer W. Kimball.

The Pearl of Great Price

The shortest volume in the LDS canon is the Pearl of Great Price, which draws its name from the treasured jewel of Jesus' parable in Matt 13:45–46. Franklin D. Richards, the early Mormon apostle who compiled the book, wrote in its preface, "It is presumed, that true believers in the Divine mission of the Prophet JOSEPH SMITH, will appreciate this little collection of precious truths as a *Pearl of Great Price*" (1851 ed., Preface; original punctuation and emphasis retained). The book is a collection of some of the writings of Joseph Smith, believed by Latter-day Saints to be revelatory in nature. The most recent edition (1981) includes the following titles: "Selections from the Book of Moses," "The Book of Abraham," "Joseph Smith— Matthew," "Joseph Smith—History," and "The Articles of Faith."

In 1830, Joseph Smith began a project that would occupy his time intermittently for the rest of his life: a revision of the Bible (Matthews, 1975: 26–28). This will be discussed below (see Joseph Smith Translation). Perhaps the most significant part of the revision is the material contained in its first few chapters, which are included in the Pearl of Great Price. Here Joseph Smith departed substantially from his King James text and added a large body of new material, which Mormons believe was revealed to him. The "Selections from the Book of Moses" consist of Joseph Smith's rendering of Gen 1:1–6:13. It is greatly expanded over the biblical text: whereas the "Book of Moses" material consists of 356 verses, the corresponding Genesis material consists of only 151. Among other things, the "Book of Moses" adds the following

to the biblical account: a lengthy introduction, in which Moses con-
verses with God prior to seeing in a vision the creation of the earth
(Moses 1); an explanation of Satan's evil motives (Moses 4:1–4); an
account of some experiences of Adam and Eve following their expulsion from Eden (Moses 5:1–16); an account of Cain's rebellion and the
spiritual degeneration of Adam's posterity (Moses 5:17–59); and a
record of the ministry of Enoch (Moses 6:22–7:69).

The second selection in the Pearl of Great Price is a five-chapter
composition entitled "The Book of Abraham," which is believed to be
the translation of part of Abraham's record as revealed to Joseph
Smith. Joseph Smith's interest in Abraham's ministry resulted in part
from his purchase of some Egyptian papyri in 1835 (Todd; 151–69).
Though the connection between the papyri and the "Book of Abraham" is unclear, it appears that Joseph Smith's possession of the
Egyptian texts influenced his attraction to things Egyptian and led to
his bringing forth of the document concerning Abraham. It deals in
part with the patriarch's experiences in Egypt. In 1842 the work was
published in serial form in the Mormon newspaper, *Times and Seasons*, at Nauvoo, Illinois.

A second selection from Joseph Smith's Bible revision is "Joseph
Smith—Matthew" (titled "Joseph Smith 1" prior to the 1981 edition).
It is the Mormon prophet's revision of Matthew 24, Jesus' prophecy of
future hardships for Jerusalem and the world. The new material in
this chapter is not as extensive as that in the "Selections from the
Book of Moses." For the most part, this work is a restructuring of the
King James Version text. In Matthew 24, Jesus responds to his disciples' question concerning the destruction of the temple and the
events that would precede his future advent (Matt 24:3). His discourse
includes elements of both issues, which are not well defined in the
disciples' thinking, according to Matthew's depiction (Harvey: 92–93).
"Joseph Smith—Matthew" rearranges the text to divide Jesus' words
into two sections: one dealing with the calamities of the near future
(destruction of the temple, false Christs and prophets, affliction and
death of the apostles), and the other foretelling the events preceding
Jesus' return in glory. Thus the immediate future of Jerusalem, its
temple, and the Christian community, is separated in Jesus' discourse
from events of a more eschatological nature.

The canonical account of Joseph Smith's visions in the early years
of his work is found in the "Joseph Smith—History" (called "Joseph
Smith 2" prior to the 1981 edition). This record, in Joseph Smith's
own words, highlights significant events from about 1816 to 1829
(Peterson: 11). He dictated it to a scribe in 1838 (Backman, 1980: 125),

but it was not published until 1842, when it appeared as part of a series in the *Times and Seasons*. The seventy-five verse account is of tremendous importance to Latter-day Saints, as it records Joseph Smith's purported visitations by God and Jesus, the angel Moroni, and John the Baptist (who gave him the power to baptize).

The final section of the Pearl of Great Price is a list of some fundamental doctrines of the LDS faith. These were written by Joseph Smith, originally in response to a request from John Wentworth, editor of the *Chicago Democrat*, for information concerning Mormonism (see Brandt: 69–71). They were published in the *Times and Seasons* on 1 March 1842. "The Articles of Faith" consist of thirteen brief statements summarizing some of the basic doctrines espoused by the Latter-day Saints. They are by no means a formal creed or confession, but an informal overview of beliefs. Nor are they considered to be complete; some of the most important doctrines of Mormonism are not mentioned at all in the "Articles." Nonetheless they endorse all of what Latter-day Saints view as revealed truth, as the ninth Article summarizes: "We believe all that God has revealed, all that He does now reveal, and we believe that He will yet reveal many great and important things pertaining to the Kingdom of God."

The Pearl of Great Price was first published in Liverpool, England, in 1851. Franklin D. Richards, a Mormon apostle, viewed with regret the paucity of LDS reading material for British members of the Church. Already there were over thirty thousand Latter-day Saints in Great Britain (Peterson: 5), though the first missionaries of the church had arrived only twelve years previously (Roberts, 2:22–26). In response to requests for new materials, Richards collected several significant writings of Joseph Smith and published them in his Pearl of Great Price. His 1851 version contained a number of items no longer found in the current editions (Peterson: 7–13), mostly consisting of revelations that were added subsequently to the Doctrine and Covenants.

The first American edition was published in Salt Lake City in 1878. By then the collection had received widespread approval by leaders and laity alike, and in a General Conference of the church in 1880 it was canonized by the membership as Scripture (Peterson: 12–13). In 1902 it underwent a revision, omitting material duplicated in the Doctrine and Covenants and dividing the text into chapters and verses (Lyon: 210). A 1921 edition added an index and set the text in a two-column format (Peterson: 13). Along with the Book of Mormon and the Doctrine and Covenants, the Pearl of Great Price was published in a revised edition in 1981, with a new "Introductory Note," new titles for some of the works (as noted above), new explanatory introductions for each, and a totally revised footnote and referencing system (Matthews, 1982: 417–22).

Though it originated in a semiofficial manner and was not canonized until late in the nineteenth century, the Pearl of Great Price holds a position equal with the other Latter-day Saint standard works. Latter-day Saint theology would not be complete without its contributions. The "Book of Abraham" and the "Selections from the Book of Moses" teach doctrines concerning the nature of God, the preearth existence of humankind, the creation, the fall of Adam, and the atonement of Christ that are found nowhere else in the Bible or other books of the LDS canon. The "Joseph Smith—History" gives Mormons the personal account of the first prophet of their faith, as well as a canonical record of its founding events. Their prophet's testimony stands in it as a challenge to believer and nonbeliever alike: "I had seen a vision; I knew it, and I knew that God knew it, and I could not deny it" (JS-H: 25). The "Articles of Faith" summarize the Latter-day Saint position with regard to the nature of God, Jesus' atoning sacrifice, baptism, divine authority, church organization, spiritual gifts, Scripture, revelation, and Christian behavior—to name a few of the doctrines mentioned. To the Latter-day Saints the book is indeed "a pearl of great price."

The Joseph Smith Translation

The four books discussed above constitute the Standard Works of the Church of Jesus Christ of Latter-day Saints. They are the canonized scriptures against which all things in the LDS faith are measured. Yet since Mormons believe "all that God has revealed" (Article of Faith 9) and that he has been at work among the prophets of their faith since its beginning, they acknowledge all that he reveals as authoritative, whether officially canonized or not. One source of what Latter-day Saints view as revealed truth, though it is not part of their officially canonized Scripture, is Joseph Smith's Bible revision. It is viewed as a major source of truth that was brought to light as part of the restoration. Over the course of the fourteen years from the time he began the revision until his death in 1844, the Mormon founder made changes in over three thousand verses of the King James Bible (Matthews, 1975: 425). The final product of his efforts, which was never published in his lifetime, is called the Joseph Smith Translation (JST) or, sometimes, the Inspired Version.

Joseph Smith believed that his role as God's spokesman included both

the authority and the ability to make changes in the Bible as God
directed. In one of his revelations he is called "a seer, a revelator, *a
translator,* and a prophet, having all the gifts of God which he bestows
upon the head of the Church" (D&C 107:92, italics added). He called
his work a "translation," though he never claimed to have consulted
any text other than his English Bible. He "translated" it in the sense
of conveying its meaning in a new form, interpreting, adding to,
taking from, and clarifying it in the changes that he made. His role as
Bible translator, as he viewed it, was to restore lost biblical material,
correct errors that had come into the text since its writing, and
otherwise make revisions that he considered appropriate. In doing so
he created a text that often goes beyond the actual original words of
the Bible to capture what he felt were its authors' original intentions.
The Joseph Smith Translation includes changes that range from small
textual revisions, clarifying individual words or passages in the KJV, to
vast additions of material found nowhere else in world literature.
Included in the latter category are additions dealing with Adam and
Eve, Enoch, and Melchizedek (see Pearl of Great Price, above).

Many of Joseph Smith's changes have the practical effect of making passages of the Bible more revelant to the immediate needs of the
Latter-day Saints of Joseph Smith's day. One such example is found in
Romans 13, Paul's admonition regarding subservience to political
authority. The Joseph Smith Translation took the emphasis from the
authority of the state and placed it on the authority of the church.
Romans 13:1 reads, "Let every soul be subject unto the higher
powers. For there is no power IN THE CHURCH but of God."

The Mormon prophet once stated, "There are many things in the
Bible which do not, as they now stand, accord with the revelations of
the Holy Ghost to me" (Smith, 1938: 310). The Joseph Smith Translation harmonizes many biblical verses to conform with the theology
that Joseph Smith had taught before the revisions were made. In 1
John 4:12 his revision reads, "No man hath seen God at any time,
EXCEPT THEM WHO BELIEVE." This change is in harmony not
only with Joseph Smith's own reported theophany of 1820, but also
with other such experiences mentioned in the Book of Mormon,
which was published before the Bible revision was begun (e.g., 2
Nephi 11:3; Ether 3:13). Also teaching that human beings can see
God is a revision made in the account of Moses' theophany in Exodus
33:

KJV, Exodus 33:20, 23	JST, Exodus 33:20, 23
(20) And he said, Thou canst not	(20) And he said UNTO

see my face: for there shall no man see me, and live.

MOSES, Thou canst not see my face AT THIS TIME, LEST MINE ANGER BE KINDLED AGAINST THEE ALSO, AND I DESTROY THEE, AND THY PEOPLE: for there shall be no man AMONG THEM see me AT THIS TIME, and live, FOR THEY ARE EXCEEDING SIN-FUL. AND NO SINFUL MAN HATH AT ANY TIME, NEI-THER SHALL THERE BE ANY SINFUL MAN AT ANY TIME, THAT SHALL SEE MY FACE AND LIVE.

(23) And I will take away mine hand, and thou shalt see my back parts: but my face shall not be seen.

(23) And I will take away mine hand, and thou shalt see my back parts, but my face shall not be seen, AS AT OTHER TIMES; FOR I AM ANGRY WITH MY PEOPLE ISRAEL.

The Joseph Smith Translation is not simply a "Mormonizing" of the Bible. Many of the characteristic theological concepts of the Latter-day Saints are the direct result of the biblical revision. The Joseph Smith Translation is, in its own right, a major contributor to LDS theology. Though the Book of Mormon had been published shortly before the new translation was begun, many of the major contributions to the codification of Mormon theology and ecclesiology took place in the years 1830 to 1833, precisely the years in which Joseph Smith was most actively involved in biblical revisions. Several fundamental Mormon beliefs are found only in the new translation. Moreover, many of the revelations that Joseph Smith claimed to receive from God during this period were the result of questions raised during the process of Bible translating. Thus rather than view-ing the Bible revisions as the product of a preexisting Mormonism, Mormonism, to a great extent, can be viewed as the product of Joseph Smith's revision of the Bible.

The use of the Joseph Smith Translation by Latter-day Saint church leaders and scholars has been varied since the volume's orig-inal publication in 1867 (Matthews, 1975: 168–69). Since the man-uscripts, following the founding prophet's death, did not fall into the hands of the LDS church, the revisions were generally unavailable for Mormon scholars to study. Moreover, the publication was produced under the auspices of a midwestern offshoot of the LDS church (Matthews, 1975: 167–75), and the Utah-based Mormons had neither the copyright nor the opportunity to compare published editions with original manuscripts. Because of these factors, even the published editions were viewed by most Mormons with considerable restraint. Over the past two decades, that restraint has waned. With the manuscripts now available for examination, comparison with published editions has shown the latter to conform to the manuscripts in almost all cases (Matthews, 1975: 177–205). In accord with this, LDS scholars and ecclesiastical leaders now use the revision—not as a replacement to the Bible, but as a supplement to it. In a similar vein, the Church's 1979 Bible publication makes liberal use of JST passages in its footnotes and in an appendix for longer revised passages.

The Function of Scripture in Mormonism

The sacred writings of Mormonism perform a *practical* function within that faith; they are not used in any kind of ritual situation. They are not used in chanting, reciting, or praying, or in any similar rite. They contain no saving powers nor powers to bless; nor is reading them a sacramental act. In Mormonism, the reading of Scripture functions as a means to achieving two important ends: education in the principles of the faith, and communion with God. In each of these areas, the sacred literature plays an important role.

To Latter-day Saints a primary purpose for reading sacred writings is to learn about God. By examining the chronicles of his dealings with humankind and the divinely inspired theological statements recorded concerning him, one learns the will of God so one can act in accordance with it. Joseph Smith stated with regard to the Book of Mormon that one "would get nearer to God by abiding by its precepts than by any other book" (Smith, 1938: 194). Mormons view the Book of Mormon and their other Standard Works as paradigms for human behavior. In them, the rights and wrongs of human action are displayed, as are the consequences of humankind's power to choose. They believe that one cannot be saved in ignorance to the things of God (D&C 131:6). It is necessary therefore to learn the laws of God and conform oneself to them. Though not a saving ritual in and of itself, the reading of Scripture contributes to one's salvation by teaching the divinely revealed principles, laws, and ordinances by means of which one is saved.

The reading of Scripture plays an important role in facilitating communication with God, according to Mormon belief, through what might be termed "vicarious spiritual experience." Though the reader is not physically present at the events depicted in the sacred book, reading brings those events to life and enables the reader to participate in them vicariously. This type of involvement is important in the faith as a means of bringing the things of God directly into the lives of believers. Daily exposure to sacred events—if only through reading— has power to exert tremendous influence, just as does regular exposure to any other type of impetus. Mormons view the reading of sacred texts as a means by which they can learn to pattern their lives after the examples taught in their Scriptures and thereby learn to do God's will. The vicarious involvement in the things of God also leads to what is called "personal revelation." In Mormon theology, revelation from God is not restricted to prophets and apostles. Although these are viewed as receiving revelation on behalf of the church and the entire world, each individual church member claims the right to receive divine revelation for his or her own needs. Mormons believe that in all areas of life where critical decisions must be made or where the will of God must be ascertained, prayers uttered in sincerity and faith will be answered. This is not a doctrine unknown elsewhere in Christianity (see James 1:5), but in Mormonism it is a fundamental belief (see Moroni 10:3–5). The vicarious spiritual experience enables the reception of "personal revelation" to take place by creating an environment in which divine direction can be received. When one is immersed in a sacred record and in harmony with what is revealed, one can communicate with God.

Many of the religions of the world have in their formative periods a miraculous event. Judaism has the exodus from Egypt, and Islam has the Qur'an. In these, the perceived miraculous occurrences have exhibited enormous power in both the creating and the maintaining of the communities that are based upon them. In Mormonism such a miraculous event is the revelation of new Scripture. Though the holy books are not the only features of the Latter-day Saint faith that claim to be miraculous, still they, more than anything else, are held up to believer and nonbeliever alike as the test of the assertions of Joseph Smith and the Church of Jesus Christ of Latter-day Saints. Mormonism must stand or fall on its claim to modern revelation. The belief that God has spoken to humankind in modern times, and does so still in the church, is central to the existence of that faith. This belief, possibly more than any other thing, defines the Latter-day Saint community among other religions and provides its sustaining identity.

WORKS CONSULTED

Allen, James B., and Glenn M. Leonard 1980 *The Story of the Latter-day Saints*. Salt Lake City: Desert Book.

Backman, Milton V., Jr. 1980 *Joseph Smith's First Vision*, 2d ed. Salt Lake City: Bookcraft.

1983 *Eyewitness Accounts of the Restoration*. Orem, UT: Grandin Book.

Brandt, Edward J. 1976 "The Articles of Faith: Origin and Importance." *Pearl of Great Price Symposium, . . .* ed. (69–77). Provo, UT: Brigham Young University Publications.

Cook Lyndon W. 1981 *The Revelations of the Prophet Joseph Smith*. Provo, UT: Seventy's Mission Bookstore.

Ehat, Andrew F., and Lyndon W. Cook 1980 *The Words of Joseph Smith*. Provo, UT: Religious Studies Center, Brigham Young University.

Harvey, A. E. 1973 *Companion to the New Testament*. Cambridge: Oxford University Press and Cambridge University Press.

Hill, Donna 1977 *Joseph Smith, The First Mormon*. Garden City, NY: Doubleday.

Howard, Richard P. 1969 *Restoration Scriptures*. Independence, MO: Herald Publishing.

Kimball, Edward L., ed. 1982 *The Teachings of Spencer W. Kimball*, Salt Lake City: Bookcraft.

Larson, Stanley R. 1977 "Textual Variants in *Book of Mormon* Manuscripts." *Dialogue: A Journal of Mormon Thought* 10/4 (Autumn, 1977): 8–30.

Lyon, T. Edgar 1948 *Introduction to the Doctrine and Covenants and the Pearl of Great Price*. Salt Lake City: Deseret News Press.

Matthews, Robert J. 1975 *"A Plainer Translation": Joseph Smith's Translation of the Bible*. Provo, UT: Brigham Young University Press.

1982 "New Publications of the Standard Works—1979, 1981." *Brigham Young University Studies* 22:387–423.

McConkie, Burce R. 1966 *Mormon Doctrine*, 2d ed. Salt Lake City: Bookcraft.

Mortimer, W. James 1983 "The Coming Forth of the LDS Editions of Scripture." *The Ensign* 13/8 (August, 1983): 34–41.

Packer, Boyd K. 1982 "Scriptures." *The Ensign* 12/11 (November, 1982): 51–53.

Peterson, H. Donl 1976 "The Birth and Development of the Pearl of Great Price." *Pearl of Great Price Symposium, . . .* ed. (3–13). Provo, UT: Brigham Young University Publications.

Roberts, Brigham H. 1930 *A Comprehensive History of the Church of Jesus Christ of Latter-day Saints,* 6 vols. Salt Lake City: Deseret News Press.

Smith, Joseph Fielding, ed. 1938 *Teachings of the Prophet Joseph Smith*. Salt Lake City: Deseret Book.

1956 *Doctrines of Salvation: Sermons and Writings of Joseph Fielding Smith*, vol. 3. Bruce R. McConkie, comp. Salt Lake City: Brookcraft.

Stocks, Hugh G. 1979 *The Book of Mormon, 1830–1879: A Publishing History*. M.A. thesis, UCLA; 1979.

Talmage, James E. 1924 *The Articles of Faith*. Salt Lake City: The Church of Jesus Christ of Latter-day Saints.

Todd, Jay M. 1969 *The Saga of the Book of Abraham*. Salt Lake City: Deseret Book.

Widtsoe, John A. ed. 1971. *Discourses of Brigham Young*. Salt Lake City: Deseret Book.

VIII

Science and Health with Key to the Scriptures
". . . to gyve science & helthe to his puple . . ."

Luke 1:77 (Wyclif)

Robert Peel

In 1875 a privately printed book by a little-known writer, Mary Baker Glover, then in her middle fifties, appeared in Boston in a modest edition of one thousand copies. The book, *Science and Health,* undistinguished in appearance though challenging in content, attracted little immediate attention. Three years later the first edition was still not exhausted.

In another ten years, however, when the book had been revised several times and its title expanded to *Science and Health with Key to the Scriptures,* its author (now Mary Baker Eddy) was arousing widespread public interest as the leader of a striking new religious movement, and the sales of the book had mounted to some thirty-eight thousand copies. By the time of her death in 1910, the number of copies sold or distributed was well on the way toward the million mark, and a German translation was being prepared as the first of many others to follow.

William Dana Orcutt, for many decades director of Oxford University Press in Cambridge, Massachusetts, wrote in 1950 of the book which that highly reputable press had printed since 1881: "With the exception of the Holy Bible, the Christian Science textbook, 'Science and Health with Key to the Scriptures' by Mary Baker Eddy, holds every printing and publishing record. Written by an unknown author, privately printed in 1875 without benefit of publishers' promotion or even booksellers' interest, this volume has gone through hundreds of editions, comprising several million copies, bought by individuals all over the world" (1950: 3).

The term "Christian Science textbook" used by the Episcopalian Orcutt was borrowed from general Christian Science usage, but less sympathetic writers have sometimes referred to Mrs. Eddy's book as "the Bible of Christian Science." She herself called it only a "key" to the Scriptures and always maintained that the Bible (in the King James Version which she habitually but not exclusively used) was her "sole teacher" (1911a: viii). Typically she wrote in *Science and Health:* "The Bible has been my only authority. I have had no other guide in 'the straight and narrow way' of Truth" (126). The first of the six religious tenets to which all members of the Church of Christ, Scientist must subscribe states categorically, "As adherents of Truth, we take the inspired Word of the Bible as our sufficient guide to eternal Life" (1911a: 497).

In view of the objections that have frequently been raised concerning the accuracy of such statements, a critical examination of the way in which this self-proclaimed key to the Scriptures came into existence is called for. And this in turn requires a preliminary glance at the religious atmosphere into which Mary Baker of Bow, New Hampshire, was born in 1821.

Genesis

Although Calvinism no longer dominated New England thought, it remained a powerful influence in the conservative countryside among such pious farm families as the Congregationalist Bakers. A Baker child would be early indoctrinated in its basic tenets: the absolute sovereignty of God, the total depravity of humankind, and the supreme authority of the Scriptures as the word of God. Though the youngest Baker child, Mary, rebelled in her teens against the doctrine of predestination as incompatible with the God revealed through Jesus as an infinitely loving Father, the Bible remained the bedrock of her faith to the end of her life. Later she was to see the ill health that marked the first half of her life as resulting largely from her struggle to reconcile a God of infinite love and power with the sorrows and sufferings of human existence. But through those troubled years the Bible remained, in words that recur in her poems of that period, the one sure "chart and compass . . . anchor and helm" (Peel, 1966: 98, 103) to which she turned for comfort.

At the same time, with an education limited by the country academies of those days, a certain intellectual liveliness led her into metaphysical speculations not usual among young women of her day and age. As a twenty-five-year-old widow, meditating on the immortality of the soul, she wrote in an obscure magazine in 1847:

> Who does not sometimes conjecture what will be his condition and employment in eternity: Will the mind be continually augmenting its stock of knowledge, and advancing toward complete perfection? It cannot be otherwise.
>
> We shall there apprehend fully the relations and dependencies

incomprehensible to understandings encircled by clay. . . . The result of all experiments will then be satisfactory, since they will accord with the deductions of enlarged and enlightened reason. . . .

The imperfection of language will be no hindrance to the acquisition of ideas, as it will no longer be necessary as a medium of thought and communication. Intelligence, refined, etherealized, will converse directly with material objects, if, indeed, matter be existent (1847: 25).

The rather startling doubt expressed so casually in the last five words of this passage was reinforced by her search for health during the next two decades of her life. At times she was in a state of almost helpless invalidism vaguely defined as "spinal inflammation." Experiments in homeopathy, hydropathy, animal magnetism, and other forms of unorthodox treatment led her increasingly to suspect that the cause of all disease was mental rather than physical.

In her 1891 autobiography, *Retrospection and Introspection*, Mrs. Eddy would sum up in a single sentence that long quest for both health and metaphysical certainty: "From my very childhood I was impelled, by a hunger and thirst after divine things—a desire for something higher and better than matter, and apart from it—to seek diligently for the knowledge of God as the one great and ever-present relief from human woe" (39). It is not surprising that with her deeply rooted feeling for the Bible, the goal she was seeking should be linked in her mind with the healings of Jesus and his promise to his disciples—of all time?—that "ye shall know the truth, and the truth shall make you free" (John 8:32).

It is equally unsurprising that in 1862 at the lowest ebb of her health she should have responded with eager hope to the circular of a Portland (Maine) healer, Phineas Parkhurst Quimby, announcing that this self-proclaimed doctor". . . gives no medicines and makes no outward applications, but simply sits down by the patients, tells them their feelings and what they think is their disease. If the patients admit that he tells them their feelings, etc., then his explanation is the cure; and, if he succeeds in correcting their error, he changes the fluids of the system and establishes the truth, or health. The Truth is the Cure (Dresser, 1921: 144).

Quimby was a former mesmerist who still retained some of the practices of mesmerism but was exploring his way toward a crude form of mind-cure and attempting to identify his evolving system of suggestion with the healings of Jesus—as several prominent mesmerists had already done in regard to their own therapeutic methods. Full of faith, Mrs. Eddy experienced a remarkable (though temporary) recovery of health when she journeyed to Portland for treatment. Immediately she became one of Quimby's most ardent supporters, reading her own Christian convictions into his psychological system—rather to his surprise but also to his gratification.

The attempt to fuse the two approaches was doomed to final failure. Among the voluminious manuscript material that Quimby left at his death is a statement by him which makes clear the basic reason: "My foundation is animal matter, or life. This, set in action by wisdom, produces thought" (Dresser, 1895: 878). Mind, to him, was "spiritual matter"—a vapor or aura rising from the fluids of the body and containing the individual's spiritual "identity." This basically materialistic concept was the exact opposite of the conclusion the founder of Christian Science was to reach a few years later, as summed up in her "scientific statement of being" with its concluding words: "Spirit is God, and man is His image and likeness. Therefore man is not material; he is spiritual" (1911a: 468).

There is no doubt that the visits and correspondence she had with Quimby during the next three years stimulated the future Mrs. Eddy greatly and strengthened her conviction that the mental factor in health was all-important, but it left her religious development basically unaffected. The Portland healer's son and champion, George Quimby, recognized this when in 1901 he wrote unflatteringly but honestly, "The *religion* which she teaches certainly *is hers*, for which I cannot be too thankful; for I should be loath to go down to my grave feeling that my father was in any way connected with 'Christian Science'" (Dresser, 1921: 436).

Mrs. Eddy's own account many years later puts the three-year Quimby episode into perspective as a formative influence but by no means the source of Christian Science or of *Science and Health*, as some of her biographers have claimed it to be:

> I tried him as a healer, and because he seemed to help me for the time, and had a higher ideal than I had heard of up to that time, I praised him to the skies, wrote him letters—they talk of my letters to Quimby, as if they were something secret, they were not, I was enthusiastic, and couldn't say too much in praise of him; I actually loved him, I mean his high and noble character . . . but when I found that Quimbyism was too short, and would not answer the cry of the human heart for succor, for real aid, I went, being driven there by my extremity, to the Bible, and there I discovered Christian Science; and when I had found it, I deserted Quimby and his scheme of healing just as I had in turn deserted everything else . . . and I have built Christian Science upon the Petra of the Scriptures (Peel, 1977: 234).

She later placed the decisive event that led to that discovery in early 1866, a few weeks after Quimby's death, when she was living near Lynn, Massachusetts. Meeting with an accident that left her in "a critical condition," according to a Lynn newspaper at the time, she suddenly experienced what seemed to her friends a "miraculous" recovery while reading one of Jesus' healings in the New Testament. Many years later she wrote, "That short experience included a glimpse of the great fact that I have since tried to make plain to others, namely, Life in and of Spirit; this Life being the sole reality of existence" (1897: 24).

Since then questions have been raised about various physical details of the incident, but there can be no doubt whatever of the religious experience it occasioned. As the great German church historian Karl Holl wrote, "If one tries, even for a moment, to erase this religious experience from her life as a fable invented by her later on, then her entire struggle in the following years becomes incomprehensible, especially her opposition to mesmerism" (3: 464). While Mrs. Glover (as she then was) did not wholly throw off the influence of Quimby for another six years, 1866 remains the definitive "year of discovery."

Development

Her next nine years were spent in Bible study, writing, teaching, healing, and occasional public speaking. This formative period, with its exploration and experimentation in what she called "the newly discovered world of Spirit" (1911a: viii), culminated in the publication of *Science and Health,* to be followed four years later by the founding of the Church of Christ, Scientist.

The precursor of *Science and Health* was a short manuscript with a long title: "The Science of Man, By Which the Sick are Healed, Embracing Questions and Answers in Moral Science." This metaphysical essay, which Mrs. Glover had written for her earliest classes, has sometimes been confused with a short Quimby manuscript called "Questions and Answers," which she at first had tried to adapt to her own views by means of rewriting (Peel, 1966: 230–33; 1977: 458–60). When the task proved impossible, she wrote "The Science of Man" as a completely fresh venture of her own and did all her teaching from that. Quimby's manuscript had begun with the question: "You must have a feeling of repugnance toward certain patients. How do you overcome it and how can I do the same?" Mrs. Glover's began: "What is God?" The two questions mark the distance between a pragmatic psychology and a searching theology.

"The Science of Man" was copyrighted in 1870 but not actually published until 1876—and then in a considerably revised form. In a still later version it was incorporated in 1881 into the third edition of *Science and Health* as the chapter "Recapitulation," which in an even later version is still the basis of all Christian Science class instruction. This chapter contains the brief but now famous "scientific statement of being" which is at the heart of Christian Science metaphysics, as the six religious tenets with which the chapter ends is at the heart of its theology.

The author's name had changed in 1877 with her marriage to one of her students, Asa Gilbert Eddy, and the title of her book changed in 1883 when for the first time she included a short section called "Key to the Scriptures" and added the phrase to the book's title.

The new section consisted of a glossary of biblical names and terms, defining the metaphysical or spiritual significance that Mrs. Eddy felt they possessed beyond their literal and historical meaning. The idea of such a glossary may possibly have been suggested to her by an 1847 *Dictionary of Correspondences* drawn from Swedenborg's writings,[1] but what came forth was very much her own. As early as 1866 she had been engaged in writing a detailed "spiritual interpretation" of the book of Genesis. That bulky manuscript, with its constant deletions, corrections, interlineations, and fresh starts, shows her groping for language to express her unfolding thoughts, but it already reveals a startling originality in its treatment of the two biblical accounts of creation. Later this interpretation would be developed in a chapter entitled "Genesis" and incorporated in the "Key to the Scriptures."

Actually Mrs. Eddy always considered that this four-word descriptive phrase was not merely the title of one section of the book; in a wider sense it applied to the whole of *Science and Health*. The title of the Christian Science textbook, like the book itself and like the once-memorable and still-quotable Topsy, just "growed" out of the author's developing experience. She had concluded early that inspired vision might require painstaking revision of its written expression if it was to communicate itself adequately to others. Between the publication of *Science and Health* in 1875 and the author's death in 1910, the book would have at least six major revisions, with innumerable smaller changes made in the printings that occurred between these landmark editions.[2]

One significant step occurred in 1885, when she engaged a Boston man of letters—ex-Unitarian minister, J. Henry Wiggin—to help her with the sixteenth edition on which she was then working. He turned out to be a mixed blessing. His aid was invaluable on those matters of

"punctuation, capitalization and general smoothing out as to construction of sentences" for which he had been engaged (Orcutt, 1950:
29). In some ways his general literary advice was also helpful, but the
limitations of his Boston Brahmin culture showed up in some of his
recommendations, such as the quotations from assorted authors which
he persuaded Mrs. Eddy to sprinkle through the book. These surface
touches of sophistication diluted by the genteel tradition would soon
have dated the book, and Mrs. Eddy wisely removed them in later
revisions, a fact which supports her statement that in "almost every
case where Mr. Wiggin added words, I have erased them in my
revisions" (1913: 318).

Her own view of his basic function was expressed in her comment
years later: "I engaged Mr. Wiggin so as to avail myself of his criticisms of my statement of Christian science, which criticisms would
enable me to explain more clearly the points that might seem ambiguous to the reader" (1913: 317). Extravagant claims have been made
that he "rewrote" *Science and Health*, but Wiggin himself claimed
only to have "polished" it, and a close comparison of the sixteenth
edition with those immediately preceding it bears out his estimate.
While he remained skeptical of Christian Science, his admiration of
its founder in their early years of association was outspoken. In an
1886 pamphlet, *Christian Science and the Bible*, writing under the
pseudonym "Phare Pleigh," he defended her Christianity, paid tribute to her sincerity, and gave a useful picture of the birthing of the
new edition:

> Whatever is to be Mrs. Eddy's future reputation, time will show. . . .
> Within a few months she had made sacrifices, from which most authors
> would have shrunk, to ensure the moral rightness of her book. . . . Day
> after day flew by, and weeks lengthened into months; from every quarter
> came importunate missives of inquiry and mercantile reproach; hun-
> dreds of dollars were sunk in a bottomless sea of corrections; yet not till
> the authoress was satisfied that her duty was wholly done, would she
> allow printer and binder to send forth her book to the world (65).

During the next five years Wiggin performed various other literary services for Mrs. Eddy, including—for part of that time—the
editorship of *The Christian Science Journal*, the monthly periodical of
the growing movement. Disagreements arose, however, when he
tried to influence her in matters affecting the substance and basic
vocabulary of Christian Science. Young William Dana Orcutt, then
new to Oxford University Press in Cambridge with which Wiggin had
connections, described him as "a vainglorious, pompous man, with a
very high opinion of his own ability," who frequently complained of

"the difficulty he had in trying to persuade Mrs. Eddy to accept his suggestions" (1950:3). This contrasted with Orcutt's own response to her in his business dealings through the years: "At first one might have been deceived by her quiet manner into thinking that she was easily influenced. There was no suggestion to which she did not hold herself open. If she approved, she accepted it promptly; if it did not appeal, she dismissed it with a graciousness that left no mark; but it was always settled once and for all. There was no wavering and no uncertainty" (1926: 53).

The result of Wiggin's wounded self-esteem was a growing cynicism about Christian Science and its leader. Mrs. Eddy commented on the "shocking flippancy" in his notes on her proofs, though she wrote him mildly enough, "My faith in your criticism continues, but you know faith sometimes needs Mr. Wiggin's notes, and his notes, occasionally, need my metaphysics" (Peel, 1971: 282). By the middle 1890s she made no further use of his services, but after his death she wrote appreciatively, "I hold the late Mr. Wiggin in loving, grateful memory for his high-principled character and well-equiped scholarship" (1913: 319).

The fiftieth edition of *Science and Health*, which represented perhaps the most important revision of all of them, had appeared in 1891. Wiggin had been called in to help only toward the end of its preparation and played a considerably lesser role than with the 1885–1886 revision. The fiftieth has been called the first edition of *Science and Health* with which the present-day Christian Scientist can feel really at home. Its easier, more authoritative tone is to be found also in many of the articles Mrs. Eddy wrote for her own and other periodicals during the 1890s and gathered into her *Miscellaneous Writings* in 1897.

A good example of the style she had achieved in this later period of her life is a paragraph in which she summed up the earliest stage in her development of Christian Science. It occurs in the opening chapter, "Science, Theology, Medicine," of the fiftieth edition and is given here in essentially the form it had in that edition but with a few small verbal refinements which she added in later revisions:

> For three years after my discovery, I sought the solution of this problem of Mind-healing, searched the Scriptures and read little else, kept aloof from society, and devoted time and energies to discovering a positive rule. The search was sweet, calm, and buoyant with hope, not selfish nor depressing. I knew the Principle of all harmonious Mind-action to be God, and that cures were produced in primitive Christian healing by holy, uplifting faith; but I must know the Science of this healing, and I won my way to absolute conclusions through divine revelation, reason,

and demonstration. The revelation of Truth in the understanding came to me gradually and apparently through divine power. When a new spiritual idea is borne to earth, the prophetic Scripture of Isaiah is renewedly fulfilled: "Unto us a child is born . . . and his name shall be called Wonderful" (1911a: 109).

There were further major revisions in 1903 and 1906, with innumerable smaller changes in the intervening printings and in the four years following the 1906 revision. In her ninetieth year, only a month or two before her decease, Mrs. Eddy authorized a few final refinements for future printings. These were incorporated in new printings just before her passing but with a 1911 date on the title page.[3] Except for changes in format, corrections of misprints, and other such minor adjustments, the book remains today as its author left it.

Her explanation of the extensive changes she made through thirty-five years is to be found in the Christian Science textbook itself: "I have revised *Science and Health* only to give a clearer and fuller expression of its original meaning. Spiritual ideas unfold as we advance. A human perception of divine Science, however limited, must be correct in order to be Science and subject to demonstration" (1911a: 361).

Controversy

Since it first gained public notice, the book on which Mrs. Eddy lavished such continuous care has been the subject of intense controversy. By some critics of Christian Science it has been labeled as blasphemous, incoherent, unintelligible, tedious, heretical, and offensive in a dozen different ways. To some readers it has seemed to be a revelation second only to that of the Bible. But the line of division has not always been so clear-cut nor the judgments so simplistic.

From the beginning some readers simply dismissed the book as unworthy of serious consideration. Some found it admirable but too transcendental. Some liked it in patches and snatches but could not take it as a whole. Some admired it for the wrong reasons and used it as a springboard for various forms of mind-cure and positive thinking, a misuse that was positively abhorrent to Mrs. Eddy. And then there was Mark Twain, who lit into the book with ferocious hilarity but with an underlying ambivalence that bears closer examination.

In 1899 he wrote that "of all the strange and frantic and incomprehensible and uninterpretable books which the imagination of man has created, surely this one is the prize sample"—a judgment that has set the pattern for much subsequent criticism. This particular passage has been quoted with approval by literally scores of writers, many of whom give no evidence of ever having read *Science and Health* for themselves and all of whom appear to have missed entirely the footnote Twain added four years later to his pages on the Christian Science textbook: "January, 1903. The first reading of any book whose terminology is new and strange is nearly sure to leave the reader in a bewildered and sarcastic state of mind. But now that, during the past two months, I have, by diligence, gained a fair acquaintanceship with 'Science and Health' technicalities, I no longer find the bulk of that work hard to understand" (29, 32).

Nor was that all. Later he went on to describe the language of *Science and Health* as "clean, compact, dignified, almost perfect," then added that this was not merely the result of expert editing by literary aides in recent years; the language of the third edition, years before Wiggin hove into view, was "very nearly as straight and clean and competent as is the English of the latest revision." In other words, he concluded, the English "was good at the outset and has remained so" (114, 117). Furthermore, his change of heart extended to the contents of *Science and Health*. With surprising sympathy though less than perfect accuracy he could write:

> The Christian Scientist believes that the Spirit of God (life and love) pervades the universe like an atmosphere; that whoso will study *Science and Health* can get from it the secret of how to inhale that transforming air; that to breathe it is to be made new; that from the new man all sorrow, all care, all miseries of the mind vanish away, for that only peace, contentment and measureless joy can live in that divine fluid; that it purifies the body from disease, which is a vicious creation of the gross human mind, and cannot continue to exist in the presence of the Immortal Mind, the renewing Spirit of God (226).

It was hard for Twain to reconcile such teaching with an author whom he insisted on seeing as grasping for money, power, glory; as vain, untruthful, jealous, despotic, arrogant, illiterate, and so on at great length. He was understandably puzzled about how such a character could have had an *interest* in what he considered to be the really "great idea" in her book:

> For the thing back of it is wholly gracious and beautiful: the power, through loving mercifulness and compassion, to heal fleshly ills and pains and griefs—*all*—with a word, with a touch of the hand! This power was given by the saviour to the disciples, and to *all* the converted. All— every one. It was *exercised* for generations afterwards. Any Christian who was in earnest and not a make-believe, not a policy-Christian, not a Christian for revenue only, had that healing power, and could cure with it *any disease or any hurt or damage possible to human flesh and bone.* These things are true, or they are not. If they were true seventeen and

eighteen hundred years ago it would be difficult to satisfactorily explain
why or how or by what argument that power should be non-existent in
Christians now (284).

The only way Mark Twain could escape the dilemma presented by
linking such a benign power and purpose with the monstrous fantasy
figure he had posited was to conclude that someone else must have
written *Science and Health* for her from the beginning!

This would have been news to Samuel Putnam Bancroft, who in
1870 had been in one of her first classes and fifty years later wrote a
book of reminiscences documented with copies of early manuscripts
she had written for those classes. Whenever asked whether she was
indeed the author of *Science and Health*, he would answer impa-
tiently, "I heard her talk it before it was ever written." Part of the time
while she was working on the book she actually lived with Bancroft
and his wife. "I have known her when [she was] nearly crushed with
sorrow," he recalled after half a century, "but she wrote on. I have
known her when friend after friend deserted her, but she wrote on. I
have seen student after student bring ridicule and reproach upon her,
but she still wrote on" (127).

Yet Mark Twain was right in one thing: it was not the Mrs. Eddy of
his imagining who wrote or could have written the book he ended by
praising. Nor was he alone in his dilemma. In varying ways other
severe critics of the Christian Science leader have also found it difficult to reconcile their views of her with the religious depth-dimension
of *Science and Health*, which is not easily explained away by any
theory of literary borrowing or psychobiographic interpretation.

A useful example is Lyman P. Powell, an Episcopalian rector and
educator who early looked into the Quimby manuscript controversy
and in 1907 wrote a book castigating Christian Science and its
founder. By 1921, however, when he was asked to write an objective
analysis of *Science and Health* for the *Cambridge History of American
Literature*, further study and investigation had led him to a considerable modification of his early views, and he concluded: "Christian
Science as it is today is really its founder's creation. Where she got this
idea, or where that, little matters. As a whole the system described in
Science and Health is hers, and nothing that can ever happen will
make it less than hers" (526). Nine years later he had swung around
even further and wrote a highly laudatory biography of the woman he
had once excoriated but had now come to consider a great Christian
leader.

Another form of ambivalence is illustrated by H. A. L. Fisher, an
Oxford historian of some distinction, whose caustic popular study of

Christian Science and Mrs. Eddy is strewn with occasional tributes which seem to contradict much that had gone before—but are also tributes to the honesty of the trained historian. Quimby, he conceded, "would certainly never have written *Science and Health;* and in the development of Christian Science that book, and that book only, has been of decisive importance." Moreover, he added, the author was a religious woman:

> If the metaphysical promptings of her mind impelled her to search for a system of the universe, the religious side of it gave to that system its emotional quality and content. Prayer, meditation, eager and puzzled interrogation of the bible, had claimed from childhood much of her energy, so that those who met her in later times were conscious of a certain quiet exaltation, such as may come to a woman nursing a secret spiritual advantage. . . . When we ask what was the inner source of her power, the answer can only be that it was religion. . . . The great ideas of god, of immortality, of the soul, of a life penetrated by Christianity, were never far from her mind (44, 61).

The daring metaphysical bent of her thinking—hinted at already in her 1847 article on the immortality of the soul—has also had to be accounted for by those who have assumed her to be incapable of original thought. This position is neatly summed up in a comment in a midwestern religious journal in 1937: "At one time I believed . . . that she [Mrs. Eddy] got it [Christian Science] from P. P. Quimby. But when the Quimby manuscripts were published, I concluded that there was not enough similarity between Quimby's ideas and Mrs. Eddy's for his to constitute a basis for hers. . . . I was convinced, however, that she was enslaved to some brilliant mind to whom she was indebted for both thought and terms" (Johnsen: 5).

This comment occurred in a favorable review of a book entitled *Mrs. Eddy Purloins from Hegel* by Walter W. Haushalter, which attempted to prove that the basic ideas and language of *Science and Health* had been stolen from an alleged essay on Hegel's philosophy by Francis Lieber, a nineteenth-century German-American political scientist. The whole thing turned out to be the crudest sort of forgery, used in an unsuccessful blackmail attempt to persuade the Christian Science church to pay for its suppression.

As soon as the book received serious, detailed attention from competent scholars, the fraudulence of the so-called "Lieber" document become overwhelmingly evident.[4] But the initial response of the academic community was one of general credulity—and over the years the myth has died hard. Even today it is circulated by various fundamentalist pamphleteers.

The whole shabby history of gullibility on this forgery is detailed in an article in the *New England Quarterly,* which points out that the Haushalter book "addressed itself to its readers' preconceptions, and these preconceptions were powerful enough to condition the reception of the book. Thus, more than one reviewer indicated that he held the legitimacy of the plagiarism charge to be a foregone conclusion" (Johnsen: 5).

Obviously the origin of *Science and Health* and the originality of its author are, to say the least, closely related. Mrs. Eddy's own view of the book that she wryly described as "hopelessly original" is indicated by her reply to a dinner guest—a friendly unbeliever—who said to her, "Christian Scientists called *Science and Health* a kind of revelation from God, but I think you originated it from your own superior talent." Her reply was quick: "Oh dear, no! I could not originate such a book. Why, I have to study it myself in order to understand it." (Peel, 1977: 23).

Authority

Christian Science is first of all a study, and *Science and Health* remains its authoritative textbook. Christian Scientists are apt to speak of themselves as "students of Christian Science," and normally they devote time each day to studying the Bible and the textbook that they believe helps them to relate the "inspired Word of the Bible" more practically—more "scientifically" even—to their lives.

Thus Christian Science is also a "practice"—a way of life as well as a way of thinking and praying. In one sense all Christian Scientists are expected to be "practitioners" of their faith, although the terms is ordinarily reserved for those who are devoting themselves full-time to the ministry of healing. Truth is to be practically "demonstrated" through the regeneration and healing of human lives and bodies. Inspiration is to be validated by experience.

It was with this practical purpose that Mrs. Eddy and a small group of her students voted in 1879 to organize "a church designed to commemorate the word and works of our Master, which should reinstate primitive Christianity and its lost element of healing" (Eddy, 1911b: 17). In its final form the resulting organization consisted of The Mother Church, The First Church of Christ, Scientist in Boston, together with its branch churches and societies around the world.

In 1895 Mrs. Eddy ordained the Bible and *Science and Health with Key to the Scriptures* as "pastor" of The Mother Church and its branches. She also instituted a system of weekly Bible lessons covering twenty-six topics and composed of correlative passages from the Bible and the denominational textbook. The topics of these "lesson-sermons" recur twice a year; the passages to illustrate them are chosen afresh each time by a committee.

Thus, every Sunday, Christian Scientists who have been individually and daily studying a given lesson during the preceding week meet together as a congregation to hear it read as a sermon by two lay readers. In every Christian Science church service throughout the world the same lesson is read on the same day and is introduced with the same explanation from the *Christian Science Quarterly:* "The Bible and the Christian Science textbook are our only preachers. We shall now read Scriptural texts, and their correlative passages from our denominational textbook; these comprise our sermon."

The rationale of this system of combined study and worship is clear, if unusual. Pulpit eloquence was to give way to spiritual education; ritual to shared understanding; outward sacraments to inner commitment; audible to silent prayer.

The Sunday service in a Christian Science church mingles something of the bare simplicity of the New England church services that Mrs. Eddy knew as a girl with a touch of the Quaker quietism and the Unitarian rationalism with which she came in friendly contact later. The midweek meeting, for which the First Reader in each church prepares a lesson composed of passages from the Bible and *Science and Health* on a topic of his or her own choosing, is chiefly known for the spontaneous "testimonies of healing" given by members of the congregation—and in this respect at least bears some resemblance to a Methodist testimony meeting. For Christian Scientists the midweek meeting is, in some sense, a witness to—and a test of—the spiritual effectiveness of the Sunday service. In the age-old controversy in regard to salvation by faith or by works, Mrs. Eddy committed her followers squarely to the position of Jas 2:18, "Show me thy faith without thy works, and I will show thee my faith by my works."

The central place of the Bible in this worship system is notable, although often overlooked because of its linkage with *Science and Health*. In few if any other churches is one-half of the sermon composed of readings from the Bible and preceded by an additional scriptural reading. On the other hand, the authority given to *Science and Health* is also unmistakable and raises a question as to whether Christian Scientists give it equal authority with the Bible.

Certainly it has for them an authority at least equal to that which traditional Christians give the great historic creeds. But like those creeds it claims only to be making explicit what is inherent in the Scriptures—and to derive its authority directly from the Scriptures.

Science and Health itself contains more than seven hundred quotations from the Bible, plus innumerable other references to scriptural teachings, events, characters, figures of speech, textual and theological problems. Verbal echoes from the Bible abound throughout the book, often missed entirely by secular critics looking for influences on Mrs. Eddy's writing. *Science and Health* without the Bible would be, in its author's eyes, as anomalous as a key without a door to unlock.

In her 1902 revision of the textbook, Mrs. Eddy made two major changes. In the first place, she moved two chapters—"Prayer" and "Atonement and Eucharist"—up to the front of the book, thereby establishing at once the Christian spirit and theology that she considered essential to an understanding of the metaphysics that followed. The spirit is well illustrated in the following typical passage from the second chapter: "While we adore Jesus, and the heart overflows with gratitude for what he did for mortals—treading alone his loving pathway up to the throne of glory, in speechless agony exploring the way for us,—yet Jesus spares us not one individual experience, if we follow his commands faithfully; and all have the cup of sorrowful effort to drink in proportion to their demonstration of his love, till all are redeemed through divine Love" (26).

Characteristically, the sentences immediately preceding and following this passage introduce in an almost casual way a crucial theological point that is elaborated in various other contexts later in the book: "The divinity of the Christ was made manifest in the humanity of Jesus. . . . The Christ was the Spirit which Jesus implied in his own statements: 'I am the way, the truth, and the life;' 'I and my Father are one.' This Christ, or divinity of the man Jesus, was his divine nature, the godliness which animated him."

In a later chapter entitled "Science of Being" this point is amplified, with the addition of metaphysical terms which further extend its meaning:

> The advent of Jesus of Nazareth marked the first century of the Christian era, but the Christ is without beginning of years or end of days. Throughout all generations both before and after the Christian era, the Christ, as the spiritual idea,—the reflection of god,—has come with some measure of power and grace to all prepared to receive Christ, Truth. Abraham, Jacob, Moses, and the prophets caught glorious glimpses of the Messiah, or Christ, which baptized these seers in the divine nature, the essence of Love. The divine image, idea, or Christ was, is, and ever will be inseparable from the divine Principle, God (333).

This in turn gains a further dimension from the answer to the question "What is God?" in the chapter "Recapitulation": "God is incorporeal, divine, supreme, infinite Mind, Spirit, Soul, Principle, Life, Truth, Love" (465).

The second change made in the 1902 revision was the addition of a final one hundred-page chapter entitled "Fruitage" and introduced by the words of Jesus: "Wherefore by their fruits ye shall know them" (Matt 7:20). This was made up entirely of testimonials from people who had been healed simply by reading or studying *Science and Health*. The chapter includes healings of cancer, tuberculosis, heart disease, kidney ailments, broken bones, cataracts, eczema, alcoholism, insanity, and a host of other ills. They are not unlike the testimonials that have been published in the Christian Science periodicals monthly and weekly during the past one hundred years, except for the fact that *Science and Health* itself appears to have been the sole "practitioner" in each of these cases.

What is likely to strike the reader of this chapter, however, is how often the physical healing is presented as subordinate to an influx of light, a "new birth" or awakening to a fresh sense of life and its possibilities. Very often the chief gratitude expressed is for a higher understanding of God—and a deeper appreciation of the Bible. A frequent refrain is that the Bible is now a new book to the testifier. One woman writes that after her healing through her "illumined" study of *Science and Health*, the Bible became "my constant study, my joy, and my guide," and she continues: "The copy which I bought at the time of my healing is marked from Genesis to Revelation. It was so constantly in my hands for three years that the cover become worn and the leaves loose, so it has been laid away for a new one. Two and three o'clock in the morning often found me poring over its pages, which grew more and more sacred to me every day, and the help I received therefrom was wonderful, for which I can find no words to express my gratitude" (691).

This biblical emphasis is possibly the aspect of Christian Science to which the least academic attention has been paid—an oversight helped along by a gnostic strain among some of Mrs. Eddy's followers who tend to stress the letter of her teachings (i.e., its absolute metaphysics) at the expense of its Christian spirit and its biblical roots.

Mrs. Eddy told WIlliam Dana Orcutt in 1893 that it had always been her desire that her book should encourage more and more people to turn to the Bible. There was soon an interesting bit of practical evidence that it was doing just that. Recognizing how much the circulation of the Christian Science textbook was helping to stimulate the demand for Bibles, the Oxford University Press in 1894 agreed to furnish the Christian Science Publishing Society—and them alone—the much-desired Oxford India paper hitherto reserved for the printing of Bibles and prayer books, in order that Christian Scientists might have copies of their textbook with pages similar to those of the Bible as an aid in studying them together.

Prolepsis

The world has been catapulted into a new age since the first edition of *Science and Health* appeared in 1875. Yet the woman who could write of the coming age, "The astronomer will no longer look up to the stars,—he will look out from them upon the universe" (1911: 125), cannot be simplistically written off as a nineteenth-century religious fanatic.

When asked by a reporter from the *New York Herald* in 1901 what she thought of "modern material inventions," Mrs. Eddy replied in part: "We use them, we make them our figures of speech. They are preparing the way for us" (1913: 345). This was illustrated by her statement in an article, "The Christian Science Textbook," in which she wrote: "Hidden electrical forces annihilating time and space, wireless telegraphy, navigation of the air; in fact, all the *et cetera* of mortal mind pressing to the front, remind me of my early dreams of flying in airy space, buoyant with liberty and the luxury of thought let loose. . . ." To which she added that the "night thought . . . should unfold in part the facts of day, and open the prison doors and solve the blind problem of matter. The night thought should show us that even mortals can mount higher in the altitude of being. Mounting higher, mortals will cease to be mortal" (1913: 110).

If this was not mere day-dreaming, neither was it the utopian vision of self-confident twentieth-century scientism. Beside it one must put Mrs. Eddy's stark pronouncement that earth will become "dreary and esolate" until "the final spiritualization of all things," with her further less-than-roseate prediction: "This material world is even now becoming the arena for conflicting forces. . . . The breaking up of material beliefs may seem to be famine and pestilence, want and woe, sin, sickness, and death, which assume new phases until their nothingness appears. . . . This mental fermentation has begun, and will continue until all errors of belief yield to understanding. . . . The more destructive matter becomes, the more its nothingness will appear, until matter reaches its mortal zenith in illusion and forever disappears" (1911a: 96, 97).

Mrs. Eddy's conviction that "incredible good and evil elements"

(89) were coming to the surface in the relatively stable world of the late nineteenth century might be said to have pointed proleptically to a world that would include both the adventure of space exploration and the mushroom cloud of nuclear devastation. Long before 1914 she had broken with the optimistic American faith in automatic linear progress. There was room for Armageddon in her theology, and this decisively separates Christian Science from the success philosophies with which it has often been confounded.

Not that it has been free from the secularizing tendencies that have eroded the spiritual force of so much American religion. Mrs. Eddy's publisher in the early 1890s had warned, "When the founder of Christian Science is taken away, its Christianity will disappear with her" (Peel, 1977: 336). That has not happened, but a perceptive academic study in 1973 took note of a strong tendency in that direction in the early years of this century and made the pungent comment:

> To the degree that Christian Science was secularized in practice—and there is some evidence that it was—its character as a pragmatic grasp of Christian revelation was vitiated. The point can be stated in terms of two ways in which the term *pragmatic* may be used. In its larger and philosophic sense, *pragmatic* signifies a quality of being experientially meaningful. But in its lesser and more popular usage, it connotes convenience and mere experiency. The secularized practice of Christian Science amounts to the reduction of a pragmatic religious teaching in the larger sense to a pragmatic problem-solver in the lesser sense (Gottschalk, 292).

This latter position, Gottschalk goes on to say, must be distinguished from "Mrs. Eddy's basic vision." The position of authority given to the Bible and *Science and Health* in the Church of Christ, Scientist has been crucial in preserving that vision as the guiding force in the Christian Science movement. Over the years an occasional small segment of the movement has dropped away to pursue its own pragmatic or ideational goals, but by and large the church has held to the Christian ideals and disciplines spelled out by *Science and Health* and the *Manual of The Mother Church*.

At the same time the ecumenical movement and the Christian healing movement have helped to abate old rigors of separation between Christian Science and the traditional churches. Mrs. Eddy expressed the hope that spiritual healing would increasingly spread to other denominations, and that has been notably the case in the past two or three decades. It is difficult to know how much direct or indirect influence *Science and Health* may have had in this development, but its concept of healing as a witness to the supremacy of spiritual power is certainly to be found in much of the interdenominational literature on the subject.

This point is made in an official publication of the Church of Christ, Scientist, issued in 1966, the centenary of Mrs. Eddy's "discovery" of Christian Science:

> "The healing of physical disease is one of the most concrete proofs that can be offered of the substantiality of Spirit. It is not of itself conclusive, and in the nature of things it cannot be offered under the conditions of controlled experiment. But in conjunction with all the other evidences of spiritual power furnished by Christianity understood as Science it offers a substantial challenge to materialistic assumptions" (Committee: 254).

The word "Science" used in this way remains an offense to many and an enigma to most. The audacity of its challenge to the sophisticated scientism of our age is beyond the scope of this article. Its relation to the challenge of New Testament Christianity has already been touched upon. The challenge it has for Christian Scientists goes back to Mrs. Eddy's "basic vision." This is brought out in a very simple passage in an article written for the centenary of the publication of *Science and Health:*

> "Catch the vision that wrote the book," Christian Scientists in the early days sometimes said to those who were just beginning to study *Science and Health*. It was plain to these Christian Scientists that a tremendous new understanding of reality had brought the book into being. Through reading it they, too, were catching a glimpse of this reality. So assuring, self-evident, and powerful was this new view of life that it seemed perfectly natural for sickness of many years' duration and even the shadow of death to melt away as part of some previous ignorance (Phinney, 1975: 663).

To the extent that any biblically-inspired book produces such results it may be said to participate in the spirit of the tremendous announcement that issued from the throne of God in Revelation 21: "Behold, I make all things new."

NOTES

/1/   This claim was advanced in an article by Hermann S. Ficke in *Bibliotheca Sacra*, October 1928. For comment see Peel 1966: 348, n. 52.

/2/   At first each printing (usually about one thousand copies) was numbered and referred to as a new "edition." This continued until 1906 when the numbering was stopped at the 418th printing.

/3/   The changes made in new printings between the 1906 revision and Mrs. Eddy's death were not sufficient to justify a new copyright; hence these printings all came out under the 1906 copyright, which gave adequate protection and was renewed in

1934. Normally this protection would have extended only to 1962, but in that year all renewal copyrights received the first of six interim extensions pending Congressional consideration of a general revision of U.S. copyright laws. By a special bill enacted by Congress in 1971, additional protection was given to *Science and Health* through the year 2046.

/4/   The first such study was by Moehlman in 1955. As a Baptist scholar and church historian, Moehlman on internal evidence alone became convinced of the fraudulence of the Haushalter claim. His assumptions have been borne out and amplified by later documented studies.

WORKS CONSULTED

Bancroft, Samuel Putnam
    1923   *Mrs. Eddy As I Knew Her in 1870*. Boston: Longyear Foundation.

Clemens, Samuel [Mark Twain, pseud.]
    1907   *Christian Science*. New York: Harper & Bros.

Committee on Publication
    1966   *A Century of Christian Science Healing*. Boston: Christian Science Publishing Society.

Dresser, Annetta G.
    1895   *The Philosophy of P. P. Quimby*. Boston: George H. Ellis.

Dresser, Horatio W.
    1921   *The Quimby Manuscripts*. New York: Thomas Y. Crowell.

Eddy, Mark Baker
    1847   "The Immortality of the Soul," *The I.O.O.F. Covenant* 6/5 (May).
    1891   *Retrospection and Introspection*. Boston: W. G. Nixon.
    1897   *Miscellaneous Writings*. Boston: Joseph Armstrong.
    1911a   *Science and Health with Key to the Scriptures*. Boston: Allison V. Stewart.
    1911b   *Manual of The Mother Church*. Boston: Allison V. Stewart.
    1913   *First Church of Christ Scientist and Miscellany*. Boston: Allison V. Stewart.

Fisher, H. A. L.
    1929   *Our New Religion*. London: Ernest Benn.

Gottschalk, Stephen
    1973   *The Emergence of Christian Science in American Religious Life*. Berkeley: University of California Press.

Haushalter, Walter M.
    1936   *Mrs. Eddy Purloins from Hegel*. Boston: A. A. Beauchamp.

Holl, Karl
    1928   *Gesammelte Aufsätze zur Kirchengeschichte*. Tübingen: Mohr.

Johnsen, Thomas C.
    1980   "Historical Consensus and Christian Science; The Career of a Manuscript Controversy," *New England Quarterly* 53/1 (March).

Moehlman, Conrad H.
    1955   *Ordeal by Concordance.* New York: Longmans Green.

Orcutt, William Dana
    1926   *In Quest of the Perfect Book.* Boston: Little, Brown.
    1950   *Mary Baker Eddy and Her Books.* Boston: Christian Science
                           Publishing Society.

Peel, Robert
    1958   *Christian Science: Its Encounter with American Culture.* New
                           York: Henry Holt.
    1966   *Mary Baker Eddy: The Years of Discovery.* New York: Holt,
                           Rinehart & Winston.
    1977   *Mary Baker Eddy: The Years of Authority.* New York: Holt,
                           Rinehart & Winston.

Phinney, Allison W., Jr.
    1975   "Science and Health with Key to the Scriptures: Its Impact on
                           Religion," *The Christian Science Journal* 93/12 (December).

Powell, Lyman
    1907   *Christian Science, the Faith and its Founder.* New York: G. P.
                           Putnam.
    1924   "Popular Bibles," *Cambridge History of American Literature,*
                           vol. 3. New York: Macmillan.
    1930   *Mary Baker Eddy, a Life Size Portrait.* New York: Macmillan.

Wiggin, James Henry [Phare Pleigh, pseud.]
    1886   *Christian Science and the Bible.* Boston: S. H. Crosse.

INDEX

INDEX TO BIBLICAL
REFERENCES AND
OTHER SACRAL WORKS